READING KRISTEVA

READING KRISTEVA

Unraveling the Double-bind

KELLY OLIVER

INDIANA UNIVERSITY PRESS

Bloomington and Indianapolis

For my family

The paper used in this publication meets the minimum requirements of American
National Standard for Information Sciences—Permanence of Paper for Printed
Library Materials, ANSI Z39.48-1984.

⊗ ™

Manufactured in the United States of America

Library of Congress Cataloging-in-Publication Data

Oliver, Kelly, date.
  Reading Kristeva : unraveling the double-bind / Kelly Oliver.
      p.   cm.
  Includes bibliographical references and index.
  ISBN 0-253-34173-6 (cloth : alk. paper). — ISBN 0-253-20761-4
(pbk.)
    1. Kristeva, Julia, date. 2. Feminist literary criticism.
3. Psychoanalysis and literature. 4. Feminism and literature—
France. I. Title.
PN75.K75045 1993
801'.95'092—dc20   92-9543

1 2 3 4 5   97 96 95 94 93

CONTENTS

ACKNOWLEDGMENTS

I would like to thank Rosemarie Tong for her encouragement and understanding; without it, I would not have written this book. I would also like to thank Judith Butler, Michele Ginsberg, Elissa Marder, Janet Rabinowitch, Linda Singer, Hugh Silverman, Teri Stratton, Iris Young, and Ewa Ziarek, for extremely useful comments on various sections, at various stages, of my manuscript. I especially want to thank Elizabeth Grosz for her careful reading of the entire manuscript; her detailed comments made this a better book. For help with French texts, I would like to thank Nadja Hofman. For research assistance, I would like to thank Holly Dawson, Honor Fagen, and Peter Shoemaker. For financial support for the summer of 1989 I am grateful to Miami University Faculty Fellowships. For financial support for the summer of 1991 I am grateful to George Washington University and the Dilthey Foundation.

I would also like to thank all of my friends who listened to my trials and triumphs and often gave me advice, much of it useful: Kim England, Elissa Marder, Peter Heckman, David Buller, Doug Tobias, Doug Kellner, Robert Bernasconi, Tamsin Lorraine, Lisa Heldke, Debra Silverman. A special thanks to Linda Singer, whose advice was always good, who always put things into a useful perspective. She was the best colleague and mentor that I could ever hope to have. I miss her.

Finally, I would like to acknowledge the support of my family, especially my mother, Virginia, for her loving ear and her adventurous spirit; Grandma Ellen, for spoiling me and insisting that I not settle for less; Grandma Ruth, for showing me how to be strong and work hard; my father, Glen, for always telling me to finish what I start and for giving me determination; Grandpa Mel, for showing me laughter, kindness, and how to tell evergreens apart; Grandpa Russell, for being a true philosopher and talking with me about the meaning of life way past my bedtime; Doug, for setting a challenging research pace; Ruthy, for being strong and sweet; and Bucky, for scouting out great camping spots and appreciating that without regular sojourns to the mountains of northern Idaho I would suffocate.

I wrote the essay that became the seed for this project after encouragement from Nancy Fraser. I would like to thank Nancy for her continued support. Without it, none of this would have been possible. I wrote that first essay, electrically charged, under the green light in the kitchen on Kentucky Street. A loving thanks to its inhabitants and their familiars, creatures of the night, who always make me smile, Kaos, Wizard, and Skeeter.

INTRODUCTION
OSCILLATION STRATEGIES

At the start of this project I began a fairly straightforward critique of Kristeva's theories. But the more that I read and the more that I wrote, the more sympathetic I became to her project. As soon as I came to some conclusion about one of her theories, I would read a passage that would convince me of something else. In terms of traditional philosophical discourse I might say that Kristeva's writing is full of contradictions. But hers is not a discourse that strictly adheres to the logic of noncontradiction. Rather, hers is a discourse that breaks the law of noncontradiction upon which traditional notions of identity are built. Kristeva's writing challenges traditional notions of identity. This is what opens up the possibility of interpretation.

The extreme views expressed in the secondary literature on Kristeva's writing are evidence of the way in which her writing opens itself to interpretation. For example, some of her critics argue that Kristeva's theory presents an essentialist notion of woman and the feminine (Silverman, Stone, Kuykendall, Grosz); others argue that it undermines any essentialist notion of woman (Ainley, Rose). Some of Kristeva's critics argue that her theory is founded on an essentialist conception of maternity (Grosz, Jones, Butler, Kuykendall, Fraser, Stanton); others argue that her notion of maternity is double and indeterminate (Ainley, Ziarek, Chase). Some critics argue that she promotes anarchy (Smith, Eagleton); others argue that her theories are conservative or even fascist (Fraser, Jones, Leland, Gidal). Some critics argue that her theories open up the possibility of change (Ainley, Chanter, Rose, Jardine); others argue that they close off the possibility of change (Fraser, Leland, Grosz, Gidal). Some critics argue that her theories are ahistorical (Fraser, Butler); others argue that her work is fundamentally concerned with the history of social structures (Lechte, Chanter). Some critics argue that Kristeva does not provide for a female or political agency (Kuykendall, Fraser); others argue that she does (Jardine, Rose). Some critics argue that her theories are useful for feminism

1

(Chanter, Rose, Ziarek); others argue that they are not (Butler, Fraser, Leland, Grosz, Jones, Stone, Kuykendall).

Alice Jardine provides an insightful diagnosis of Kristeva's critics:

> Kristeva's thought is peculiar: it is transparent enough that it tends to be reduced very quickly to a set of bipolar opposites by her critics (and thereby criticized as being everything from ultraanarchistic to ultraconservative); but at the same time, it is opaque enough to be uncritically idealized by her most fervent admirers. (1986, 106)

Like Jardine, I attempt to avoid both of these extremes. Although I offer a sympathetic, recuperate reading of Kristeva in order to use her theories in a feminist context, I am also critical of those theories. The ambiguities in her writing that open up the possibility of interpretation can also frustrate interpretation. They make her writing both trying and exciting at the same time.

The frustration and excitement of reading Kristeva's writings makes my own relationship to them similar to what she describes as the relation to the abject mother. I am both attracted to and repelled by her writings at the same time. Like the abject mother, her writings are both sublime and repulsive. And I am fascinated by them. I am drawn to them in a struggle to control them by interpreting them, by understanding them, by making sense out of them. What you will read is the result of my struggle to understand and interpret Kristeva's writings.

For some feminists, the most troubling aspect of Kristeva's writing is her hostile relation to feminism. Kristeva claims that she turns away from feminism because feminists are merely rushing after "phallic power." She objects to a feminism that merely wants to possess power. She is concerned to transform the logics of power that give rise to women's marginalization in general. Specifically, she is concerned with representations of difference that allow individuals to express their individuality without being marginalized in society. She claims, however, that feminism works with traditional representations of difference that insure that difference will always be marginalized. She sees a feminism that merely wants to make women's difference central and move everything traditionally central to the margins. And certainly many Anglo-American feminists would also object to the kind of feminism that Kristeva rejects.

Kristeva much too quickly dismisses feminism without investigating the differences within feminisms. It is an unfortunate irony that while Kristeva is concerned with difference and individuality, she denies the differences and individuality of multitudes of feminists writing and working all over the world. It is especially unfortunate that with her hasty dismissal of feminism, Kristeva has alienated many Anglo-American feminists; it is unfortunate because many of her theories provide an important challenge to traditional psychoanalytic and linguistic theory than can be useful for feminism.

For example, from her earliest writings Kristeva has attempted to bring the semiotic body, replete with drives, back into structuralism. This attempt has also marked her point of departure from Lacanian theory. She argues that Lacan's bracketing of the drives "castrates" Freud's discovery. Kristeva, protecting the father of psychoanalysis from this castration threat by his most prodigal son, reinscribes the drives in language. She attempts to protect Freud's body from Lacan's desire.

In order to bring the body, replete with drives, back into structuralism, Kristeva employs two very different strategies. First, she brings the speaking body back to signification by maintaining that bodily drives make their way into language. She developed the notion of the semiotic element in signification in order to bring the body back into the very structure of language. Bodily drives make their way into signification through the disruptive but necessary force of this semiotic element. Most commentators concentrate on Kristeva's theory of the semiotic in signification.

Kristeva, however, employs a second perhaps more interesting strategy for bringing the speaking body back into structuralism. Her tactic is to reinscribe language within the body, arguing that the dynamics that operate the Symbolic are already working within the material of the body and the presymbolic imaginary. She concludes that these dynamics must therefore be material or bio-logical as well as symbolic. In other words, her strategy is to trace the signifier through the body in order, at the same time, to reinscribe the body in language. She argues that the *logic* of signification is already present in the material body.

For Kristeva this body that sets up and harbors the Symbolic (at the same time that it threatens it) is the maternal body. The maternal body *prefigures* the Law of the Father and the onset of the Symbolic. What Kristeva calls the "maternal function" contains both a negation and an identification that precede Lacan's mirror stage. This is to say that both the negation and the identification that are essential to human subjectivity are already operating within the maternal function prior to the subject's entrance into language. This has tremendous consequences for psychoanalysis. In traditional Freudian and Lacanian psychoanalysis it is the paternal function that initiates the negation and identification that finally propels the infant into both language and subjectivity. Kristeva's theory challenges the traditional notion of the paternal function. In addition, it challenges Lancanian theories of subjectivity.

Unlike either Freud or Lacan, Kristeva is concerned with analyzing the complexities of the maternal function, which she maintains have been left out of traditional psychoanalytic theory. Her texts take us deeper and deeper within the maternal function, and thereby take us deeper and deeper into the maternal body. In her earlier work Kristeva discusses the infant's relationship to the surface of the mother's body, to the mother's breast. She describes the ways in which negation and identification are already operating in this relationship. She identifies a maternal prohibition, which precedes any paternal prohibition, that regulates what goes into and comes out of the infant's body; eventually the mother weans the infant by denying or prohibiting the breast altogether. So the child's relation to its mother's breast is already operating according to a logic of negation.

In addition, the infant's body itself is already operating according to a logic of negation. It already experiences privation—as excess—through its anality; when there is too much matter, some is expelled. Both the primary maternal prohibitions and the infant's experience of material negation point to a rejection that Kristeva argues operates on a material level prior to symbolic rejection. This material rejection sets up the possibility of symbolic rejection, negation, and separation. Even birth itself, with one body expelled from another, becomes a prototype for negation and separation.

Kristeva describes another phase of the child's relation to its mother's body as an abject relation, which operates in between material rejection and symbolic rejection. The phase of the maternal function that she identifies with abjection is also identified with the mother's "sex." For Kristeva, the mother is "alone of her sex." This is because for the child the mother's sex represents the canal through which it entered the world. This phase of abjection within the maternal function marks the transition between material rejection and symbolic rejection. For the child, it marks the transition between dependence on the maternal body and independence from the maternal body. In this phase of abjection, however, the borders between them—between child and mother, between nature and culture, between subject and other—are called into question.

Kristeva maintains that in order to support the transition through abjection into the Symbolic order the infant needs a fantasy of a loving imaginary father. This fantasy is a matter of a primary identification that offsets, counterbalances, the primary negation. Just as she argues that there is a primary negation that precedes and sets up symbolic negation, so too she argues that there is a primary identification that precedes and sets up symbolic identification. There is what Kristeva calls a primary "reduplication" that operates within the semiotic in order to set up the pattern of identification. Like the logic of negation, the logic of identification is already operating on the level of the semiotic body prior to the child's entrance into the Symbolic order.

My book can be read as the story of Kristeva's double strategy for bringing the speaking body back into structuralism: putting symbolic logic within the body, and putting semiotic bodily drives within the Symbolic.

I describe *Revolution in Poetic Language* (1974) and *Powers of Horror* (1980a) as her attempts to bring back the speaking body by placing the logic of symbolic negation within that body and by putting material *negation* into the Symbolic. *Revolution in Poetic Language*, with its description of primary material rejection in the infant's own body and in its relation to the surface of the mother's body, points to a material semiotic rejection operating both to set up the Symbolic and as the driving force within the Symbolic. *Powers of Horror*, with its expansion of primary rejection to include the child's relation to its mother's sex and its own birth, points to a semiotic structure inherent in the continuation of the species that prefigures the separation and rejection required in order to enter the Symbolic.

I describe *Tales of Love* (1983) and *Black Sun* (1987) as Kristeva's attempts to bring back the speaking body by placing the logic of symbolic *identification* within the body and by putting material reduplication into the Symbolic. *Tales of Love*, with its primary identification engendered by the child's fantasy of its conception, sets up the possibility of symbolic identification. *Black Sun*, and its semiotic identification with what Kristeva calls the maternal "Thing," makes identification with the maternal body the flip side of rejection of the abject maternal body.

Kristeva continues to employ her double strategy in *Strangers to Ourselves* (1989) when she argues that the subject can relate to an other because the other is within the subject. Just as Kristeva attempts to bring the speaking body back into language by putting the logic of language into the body, she attempts to bring the subject into the place of the other by putting the other into the subject. Just as she sees the pattern and logic of language within the body, she sees the pattern and logic of alterity within the subject. Through her double strategy, she makes the social relation interior to the psyche.

Kristeva's analysis of primary negation and primary identification takes us further into the maternal function. With her analysis in *Revolution* of the child's relationship to the maternal body as regulator, giving and taking away the breast, and her analysis in *Powers of Horror* of the child's relationship to its birth and its mother's sex, and her analysis in *Tales of Love* of what I read as the child's relationship to its conception, she takes us from the surface of the mother's body through the mother's sex into the mother's womb. At its limit, Kristeva's journey into the maternal function can be traced as a journey into the maternal body.

My book can also be read as the story of Kristeva's trip through the maternal body, the story of her challenge to traditional psychoanalysis pushed to its borders. Kristeva argues that traditional psychoanalysis, starting with Freud and continuing through Lacan, ignores the significance of the maternal function. For both Freud and Lacan it is the paternal

that functions to initiate the child into language and the social. Kristeva
suggests that both Freud and Lacan overlook the complexities of the maternal function prefiguring the paternal Law.

Kristeva's analysis of the maternal function fills in a conspicuous gap
in both Freudian and Lacanian theory. Her emphasis on the maternal
function transforms Lacanian theory of language and the Unconscious. It
transforms traditional notions of analytic practice. And it has significant
implications for political theory, especially feminist theory. In spite of her
dismissal of feminism, Kristeva's analysis of the maternal function and
women's oppression is thought provoking. I take what is merely a suggestion about the relation between traditional representations of the maternal
function and women's oppression in her thought and develop it.

She suggests that within Western culture, discourses on maternity do
not separate the maternal function from women. Within our traditions,
both women and femininity have been associated with motherhood in
spite of the facts that for much of their lives women cannot bear children,
some women cannot or choose not to bear children, and mothers are also
women apart from their fulfilling the maternal function. Kristeva suggests
that women's oppression can be partially attributed to our discourses on
motherhood and misplaced abjection.

Kristeva describes a phase in which the child must abject its mother in
order to separate from her. Actually, what the child must abject is the
"maternal container." It does not need to abject the mother's body as the
body of a woman. It does not need to abject its mother herself as a person.
Rather, it needs to abject the maternal container upon which it has been
dependent in order to be weaned from the mother. In our culture, however,
since the maternal function is not separated from our representations of
women or the feminine, women themselves have become abjected within
our society. Kristeva begins to develop an alternative discourse of maternity in her essay "Stabat Mater." (1976a) Her analysis of the maternal
function, which permeates all of her work, is in itself a new discourse of
maternity.

I find Kristeva's suggestions extremely useful for thinking about
women's oppression as a partial consequence of the representation of
women's association with reproduction. She does not, however, argue that
we should disassociate women from reproduction. For her reproduction
is not only an important aspect of human survival but also a unique
experience that women can enjoy. She suggests that we need to reconcept-
ualize and rearticulate the relationship between women and reproduction.

Some of Kristeva's critics, however, argue that she proposes a kind of
biological determinism that limits women to their reproductive function. For example, Ann Jones argues that Kristeva refuses to "assign
women any specificity beyond a widely shared position outside the
Symbolic. . . . When Kristeva does define feminine specificity, she turns

out to have a biological specificity in mind: women's role in reproduction." (1984, 62) Jones argues that Kristeva makes motherhood "woman's duty." She does not, however, indicate where she finds any textual support for this extreme claim. Jones concludes that "Kristeva still believes that men create the world of power and representation; women create babies." (1984, 63) And Jones argues that for Kristeva, this male-dominated world of power and representation is "an immovable structure." (1984, 66) She claims that the "Symbolic order is a man's world; it dominates the primary pleasures of the body and the senses, suppresses nonreproductive sexuality and any physical and psychic expenditure not aimed at profit and accumulation. Kristeva, that is, identifies the Symbolic with patriarchy, understood as the totality of culture." (1984, 58).* But Kristeva does not see the social as an immovable structure; in fact, she started her work as a reaction against the rigidity of structuralism. Also, in her best moments, especially in her latest work, Kristeva is careful to distinguish the feminine from woman and both of these notions from maternity. She suggests that the maternal operates as a function that, in principle, can be performed by both men and women. Kristeva wants to take us beyond categories that have traditionally been used to limit us, all of us, both women and men. She wants to conceive of a notion of difference that does not operate according to a dualist logic of opposition. It has become important to Kristeva's argument that both woman and the feminine are not reduced to maternity. She suggests that women's oppression is partially the result of Western culture's reduction of women to reproduction.

For Kristeva, social problems always have their core in representation; and she argues that our representations of maternity are not only detrimental to women but, since the first relation is with the mother, to all human relations. To reconceive of this relation is to reconceive of human

---

*Jones bases this conclusion on a questionable extrapolation from one of Kristeva's "lesser" works, *About Chinese Women*. In fact, most of Jones's claims are not anchored in Kristeva's texts; when they are, they are tortured out of this most questionable and often offensive text, *About Chinese Women*.

There are several problems with Jones's interpretation of Kristeva's theories. First, Kristeva is always concerned with representation. She is not in any way a biological determinist. Even her most famous notion, the semiotic, is always already tied to signification; it is the drives as they are manifest in signification. She does not talk about any experience prior to signification. Her discussion of the maternal is always framed within a discussion of *discourses* on maternity. And she tries to create her own discourse of maternity. She makes this attempt because she believes that we can change the social structure by changing representation. All of her work is an attempt to change representation and thereby change the social. If, as Jones suggests, Kristeva maintains that the social is "an immovable structure," all of her life's work would be nothing more than masochism.

Second, the Symbolic is not the order of man. Kristeva maintains that both men and women can access the semiotic and the Symbolic, although sexual difference as it is constructed in our culture does come to bear on how and how much. Still, Kristeva emphasizes that women are primarily speaking beings. And she encourages women to take up their rightful places within the Symbolic order.

relations. This is why Kristeva suggests that it is necessary for ethics to take mothers into account. She begins to articulate a new ethics, what she calls "herethics," based on a newly conceived relation between mother and child.

Maternity, however, becomes just one model for a new ethics, in which relations to the other are founded on relations to the other within oneself. Throughout Kristeva's writings there are models for a reconceived ethics. This is the explicit topic of her latest theoretical book (as of this writing), *Strangers to Ourselves*. There she maintains that psychoanalysis is also a model for ethics. Psychoanalysis teaches us to embrace the stranger within ourselves; and this, in turn, teaches us to embrace the stranger in society. The ethics of psychoanalysis, says Kristeva, implies a politics, a politics of difference. In her early work she argues that poetic language is another model for ethics, an ethics that includes negativity that challenges any fixed identity in order to prevent totalitarianism of symbolic Law. The ethics of poetic language also implies a politics.

Kristeva is most well known for her theory of revolutionary language. She argues that poetic revolution is analogous to political revolution. She maintains that elements of material rejection and identification that she associates with the maternal "semiotic" make their way into language. For Kristeva, all signification is driven by a dialectic between semiotic drive force and symbolic stases. This dialectic oscillation is productive insofar as it opens the possibility of new types of discourse. The infusion of semiotic elements within signification can actually change the structure of discourse. Kristeva claims that types of language or signifying practices that attend to this semiotic element can be useful in discharging drive force. One effect of this is that violent, aggressive, and antisocial drives can be discharged in a relatively harmless, perhaps even productive, way. Another, more significant effect is that our traditional or dominate discourses and representations can be changed. In *Revolution in Poetic Language* Kristeva compares this revolution in representation to a political revolution. My book, then, can be read as an analysis of the ethical-political implications of Kristeva's writings.

Some of Kristeva's critics, however, are concerned that her work has become less political because of the changing status of the semiotic and symbolic. For example, Paul Smith argues that from *Tales of Love* on, Kristeva abandons her notion of negativity and gives up the dialectic between semiotic and symbolic. (1989) Smith claims that in her later work the semiotic and symbolic show up as a mere dualism in which both parts are static; the semiotic becomes completely coopted and loses its revolutionary force.

Nancy Fraser makes a similar argument. She reads Kristeva's emphasis on the semiotic as a version of essentialism and her emphasis on the symbolic as a version of nominalism. Fraser maintains that with her semiotic/symbolic distinction, Kristeva merely oscillates between essentialism and nominalism. (1990) Fraser contends that since semiotic forces are always coopted by the Symbolic, a revolution cannot take place. She concludes that the oscillation between semiotic and symbolic elements within signification is a nonproductive oscillation. (1990) While I agree that Kristeva's revolution is not a revolution in the sense that the Symbolic is completely abolished, I do not agree that the dialectical oscillation between semiotic and symbolic elements is nonproductive.* For Kristeva, to abolish the Symbolic is to abolish society. Without the Symbolic order, we live with delirium or psychosis. More than this, how could we have any *discourse*, emancipatory or otherwise, without the Symbolic? Part of the confusion in Butler's analysis, and the analysis of several of Kristeva's feminist critics, can be traced to a confusion between the Symbolic and symbolic and Kristeva's inconsistent use of the distinction. She makes a distinction between *le symbolique* or *symbolique* and *l'ordre symbolique* or *la dimension symbolique*. The regular use of articles, however, in French makes it difficult to tell, apart from context, when *le symbolique* refers to the Symbolic order or symbolic elements within the Symbolic order. In many cases where the English translation would be simply "symbolic," the French reads *le symbolique*.

Part of the problem with Kristeva's symbolic is that although it is read as something equivalent to Lacan's Symbolic, it is not always. Whereas

---

*Judith Butler presents a similar argument against the revolutionary power of Kristeva's maternal semiotic. Butler argues that Kristeva "safeguards the notion of culture as a paternal structure and delimits maternity as essentially precultural reality." (1990, 80) She maintains that for Kristeva it is this precultural maternal realm that provides subversive force, and the source of this subversion is outside of culture; so any possibility of subversion is foreclosed. Butler claims that "a full-scale refusal of the Symbolic is impossible, and a discourse of 'emancipation,' for Kristeva, is out of the question." (1990, 86) Kristeva is not "in favor of a proliferating field of cultural possibilities," concludes Butler, because "she prescribes a return to a principle of maternal heterogeneity which proves to be a closed concept. . . ." (1990, 90)

First, Kristeva does not delimit maternity as an essentially precultural reality. In fact, Kristeva argues that maternity calls into question the boundary between culture and nature. She chooses maternity as a prototype precisely because it breaks down borders between culture and nature and subject and other. Elizabeth Grosz has a similar problem with Kristeva's notion of maternity. She argues that for Kristeva maternity is subjectless. (1990, 161–62) Once again this misses the point of Kristeva's analysis of maternity. Kristeva uses maternity as an example of an experience that calls into question any notion of a unified subject. Maternity becomes a prime example of what she calls a "subject-in-process." In addition, maternity calls into question the border between subject and other; the maternal body encloses an other. With maternity it is impossible to distinguish between subject and object without engaging in an arbitrary categorization. Kristeva analyzes maternity in order to suggest that all distinctions between subject and objects, all identifications of unified subjects, are arbitrary.

Next, I wonder why Butler wants a "full-scale refusal of the Symbolic." What does Butler mean by "Symbolic" here? Does Butler want to do away with culture altogether? Is she proposing that we can refuse language, even sociality itself? What else could it mean to refuse the "Symbolic"?

Lacan uses the Symbolic to refer to the Symbolic order, Kristeva uses the symbolic in two senses to refer not only to the Symbolic order but also to a specifically symbolic element within the Symbolic order that she opposes to the semiotic element. The Symbolic order is the order of signification, the social realm. This realm is composed of both semiotic and symbolic elements. So the semiotic is not strictly opposed to the Symbolic. Rather, the semiotic is part of the Symbolic. Which is not to say that it is confined within the Symbolic—although certainly we cannot talk about it except within the Symbolic order, because we cannot talk about anything outside of the Symbolic order. The semiotic moves both inside and beyond the Symbolic. The semiotic, however, does not move within the symbolic. Within signification, the symbolic is heterogeneous to the semiotic. The symbolic is the element within the Symbolic against which the semiotic works to produce the dialectical tension that keeps society going. I have tried to indicate the distinction by using upper case when I mean the Symbolic order and lower case when I mean the symbolic element.

Although confusing, the distinction between Symbolic and symbolic is important to understanding Kristeva's theory of revolutionary language. The symbolic is the element of signification that structures the possibility of taking a position or making a judgment. It is the element of stasis within the Symbolic, whereas the semiotic is the element of rejection. Both of these elements are crucial to signification. Without either of them there could be no signification. For Kristeva, signification, the Symbolic order, is always heterogeneous. This is why revolutions within Symbolic order are possible. The Symbolic order is not just the order of Law. Rather, for Kristeva, it is also the order of resistance to Law. Kristeva tries to analyze how change, even revolution, can take place within representation while acknowledging that all is representation. For Kristeva the operation of the semiotic within signification opens up the possibility of explaining cultural change. The operation of the semiotic within signification continually proliferates cultural possibilities.

Like any analogy, however, Kristeva's analogy between poetic revolution and political revolution breaks down at the point where we think of political revolution as a complete overthrow of the status quo. On the other hand, no political revolution is successful in *completely* abolishing the status quo. And it is doubtful that we would want it to be. Human life and human love are parts of the status quo along with death, destruction, and torture. So while Kristeva's revolution is not a complete and final upheaval, it does make a difference. I suggest that Kristeva describes something more akin to political reform than political upheaval.

More problematic than the coopting dialectical oscillation between semiotic and symbolic elements within signification is Kristeva's aestheticization of poetic revolution in *Powers of Horror*. Whereas in her earlier work Kristeva describes the revolution in poetic language as a political revolution, in *Powers of Horror* it becomes a purely aesthetic revolution. While there may be a relation between aesthetic experience and political revolution, Kristeva does not makes that relation explicit in her text. At some points in *Powers of Horror* the semiotic element seems to provoke a purely aesthetic response and politics is reduced to beauty. Keeping with her own dialectical oscillation, however, in her later work she moves away from the position of *Powers of Horror* and reasserts the importance of symbolic elements as a counterbalance to pure semiotic horror.

John Lechte argues that Kristeva's apparent move from privileging the semiotic in her earlier writings to privileging the symbolic in her later writings is the result of her concern to provide a counterbalance against a culture out of balance. Lechte claims that when discourse is denying the semiotic, Kristeva emphasizes it; and when discourse is denying the symbolic, she emphasizes that. (1990, 39) While this could be true, there is another way to read Kristeva's oscillation.

Kristeva's own oscillation on the priority of the semiotic or the symbolic can be read as a mirror of the dialectical oscillation between semiotic and symbolic that she describes. Neither the semiotic nor the symbolic is original. Each is dependent on the other. Neither completely destroys the other. Kristeva's writings can themselves be read as an oscillation between the semiotic and symbolic, between rejection and identification. For example, in *Revolution in Poetic Language* and *Powers of Horror* she emphasizes rejection and the semiotic. In *Tales of Love* and *Black Sun* she emphasizes identification and the symbolic. In *Strangers to Ourselves* and *Lettre ouverte à Harlem Désir* (1990) she emphasizes the ways in which one is always implicated in the other. Kristeva maintains that *Powers of Horror* and *Tales of Love*, for example, should be read together in order to get an overview of two sides of love, negation and identification. (1984b)

My book can be read as an account of the oscillation between the semiotic and symbolic forces in Kristeva's writing itself. Once again the problem is traversing the fine line between complete anarchy and totalitarianism; the problem is unraveling a theoretical double-bind that forces one or the other extreme. A complete overthrow of the Symbolic would be anarchy. It would be the abolition of human life. On the other hand, a complete repression of the semiotic leads to the tyranny of Symbolic law. Kristeva wants to avoid both of these extremes. This is why she proposes a dialectic oscillation between transgression and Law that can lead to changes in the socioeconomic structure. By changing the representation through which we live, Kristeva suggests that our lives can change. With any strategy, however, the consequences can never be completely predicted in advance.

What is at stake in reading Kristeva's dialectical oscillation between semiotic and symbolic elements within signification, her analysis of the maternal function, and her double-strategy with regard to the speaking body is a reconception of the relationship between identity and difference. All of Kristeva's writing is concerned with various stages of identity and difference. She insists on diagnosing the difference at the heart of identity and the stases operating within difference. The logic of identity and difference is the logic of subject and other. Alterity, otherness, and the stranger are always at the center of her texts. So my book can also be read as the story of Kristeva's difference.

Why are certain characteristics or persons excluded from society? How do these strangers come to be? Why are some characteristics or persons honored in society? How do these strangers become familiar? How can strangers live with each other without the threat of annihilation? How is ethics possible? These questions underline Kristeva's texts. She says that she concentrates on discourses that break identity. She is concerned with the limits of identity, the limits of discourse, the limits of the social. The limits interest her because at the limit, subjects enter the social or they are excluded as other.

In order to open up the possibility of redrawing the boundaries of the social, Kristeva constructs models of discourse that admit, even embrace, the alterity within them. Her primary models are poetry, maternity, and psychoanalysis. Poetic language discharges semiotic elements, negativity, alterity, into the Symbolic. In poetic language, identity is infused with alterity without completely breaking down. Maternity is a material model of alterity within identity. Once again identity is infused with alterity without completely breaking down. And psychoanalysis is the theory and practice of alterity within identity. Psychoanalysis taps the unconscious other scene that operates within every apparently unified subject.

It is important that alterity or difference can exist without being repressed or annihilated and at the same time without completely breaking down identity. Without identity we have no Symbolic order. Without the Symbolic order, we have no society, no human life, no love. We have only psychosis, delirium, or anarchy. This is why Kristeva is concerned to develop a theory of identity and difference that negotiates between the extremes, totalitarianism and tyranny or anarchy and chaos. She is concerned to develop a theory of difference that unravels the theoretical double-bind. In order to think about ethical and political theory, we have to be able to think about the relationship between identity—individual, group, and national—and difference. We need to formulate a theory of difference that accounts for oppression, marginalization, and exclusion in order to theorize how to reformulate difference so that it does not lead to oppression, marginalization, and exclusion.

In *Strangers to Ourselves* Kristeva reformulates traditional theories of foreignness in order to reformulate the notions of difference and otherness. She does this so that we might imagine a way of living with the foreigner while acknowledging her difference. For Kristeva, this is the ethical-political struggle of all people, especially oppressed peoples. Oppressed peoples want their individuality and difference recognized and respected without that recognition becoming the basis for exclusion and discrimination. The reformulation of the notion of otherness or foreigner also necessitates a reformulation of sameness or the citizen. The very distinction between citizen and foreigner or subject and other is called into question. Both the subject and the other must be reformulated.

My book can be read as the story of that reformulated subject, Kristeva's subject-in-process/on trial. Kristeva's claim that alterity is within the subject undermines any notion of a unified subject. Once again she identifies three discourses within which we find the alterity within identity, discourses that put the subject-in-process/on trial. The discourse of psychoanalysis postulates the fundamentally split subject, both conscious and unconscious, a subject-in-process/on trial. Her notion of the subject-in-process, however, challenges Lacanian psychoanalysis, with its emphasis on the mirror stage and the Name of the Father as the initiation into subjectivity. For her, subjectivity is a process that begins with the material body before the mirror stage. It is a process that has its beginnings in the maternal function rather than the paternal function. The maternal body itself is a primary model of the subject-in-process; its unity is called into question by the other within, an other-in-process. In addition to the discourses of psychoanalysis and maternity, poetic language is another discourse that calls the subject into crisis, puts the subject on trial. Undeniable within poetic language, the semiotic element disrupts the unity of the Symbolic and thereby disrupts the unity of the subject of/in language.

Kristeva looks to the borders of subjectivity in order to demonstrate that we are all subjects-in-process. Like avant-garde poets, pregnant Madonnas, analysands undergoing analysis, we are all foreigners, "extraterrestrials," subjects-in-process. (See Ziarek 1992.) We must learn to live within the flexible, always precarious borders of our subjectivity in order to learn to live within the flexible, always precarious borders of human society. We must unravel the double-bind between completely inhabiting the Symbolic—and thereby taking up a rigid unified subject position—and refusing the Symbolic—and thereby inhabiting psychosis. This is what I see as Kristeva's project. This is what I take on as my project. I tell the story of a Kristeva sensitive to borders, a Kristeva who refuses to be confined unless it is acknowledged that her confines are always only temporary. I tell the story of an extraterrestrial mourning the loss of maternal love.

All of the stories woven throughout my text are motivated by a concern for feminist theory. All of these stories can inform feminist theory. Kristeva's double strategy for bringing the speaking body back into structuralism provides a way to conceive of saying something new within a language and culture that are inherited from patriarchal forefathers. The story of Kristeva's challenge to traditional psychoanalytic theory exposes an emphasis on the paternal function as a masculinist fantasy that drastically underdetermines the maternal function. Her model discourses—poetry, maternity, psychoanalysis—for a reconceived ethics that operates according to a love of difference rather than the regulation and exclusion of difference provides the possibility of an ethics of difference, a feminist ethics. In addition, Kristeva's politics of difference can sensitize feminists to the importance of conceiving of difference as a process of continually challenging identity. The relationship between identity and negation is crucial to feminist theory. Kristeva's continual concern with negotiating between identity and negation in order to avoid both the totalitarianism of absolute identity and the delirium of complete negation is central to feminism. And her notion of a subject-in-process/on trial is implicated in some of the major issues in contemporary feminist debates over identity politics. The subject-in-process/on trial is an identity-in-process/on trial. Kristeva proposes a way to conceive of a productive but always only provisional identity, an identity whose constant companions are alterity, negation, and difference.

By providing various interpretations of the story that I tell about Kristeva, I hope to multiply interpretations and open up the possibility of difference within my own text. I call attention to an interpretation-in-process/on trial. I do so, however, from within the Symbolic. I do not write avant-garde poetry. Rather, I attempt to elaborate the crises and condensations in Kristeva's writings. To this end, I employ several different interpretation strategies. In addition to an introduction to Kristeva's theories, and criticisms of those theories, I read some of those theories "against the grain" in order to provide recuperative readings for feminist ends.

Although I do not explicitly trace the historical development of Kristeva's writings, it is important to keep in mind the evolution of her thought. Alice Jardine argues that there are three Kristevas: the Kristeva of the '60s, who develops the new science semanalysis; the Kristeva of the '70s, who tries to describe a subject that has been repressed in Western history within the limits of totalitarianism and delirium; and the Kristeva of the '80s, who explores the deep logics of psychic phenomenon. (Jardine 1986) There seems to be a fourth Kristeva developing, the Kristeva of the '90s. While the Kristeva of the '70s was concerned with the relation between politics and literature, the Kristeva of the '80s turned away from politics altogether. Now the Kristeva of the '90s turns back to politics, this time through psychoanalysis and fiction. In her latest work Kristeva analyzes the psychic structures of social ostracism; she suggests a new ethics and politics that grow out of psychoanalysis.

I very loosely follow a chronology of Kristeva's writings, starting with her writing from the '60s and '70s in the first chapter, moving to her writings from the '80s in the second and third chapters, and concluding with some of her most recent theoretical writings from the early '90s. Still, I move back and forth through her texts, developing patterns rather than chronologies. Unlike many of Kristeva's critics, I focus on her most psychoanalytic texts from the '80s and early '90s.

Most simply, the first part of my book can be read as a refigured oedipal triangle. Kristeva's prefigured oedipal situation operates between the child (the narcissistic subject), the abject mother (the mother's body), and the imaginary father (the mother's love). (1983, 374) These terms correspond to what I call the mother's breast (maternal body), the mother's sex (birth), and the mother's womb (conception). In my reading, Kristeva sets up the prefigured oedipal structure within the maternal function. Although these terms operate prior to the oedipal complex and, in one sense, prior to the onset of the Symbolic, their functions prefigure those of the three terms in the traditional oedipal situation.

In the first chapter I develop Kristeva's argument that the logic of negation, which is a prerequisite for subjectivity, is already operating within the body through material rejection prior to Lacan's mirror stage. I situate Kristeva's theory of the subject in relation to Lacan's theory of the mirror stage and castration. Here I analyze her maternal function as a regulator prior to any paternal prohibition. I describe maternal regulation as the child's relation to the mother's breast.

In the second chapter I continue to develop Kristeva's claim that the logic of negation is already operating in the body before it is taken over by the Symbolic. I most explicitly describe the maternal function and its relation to sexual difference, and the maternal semiotic *chora*, which has become extremely controversial in feminist criticism. The maternal body itself is full of alterity and negation. And the prototype for symbolic negation is the experience of birth. I describe the child's abject relation to its mother as a relation to its own birth.

In the third chapter I develop a reading of Kristeva's imaginary father in order to recuperate this concept for feminist theory. I argue that if we read the condensations and displacements in Kristeva's own texts, the imaginary father can be read as a screen for the mother's love. Here I relate her notion of the imaginary father to the maternal function. With the notion of the imaginary father, Kristeva proposes that both negation and identification are prefigured within the maternal function. I argue that her fantasy of the imaginary father is the infant's fantasy of a primary identification with its own conception. The loving imaginary father is the love through which the child imagines that it was conceived.

In the last half of the book, I sort through the implications of Kristeva's theories in order to delineate useful elements from possibly detrimental elements for feminist theory. Overall I think that her project is useful for feminist theory in spite of her specific analysis and methods, some of which are questionable if not offensive. In the last three chapters I diagnose the politics of Kristeva's theories of language, psychoanalysis, and her theory of politics itself.

In chapter 4 I analyze Kristeva's claim that revolution in language is analogous to political revolution. I conclude that although the dialectic between semiotic and symbolic elements within signification does not give rise to a revolution, it can explain how change takes place within language. My focus is Kristeva's account of the relationship between women and language and her suggestion that women are in a double-bind in relation to the Symbolic. I delineate those places where Kristeva herself becomes trapped in the double-bind and those places where she teaches us how to unravel it.

Chapter 5 is a diagnosis of the psychoanalysis of love that Kristeva begins to develop in *Tales of Love* and continues in *Black Sun*. I explain why she privileges analytic discourse. I criticize her use of Christian imagery when she is describing analytic discourse. And I attempt to turn Kristeva's theories back onto her own writings and analyze the analyst. Here I argue that she is a melancholy theorist longing for her lost mother-tongue.

In the sixth chapter I take up Kristeva's relation to political theory, especially feminism. I examine her turn away from politics in 1974 after her return from China and her return to political theory in 1989 with the publication of *Strangers to Ourselves*. In spite of her dismissal of feminism, Kristeva's construction of the ethics and politics of psychoanalysis can be useful for feminist theory.

In the last chapter I analyze the importation of Kristeva's writings, along with Cixous's and Irigaray's, to the United States. Since the late '70s when the writings of Kristeva, Cixous, and Irigaray were first being translated into English and published in America, these three theorists have been grouped together in what Toril Moi calls the "Holy Trinity" of French feminist theory. Once I began this book on Kristeva, I was repeatedly asked to compare Kristeva's positions to Cixous's and Irigaray's. Although I don't want to perpetuate the "Holy Trinity," I think that it is important to analyze the context in which Kristeva texts are read in America. In my last chapter I problematize the monolith "The French Feminists." I point out that none of them are French born and none of them have an unqualified relation to feminism. I articulate some of the differences between Cixous, Irigaray, and Kristeva's notions of desire.

I conclude by developing the implications of Kristeva's theories for a new ethics, an outlaw ethics. Kristeva suggests various models for a new ethics that is not merely an ethics regulated by law. Her notion of a subject-in-process necessitates a new ethics that is based on negativity rather than on identity. She brings the death drive back into ethics so that there might be fewer deaths. I conclude that her outlaw ethics can provide the beginnings of a feminist ethics.

My aim in this project is threefold. With a sustained analysis of Kristeva's writings taken as a whole, I hope to introduce those writings to a larger audience, especially feminists working in America. More than that, I read Kristeva with a feminist eye in order to diagnosis the usefulness of her theories for feminism. The most interesting parts of my analysis are those in which I present a recuperative reading, against the grain, of Kristeva's writings in order to make them more useful for feminism. This book is intended for both those who have read very little of Kristeva's writings and those who devote their research energy to them. I hope that this project will inspire both those who have turned away from Kristeva's writings—either because they are so difficult or because they seem anti-feminist—and those immersed in them to go back and reread those writings.

I

THE PRODIGAL CHILD

*What thou hast inherited from thy fathers,
acquire it to make it thine.*

Goethe, Faust, Part I, Scene 1[1]

Kristeva's work has been a journey through the Lacanian mirror, going behind/beyond it by virtue of its *mis en abîme* to a place where we confront the maternal body. Her writings trace the child's relationship to the outside of the maternal body through the mother's sex back inside the maternal body, the womb out of which the child was born. By examining Kristeva's theory of negativity in *Revolution in Poetic Language* and other writings from the 1970s, I analyze her account of the child's relationship to the surface of the maternal body, particularly the breast, as the mother regulates that relationship.

For Kristeva, like Lacan, what is at issue is the birth of desire, or the transition from need to desire. She is concerned with how the autoerotic body gives way to the speaking subject. At the level of desire, Kristeva agrees with Lacan's theories of the mirror stage, castration, the oedipal situation, and sexual difference. But she argues that Lacan discounts the semiotic drive force operating prior to the mirror stage and the oedipal situation. She claims that there is evidence that the logic of signification, the logic that organizes the mirror stage and the oedipal situation, is already operating within the material bodies of children prior to what Lacan identifies as the onset of the subject. Also, there is evidence of semiotic drive force on the surface of children's early language use. Semiotic drive force makes its way into language. It is not completely cut off or repressed after the mirror stage and the oedipal situation. Rather, what she calls the thetic break into the Symbolic is set up by material rejection that continues to operate within signification.

Kristeva argues that the negativity necessary in order to initiate human subjectivity is operating at the level of material negativity. As she describes it, eventually bodily excess gives way to a thetic break into the

Symbolic. Bodily patterns are taken over within the Symbolic. Bodily rejection can become symbolic rejection because maternal regulation organizes the psyche before the mirror stage and the oedipal situation. Maternal regulation prefigures the paternal prohibition that finally launches the subject into signification through the oedipal situation. All of this is to say that for Kristeva bodily drive force already includes the logic and prohibition of the Symbolic and that bodily drive force is never completely repressed within signification. Subjectivity is always in process both before and after Lacan's mirror stage and the oedipal situation.

Behind the Mirror Stage

In her essay "Place Names," Kristeva criticizes "a psychoanalytic practice that posits the subject as dating from the 'mirror stage'" because it minimizes the "function of the familial context in the *precocious* development of the child (before puberty, before Oedipus, but also before the 'mirror stage')." (1977a, 276) She maintains that subjectivity is a process that neither begins nor ends with the mirror stage; it is operative in the material body prior to the mirror stage. There are social relations prior to the mirror stage and language acquisition. These relations are not the specular relation of the mirror stage but relations of *transference* that she claims can be detected in the nonspeaking child before language acquisition and the onset of the oedipal complex (1977a, 277), but she doesn't elaborate on this preoedipal transference relationship until her later work on identification and love.[2]

In her earlier work, Kristeva is more concerned with negativity than identity. The negativity that is an essential component of the onset of the subject in Lacan's mirror stage is already moving through what she calls the "semiotic" body which is driven by unnameable drives. Kristeva complains that Lacan's all-encompassing Name of the Father removes these unnameable drives from childhood and places them in what he calls the "impossible real." (1977a, 276–77) She claims that her research demonstrates that the unnameable drives are part of childhood; they show up in several aspects of preoedipal childhood experience. Unnameable drives are not impossible. Rather, they are "real" in a way that ruptures the Symbolic. (1971, 113) Kristeva insists that human experience begins before what Lacan identifies as the Symbolic.[3]

Lacan's Mirror

For Lacan the subject enters the Symbolic through the mirror stage and castration. It is the "mirror stage" that first constitutes the child as a separate subject. (1977, 1–7; 1955, 166; 1954, 73–88) Prior to the mirror

stage, in what Lacan calls the "imaginary" phase, the child has only fragmented experiences and no unified sense of itself. In the mirror stage the
child held in front of a mirror by an adult recognizes its image in the
mirror. At first it confuses the image with reality. After some experimenta-
tion, it realizes that the image reflected is its own image and not just the
adult's. Finally, it realizes that the mirror image is not real.

The mirror stage is the first recognition of the "I." Prior to the mirror
stage the child does not conceive of itself as a unified whole. Rather,
before the mirror stage, it "conceives" of "itself" as fragmented movements. Even in the mirror stage the child sees a unified body reflected in
the mirror, but it still experiences its own body as fragmented. What is
paradoxical in the mirror stage is that the realization that the child is
unified comes through its *doubling* in the mirror. In a sense, it must
become two (itself plus its reflection) in order to become one (a unified
self); hence, Lacan's "split subject."

For Lacan the mirror stage points to the importance of the Symbolic in
the subject's construction. The origin of the subject's construction in the
mirror stage is dependent on a *representation* of the body. Here the symbol, through the image, of the body is the foundation for a realization
about the body. A symbol stands in for the real body. This substitution of
the symbolic for the real body prefigures all subsequent development.
(Lacan 1977, 5) The mirror stage prepares the child for its entry into the
Symbolic, into language.

In a particularly fascinating seminar, Lacan describes the relationship
between the Symbolic and the Imaginary as a relationship between time
and space. Lacan's description of the relation between time and space
speaks to the exemplary relationship between the Symbolic and the
Imaginary in the mirror stage. In the imaginary phase the child experiences its body as fragmented. There is, however, an imaginary spatial
unity that is sustained by the subsequent symbolic temporal unity. In the
Imaginary order, unity is based on spatial perceptions. But it is the name,
the symbol, that provides unity over time. Lacan says that "the name is
the time of the object." (1955, 169) Without the name, unity is fragmented
and cannot be sustained. This is also why it is the Symbolic order that
establishes the unity of the subject, "I." In spite of the fact that this "I" is
always established as a split and the entrance into the Symbolic is always
founded on a lack, there is the appearance of unity. "Naming," says Lacan,
"constitutes a pact, by which two objects simultaneously come to an
agreement to recognize the same object. [I]f. . . subjects do not come to
an agreement over this recognition, no world, not even a perception, could
be sustained for more than one instant." Lacan concludes that this agreement is the joint between the Imaginary and the Symbolic. (1955, 169–
70) The Imaginary provides a momentary spatial unity that gives rise to
a temporal unity with the Symbolic, which in turn supports it.

For Lacan, the entry into the Symbolic—started with the interplay between Imaginary and Symbolic in the mirror stage—is completed through castration in the oedipal situation. The transition from what Lacan calls the child's imaginary relationship with its mother to the child's separation from its mother is performed through the oedipal situation. The oedipal situation brings in a third term, the father, that both bridges the alienation from its mother that the child feels after the mirror stage and reinforces a permanent separation from her. The intervention of the father forces the dissolution of the imaginary unity with, and gratification from, the mother; yet it provides a medium, language, through which the child can maintain some contact with the estranged mother.

Anika Lemaire, in her treatise on Lacan, describes three stages of the oedipal situation. (Lemaire 1977, 82–83) First, the child desires its mother's desire. Next, the child fears castration and limits its desire. Finally, the child, at least the male, identifies with the father. In the first phase, the child wants the mother's desire.[4] Lacan says that the child wants *to be* the mother's Phallus: "the child, in his relation to the mother, . . . by his dependence on her love, that is to say, by the desire for her desire, identifies himself with the imaginary object of this desire insofar as the mother herself symbolizes it in the Phallus." (1977, 198)

It is crucial to note that for Lacan, unlike Freud, the Phallus is not an organ; it is not the penis. As he says, "it has no relation to the little thingummy that Freud talks about." (1982, 168) Rather, it is a signifier which signifies gratification. (Lacan 1982, 79) The child wants to be *the* object of its mother's desire, the Phallus. If "Phallus" signifies "gratification," then the child wants *to be* the mother's gratification. It wants to be its mother's everything. (Lacan 1982, 83) The Phallus is the object of the mother's desire because she too has gone through the oedipal situation and because the Phallus symbolizes gratification. (1977, 207) If we think in terms of Freud's description of the oedipal situation, the mother's own oedipal complex ends in penis envy. She substitutes a desire for a baby for her desire for the penis. Now the child wants to satisfy its mother's desire by being that penis, or, in Lacan's terminology, the Phallus that represents it. Ultimately, for Lacan all desire is the desire for the Phallus. It is desire for the satisfaction of desire, gratification. The child learns that the Phallus is imaginary, that its desire to be its mother's desire cannot be satisfied. So it substitutes the Law of the Father for the desire of the mother. It substitutes a symbolic Phallus for the imaginary Phallus.

It is this transition that Lemaire identifies with what she calls the "second phase" of the oedipal situation. In the second phase, the father intervenes and prevents the child from actualizing its desire. The child cannot be everything to the mother because the mother wants something other than the child. This something, of course, is the Phallus, gratification. And the father becomes a concrete representation of the Phallus in the oedipal situation. Because the child realizes that the mother also wants the father, it realizes that it cannot be her everything. This realization is partially based in the child's intuition that in order for it to have been conceived, the mother must have desired the father at some time (even if the father is not around). For Lacan, the father is an effect of a signifier and this is how the father operates in the oedipal situation:

> For, if the symbolic context requires it, paternity will nonetheless be attrib-
> uted to the fact that the woman met a spirit at some fountain or some rock
> in which he is supposed to live.
>   It is certainly this that demonstrates that the attribution of procreation
> to the father can only be the effect of a pure signifier, of a recognition, not
> of a real father, but of what religion had taught us to refer to as the Name-
> of-the-Father. (1977, 199)

The Name of the Father is what keeps the child from the mother. The name, the symbol, breaks the unmediated dyad between mother and child. Lacan suggests that the rupture of this dyad is necessary so that society can continue; this intimate bond in which two are one is antisocial. The father intervenes, in the place of the Phallus, to break it up. This func- tion—another central element of Lacan's "paternal metaphor"—is the Law of the Father. The Law of the Father must be abided so that the child can be initiated into society through its entry into the Symbolic and ultimately language. The imaginary relation to the mother is against the law; it is unmediated. And without mediation, substitution, exchange, there is no society. This is why the child must substitute the Law of the Father for the desire of the mother. This is also why the psychotic, who forecloses the Law of the Father, is an outlaw.

The mirror stage is a major step toward repressing the primary mother- child symbiosis. Following Lacan, Kristeva maintains that the mirror stage is essential to break up the mother-child dyad. While prior to the mirror stage the "music" produced in the mother-child symbiosis is what Kris- teva calls the "voiced breath" that fastens the child to an undifferentiated maternal body, after the mirror stage the child begins to distinguish its sounds from its mother's. The "voiced breath" becomes maternal lan- guage, an object for the child. (1974b, 195) Here the child realizes that it is a separate being.

At this stage the child attempts a symbolic satisfaction by substituting a socially acceptable desire for its antisocial, incestuous desire for its mother or its mother's desire. It does so because once it sees that it is separate, it is already too late for satisfaction. More importantly, it fears a complete lack of satisfaction. In other words, it settles for the symbol out of fear that it will be cut off from satisfaction altogether. This is what Lacan calls castration; in his metaphor, castration is when the Phallus is cut off, or when complete gratification is cut off. The threat of castration, then, is the threat of no gratification. Here, says Lacan, the child must settle for *having* the Phallus rather than *being* the Phallus and having versus being the Phallus is the core of sexual difference; I defer a discussion of sexual difference until later in this chapter.

In terms of the metaphor of castration, the child must settle for having the signifier rather than being the signifier. Founded on a lack and always inadequately, the child fills the gap between its previous imaginary gratification from its mother and its new separation from her with words. The child can now name itself in relation to others. It becomes, through language, a subject proper. It is through the symbol that the ego is erected. The subject imagines through the illusion of symbols that it has a unified ego, which is an actor, through which it can control its body. This is how the child appears to overcome its frustration in the mirror stage that it is not really the master over its image in the mirror.

Like Lacan, in *Revolution in Poetic Language* Kristeva maintains that the mirror stage and castration are the two points around which the subject's signification is organized. (1974, 46) The mirror stage presents the subject with an image, which, separate from itself, becomes the object, the other.[5] The construction of the Other is completed by castration. "Castration," says Kristeva, "puts the finishing touches on the process of separation that posits the subject as signifiable, which is to say separate, always confronted by an other." (1974, 47) The Other in the mirror stage is more or less "innocently" separate from the subject, while the Other that results from castration is not merely separate, but the object of desire. That is why it is castration that forces signification: the subject is painfully separated from the object of its desire and must search for "stand-ins," alternative satisfactions. Kristeva's description of the "phallic mother" illuminates this process. The mother's body is the source of all gratification:

> As the addressee of every demand, the mother occupies the place of alternity. Her replete body, the receptacle and guarantor of demands, takes the place of all narcissistic, hence imaginary, effects and gratifications. . . . [S]he is, in other words, the Phallus. (1974, 47)

For Kristeva, following Lacan, the Phallus represents gratification. (1979a, 41) And the position of the subject is determined by its relation to the Phallus. Kristeva, however, de-emphasizes sexual difference that for Lacan is determined by one's relation to the Phallus.[6] Although she addresses sexual difference in passing in most of her texts, it is not until *Black Sun* that she presents any substantial account of feminine sexuality. Until then she ignores feminine sexuality and assumes that the subject of psychoanalysis is male. Although Kristeva takes her lead in this assumption from both Freud and Lacan, she seems less troubled by sexual differ-

ence than either of them. Freud and Lacan, if they are useful to feminist
theory, have been useful by virtue of their struggles with sexual difference.
Kristeva prefers to address difference in general rather than focusing on
sexual difference. But her disregard for feminine sexuality makes her early
work skewed when it comes to the crucial issue of sexual difference. I
return to her account of sexual difference in the next chapter.

Kristeva's lack of attention to sexual difference can be recuperated
somewhat when she is concerned with the child's development prior to
the oedipal situation and therefore prior to sexual difference. In fact, she
turns some of Lacan's analysis of the oedipal situation, starting with the
mirror stage and castration, into preoedipal moments.[7] In these moments,
for Kristeva, sexual difference does not yet come into play. Kristeva argues
that for both males and females the mother, insofar as she represents/is
gratification, is the Phallus. For both males and females separation from
the mother is castration. Castration is a lack and the symbolic function is
always the result of lack, although for Kristeva it is never the result of a
lack only. She says that the gap between the mother and the demand put
on her is "precisely the break that establishes what Lacan calls the place
of the Other as the place of the 'signifier.'" (1974, 48) Castration, then,
adds the necessary feeling of lack to the mirror stage that insures the
symbolic function. Through castration the "dependence on the mother is
severed, and transformed into a symbolic relation to an other." (174, 48)

Still, in *Revolution in Poetic Language* Kristeva argues that the subject
must be "firmly posited by castration" in order to insure that the preoedipal drives are properly translated into language rather than becoming
psychoses. (1974, 50) "The analytic situation," claims Kristeva, "shows
that it is the penis which, becoming the major referent in this operation
of separation, gives full meaning to the lack or to the desire which constitutes the subject during his or her insertion into the order of language."
(1979a, 41) She recognizes the penis as the "major referent" of the Phallus.
She does not seem sensitive to the feminist concern that Lacan's penis/
Phallus distinction might collapse and leave us with a biological determinism reminiscent of Freud.

For Freud the turning point that initiates sexual difference is the sight
of the genitals of the "opposite sex." Freud claims that in addition to
other sorts of sexual excitement, infants of both sexes masturbate. Usually
children are reprimanded for masturbation; in the case of males, they are
threatened with penile castration. The threat always becomes associated
with the father. "If you don't stop touching it, your father will cut it off."
But until the male child sees the genitals of a female, he doesn't believe
the threat. When he first sees the female genitals he believes that they
have suffered the threatened castration. The boy sees the lack in the girl/
woman and imagines that she has been castrated. Now he is afraid that
he will be castrated. The combination of the castration threat and the sight

of the female genitals enforces the prohibition against masturbation for males.

It is important that the castration threat is associated with the father. In addition to the mother's and caretaker's attributions of punishment to the father, the child has another, more fundamental reason for associating the punishment with his father. For Freud, the male child's masturbatory pleasure is related to his incestuous desires for his mother. The boy "begins to manipulate his penis and simultaneously has fantasies of carrying out some sort of activity with it in relation to his mother." (1938, 155) The child, then, associates the castration threat with his incestuous desires. He sees the punishment for masturbation as a punishment levied by his father against his incestuous desire for his mother.

Insofar as the primary love object for both sexes is the mother's breast, the male comes under the influence of the oedipal complex early on. It is the castration complex that forces the resolution of the oedipal situation in the male. The boy sees castration as the punishment levied by his father for his incestuous desire for his mother. Out of castration fear, he represses his incestuous desire and gives up his masturbatory pleasure.

Prior to the castration complex, the boy originally perceived no distinction between himself and his mother: they were identical. Eventually, he identified his mother's breast as the object of his love. Subsequently, he identified his mother as his lover and his father as his rival. After the castration threat, the boy can no longer take his mother as his lover. Now he is forced to identify with his mother insofar as his passivity (no active masturbating) is encouraged. For Freud, in our culture, passivity is associated with the feminine; therefore, the boy's passivity identifies him with his mother's passivity. (1938, 189) In addition, the boy has a new dependence on his mother. Now he depends on his mother's love so that she doesn't tell his father about his masturbation (and thereby his incestuous fantasies) and subject him to the risk of castration by his father. (1938, 189) Although the boy realizes that he is no match for his father, he still harbors hostility toward him. At this point, the boy has only his fantasies, in which he now identifies with both the mother and the father in a new way.

The infant must satisfy himself that although he cannot have his mother now, when he grows up, he will take his father's place and consummate his desire with a mother-substitute. This motivates the boy's identification with his father. He can have a delayed gratification by identifying with his father. Freud cites this dynamic as an example of the reality principle overriding the pleasure principle. The boy realizes that the two primary reasons why reality prevents him from satisfying his incestuous desire are, first, that his father won't allow it because his father is stronger than him, and, second, that his penis is inadequate compared to his father's and it cannot satisfy his mother. Because reality demands it, the boy must be satisfied to wait until his penis works like his father's and he can find a mother-substitute. The infant's sexual desires remain latent until puberty when they can resurface with a more "appropriate" (socially acceptable) love object, a mother-substitute.

For Freud, the girl has a much larger task in the oedipal situation. She has to change both her love object and the site of her genital pleasure. Since the girl, like the boy, has her mother as her first love object, the oedipal complex does not begin right away for girls. Rather, it is the castration complex that gives rise to the oedipal complex in girls. Just as for the boy, the sight of the genitals of the opposite sex is important for the onset of the castration complex in the girl. The girl sees the boy's penis and feels wronged by her lack and wants one too. So the girl feels envy for the penis rather than a fear of losing the penis. (For Freud, she has already lost it.) Freud suggests that early masturbation becomes the girls unsatisfying attempt to be a boy and have his pleasure. But she is doomed to failure and gives up masturbation.[8] (1938, 193)

Freud argues that the girl blames her mother for her lack of a penis. Her love was directed toward her phallic mother, but after the discovery that her mother, too, does not have a Phallus, the girl becomes hostile toward her mother. She feels cheated by her mother both because she doesn't have a penis and because her mother doesn't have one. This hostility toward her mother motivates the girl to direct her love to her father. After all, her father has the penis that she longs for. Now she necessarily has to identify with her mother in the hope that she can have her father's penis at her disposal.[9] (1938, 193)

Freud argues that the girl's wish for the penis culminates in another wish. She wants to have a baby from her father as a gift. The girl, frustrated in her desire for a penis, substitutes a baby for a penis. Through this twist, where a baby becomes the symbolic equivalent to a penis, the female's new love object is reinforced. Now already hostile toward her mother, the child sees in her father a renewed hope for a penis/baby.[10]

So the castration complex, which appears in girls as penis envy, brings with it the oedipal complex. Freud maintains that "it does little harm to a woman if she remains in her feminine Oedipus attitude." (1938, 194) After all, she has nothing to lose and everything to gain by imagining her father as her lover. She discontinues her masturbation because it just reminds her of her inferior genitals. She will wait until she is grown and can choose a husband "for his paternal character, ready to recognize his authority" and extend her love for the penis to its bearer in the same way that she extended her love for the breast to its bearer. (1938, 194) The girl, then, must transfer her love from the breast to the penis. For the girl, whereas the mother's breast once brought satisfaction, the father/husband's penis will have to do. The female's only satisfaction will come when she has a baby by her father-substitute to fill in for the missing penis. A male baby is a double glory because it is, in a sense, a penis with a penis. It is interesting to read Freud through Lacan at this point. Lacan suggests that the child wants to be the mother's gratification. Here, by making the *boy* baby the ultimate satisfaction for the mother, Freud insures that *he* is his mother's gratification.[11]

Freud maintains that "whereas in boys the Oedipus complex is destroyed by the castration complex, in girls it is made possible and led up to by the castration complex." Freud explains the apparent contradiction:

> This contradiction is cleared up if we reflect that the castration complex always operates in the sense implied in its subject-matter: *it inhibits and limits masculinity and encourages femininity.* The difference between the sexual development of males and females at the stage we have been considering is an intelligible consequence of the anatomical distinction between their genitals and of the psychical situation involved in it; it corresponds to the difference between a castration that has been carried out and one that has merely been threatened. (1925, 256; italics mine)

Castration operates on a different level for Lacan. (See 1982, 168.) For Lacan, the castration complex is brought on when the child realizes that the mother does not have the Phallus; the mother is not self-satisfied. She too wants something more, something more than the child. Her lack makes the child's lack even more severe. The child realizes that this lack is not temporary. It sees the difference between having the Phallus and being (had by) the Phallus. The male child sees that he has the penis, but because of the father's position in relation to the mother his penis does not help him satisfy his mother's desire. So, although he has the penis, he does not have the Phallus (gratification). In what Lemaire describes as the third phase of the oedipal situation, the male child substitutes an identification with his father (through their common possession, the penis) for his identification with his mother and postpones his desire for his mother until he can find an acceptable substitute when he grows up.

Ultimately, Lacan is always a Hegelian. Although the Law of the Father replaces the desire of the mother—so that the subject may enter language, become a subject proper, and take on an ego—through the dialectic of desire, the Law of the Father becomes the desire of the mother: the Phallus. The mother desires the Phallus because she too has come under the Law of the Father. The Law of the Father is erected upon the desire of the mother. Without her desire there would be no need for the Law. The Phallus functions both as the desire of the mother and the Law of the Father. It is a signifier that signifies signification. But, of course, for Lacan signification is always the result of a chain of signifiers through which the signified is merely an effect: "the signifier has an active function in determining the effects in which the signifiable appears as submitting to its mark, becoming through that passion the signified." (1982, 78) The

Phallus is a very strange signifier and it creates a very strange effect. The effect of the Phallus—that is, the signified that it creates—is signification itself. The Phallus, then, is erected upon itself:

> For the Phallus is a signifier, a signifier whose function in the intrasubjective economy of analysis might lift the veil from that which it served in the mysteries. For it is to this signified that it is given to designate as a whole the effect of there being a signified, inasmuch as it conditions any such effect by its presence as signifier. . . . [T]he Phallus can only play its role as veiled, that is, as in itself the sign of the latency with which everything signifiable is struck as soon as it is raised (aufgehoben) to the function of signifier. The Phallus is the signifier of this Aufgehoben itself which it inaugurates (initiates) by its own disappearance. (1982, 79–80, 82)

In order to operate the Law of the Father, the Phallus must be veiled. It cannot show itself for what it is, which would be paradoxical insofar as what it is is a not-what, a no-thing, a disguise in itself, a pure signifier. Or, as Jacqueline Rose argues, the Phallus is a fraud. (1982, 40)

Symbolic satisfactions, signifiers, are always mere disguises, temporary appeasements. After the mirror stage, the Law of the Father moves the subject away from the disappointed desire of the mother because it holds out the possibility of something more. This takes us back to the desire for the mother. First the child experiences a need that is automatically satisfied. With the onset of the mirror stage, the child can no longer assume that its needs will be satisfied. Now, in order to insure satisfaction, it must make demands when it needs something. As long as the child's "needs are subjected to demand they return to him alienated." (1982, 80) Part of the need cannot be articulated in the demand. It is this primal repression that becomes desire. (1982, 80) In principle, desire can never be satisfied. Symbols are a poor substitute for immediate satisfaction; but they are better than nothing. This is the Law of the Father: break off your exclusive dyadic relation with the mother. You cannot be the Phallus, the signifier; settle instead for having it.

If females settle for not having the Phallus, isn't this settling for not having the signifier? In other words, do females enter language? For Lacan, the entry of the subject—both male and female—into language is determined by its relationship to the Phallus. Before the child substitutes symbols for its imaginary relationship to its mother, it must experience the lack of the Phallus through symbolic castration. Females experience this lack in a different way than males; this difference in their relationship to the Phallus is what constitutes sexual identity. Females, of course, not only cannot be the Phallus but, unlike males, they also cannot have the Phallus. They suffer a double lack.

For Lacan, the female's relation to the Phallus is one of nostalgia for the precastrated imaginary relation to the Phallus. Because she does not have the Phallus, Lacan suggests that she cannot resolve the desire to be the Phallus. (1982, 83) Lacan argues that the woman sells herself to the other as lack. She wants to be loved for what she is not. (1982, 84) The woman is constituted through the signifier of the Phallus as giving to man what she does not have. In other words, she appears as man's gratification because she doesn't have it, the Phallus. Woman (who, by the way, does not exist) functions as the "not-all" in the phallic function. She is the mother who didn't have it, the Phallus. She is the mother who doesn't have everything. So she is the symbol of castration. And if woman did exist, says Lacan, it would be in the place of the radical Other, the place of that nonexistent gratification that motivates all human activity.[12] (1982, 151)

In addition to functioning within signification by providing the Other for the Western subject man, woman's *jouissance*, insofar as it is not phallic, mystifies signification.[13] Lacan calls this a supplementary *jouissance* because it does not complement man's. In other words, it is precisely *not* the missing complement to man's desire, that which will put man back together again. Rather, as Irigaray, Cixous, and, to some extent, Kristeva maintain, it is what has been left out of signification. In the words of Lacan, "I believe in the *jouissance* of the woman insofar as it is something more, on the condition that you screen off the *something more* until I have properly explained it." (1982, 147) For Lacan, this *jouissance*, which is proper to the woman who does not exist and signifies nothing, is not something that she can know. She merely experiences it, like the mystic. ". . . [T]hey don't know what they are saying," spouts Lacan, "which is all the difference between them and me." (1982, 144)

This *jouissance* is a "*jouissance* of the body . . . a *jouissance* beyond the Phallus." (1982,l 145) Yet, as he describes it, it too is one face of the Other, perhaps the most frightening face (the non-phallic mother who has her own pleasure?). "Might not this *jouissance* which one experiences and knows nothing of," asks Lacan, "be that which puts us on the path of ex-istence? And why not interpret one face of the Other, the God face, as supported by feminine *jouissance*?" (1982, 147) In spite of the *jouissance* beyond the Phallus, however, it seems that we are back to, if not within, the phallic economy.

We may wonder, with many feminists, why a *phallic* economy? Why not, for example, an economy of the breast? Why not a weaning complex instead of a castration complex? Why not the being versus the having of the breast that Freud talks about? The distinction between being and having is first used by Freud in relation to the mother's breast. In a note dated July 12, 1938, Freud makes the distinction between "being" and "having":

"Having" and "being" in children. Children like expressing an object-relation by an identification: "I am the object." "Having" is the later of the two;

> after the loss of the object it relapses into "being." Example: the breast.
> "The breast is part of me, I am the breast." Only later: "I have it"—that is
> "I am not it".... (1938b, 299)

Could it be because, as Teri Stratton suggests, at the age of 3 or 4 the
breast, unlike the penis, is not a sign of difference; after all, in the bodies
of children breasts do not differentiate sexes.[14] We might wonder, however,
why the mother's breasts, with which the child is intimately familiar and
which are definitely different than the child's own, could not be a sign of
difference. Why isn't this early sign the sign of difference?

For Lacan, and Freud in his better moments, breasts aren't the sign of
difference ultimately and primarily because we live in a phallocentric
culture. The phallocentrism produced by the dialectic identified by psychoanalysis, says Lacan, is "entirely conditioned by the intrusion of the
signifier in man's psyche, and strictly impossible to deduce from any pre-
established harmony of this psyche with the nature that it expresses."
(1977, 198) Lacan gives a less politically sensitive interpretation of why
the Phallus becomes a symbol of gratification:

> One might say that this signifier is chosen as what stands out as most easily
> seized upon in the real of sexual-copulation, and also as the most symbolic
> in the literal (typographical) sense of the term, since it is the equivalent in
> the relation of the (logical) copula. One might also say that by virtue of its
> turgidity, it is the image of the vital flow as it is transmitted in generation.
> (1977, 198)

Lacan argues that these propositions cover over the functions of the
Phallus in signification. In any case it is once again the sight of the penis
that gives rise to its privilege. The penis is the copula that unites the two
halves, man and woman. So its signifier, the Phallus, is what symbolizes
gratification. Also, as the symbolic copula (X is Y), the Phallus insures
that the signifier refers to a signified. It is the turgid link between the two.
It insures that symbols really do stand for the thing—the thing is not
lacking, even if it is one step removed. And this is the illusion. This is
the veil over the Phallus that psychoanalysis pulls away in order to expose
the hole in the place of the Phallus.[15]

In this scenario, what is the relationship between the penis and the
Phallus? Is it, as Nancy Fraser suggests, that the Phallus and penis have
been collapsed? (Fraser 1990) What does Lacan mean when he says that
the mother does not have the real Phallus, or that Claudius, Hamlet's
mother's lover, does have the real Phallus? (1982, 83; 198 – 77, 50) Is the
penis the real Phallus? If Lacan's Phallus is erected on the penis, then are
we back to Freud's suspect biologism? The identity of the Phallus and
penis has ben a significant bone of contention in contemporary feminist
theory.

Ellie Ragland Sullivan argues that "from an Imaginary perspective, the Phallus is the signifier of the lack inherent in Desire." (1982, 12) The Phallus as "the first metaphorical or 'pure' signifier is the Name-of-the-Father which spells out prohibition, separation, difference, compromise: i.e., Castration." (1982, 12) Oddly enough, according to Sullivan the Phallus signifies castration. This seems to separate the Phallus from the penis in its bodily presence. Jane Gallop argues, however, that the Phallus "*also* always refers to *penis*." (1982, 246) Gallop suggests that although within Lacanian theory the Phallus is not equivalent to the penis, "*Phallus* cannot function as signifier in ignorance of *penis*." (1981, 248) Phallus only takes on its significance as a sign of difference once the bodily difference between having and not having the penis has been spied. Gallop maintains that the confusion between Phallus—associated as it is with power—and penis in Lacanian theory can lead to a confusion in the association of the penis (men) with power and the lack of penis (women) with a lack of power. (1981, 246)

Teri Stratton takes a position in relation to Lacan's Phallus somewhere between Sullivan's and Gallop's. Stratton argues that "[w]hile the Phallus is not the penis, there is a representational juncture, a symbolic knotting ... which links them together and signals their mutual implication." (1990, 7) She maintains that the Phallus designates both the penis-object and what the penis-object is not. She presents a diagnosis of Lacan's use of "real Phallus" as a "rhetorical decoy which aims as much to cloak the signification of the Phallus as (only) a signifier as it does to promote its signifying ambivalence." (1990, 17) She claims that Lacan uses the Phallus and its "glaring reference to the penis" as a "lure." (1990, 14) Stratton seems to suggest that Lacan intends to make his readers think that the Phallus is the penis. He lures them into this belief. Stratton believes that Lacan does this in order to bait his women readers.[16] But why does he want to antagonize women by showing them his Phallus and tricking them into believing that it is a penis? Is Lacan just an exhibitionist? This is only the beginning of the problems with Lacan's Phallus.

Unlike Lacan, Kristeva does not seem concerned to distinguish the Phallus from the penis or to reveal the Phallus as a fraud. Rather, she unproblematically maintains that the penis is the major referent of the Phallus in the oedipal situation. The penis "gives full meaning to the lack or desire which constitutes the subject during his or her insertion into the order of language." (1979a, 41) Without concern for any apparent biological determinism, without concern for sexual difference, Kristeva takes over a simplified version of the Lacanian Phallus. For her, it is the positing of the subject through castration, fear of losing the Phallus, that enacts the transition between the preoedipal and the Symbolic. The result of this transition is language. And the acquisition of language is the result of the process of becoming a subject, moving from preoedipal to oedipal stages. Unlike Lacan, however, Kristeva suggests that the preoedipal drives never remain completely repressed. She maintains that we can find traces of this preoedipal phase in language. The transition between the preoedipal and the Symbolic is never finished.

Kristeva's Drives

Between the preoedipal and the oedipal, the autoerotic body somehow becomes the body proper, and this is what Kristeva sets out to describe. (1975a, 285) The autoerotic, preoedipal body is what she calls the "semiotic" body.[17] Semiotic activity is the mark of drives that stem from the body. (1975, 136) These drives are prior to Lacan's mirror stage in which the infant first recognizes itself as a body proper. It is this realm of bodily drives that Kristeva wants to bring back into Lacanian theory. (1974, 30)

The material signifying process, or drive process, is both biological and social. For Kristeva, it cannot be reduced to either one or the other. She returns to the Freudian theory of drives, which she maintains provides "a bridge between the biological foundation of signifying functioning and its determination by the family and society." (1974, 167) She is interested in this drive heterogeneity and how through jolts of matter it eventually produces the speaking subject. "Drives," says Kristeva, "are the repeated scission of matter that generates significance, the place where an always absent subject is produced." (1974, 167) This absent subject is also heterogeneous. First, it is the absent subject of Lacanian analysis—the apparently transcendental subject who, carried away by language, is able to "step out" and "take a look." Second, it is the absent semiotic subject, the semiotic body, that is repressed in the signifying process that produces the transcendental subject.

Kristeva claims that the onset of the Lacanian subject is completed at the cost of repressing drives. The drives are what Lacan calls the "impossible real." This is why she claims that for Lacan we have no access to drives in themselves; drives are always and only representations of drives.[18] (1954, 80, 87, 239) They are always already symbolic. Kristeva argues that her theory is distinguished from Lacan's because for her the drives operate on a material level that is both logically and chronologically prior to the onset of the Symbolic. More importantly, these drives are social, not because they are already symbolic, but because within the semiotic body there is already an experience of otherness that prefigures the other in the mirror even as it sets it up.

Kristeva argues that Lacan's account of desire covers over its relationship to the semiotic body, full of drives, out of which it comes. She complains that for Lacan the subject is constituted at the expense of "the real," the drives, from which this subject will be forever cut off. (1974, 131) This, she says, leads to a "Kantian agnosticism" where the real cannot be known; it is impossible. Lacan's Kantian agnosticism, objects Kristeva, "castrates" the Freudian discovery. For her, the Lacanian notion of desire combines Freud's topography with Hegelian negativity "but raises them out of their biological and material entrenchment into the domain of social praxis where 'social' means 'signifying.'" (1974, 130) The result is that desire's basis in drives is "dismissed and forgotten." (1974, 131) Attention is focused on desire itself, which is merely a reactivation on the symbolic level of a negativity that takes place in the body.[19] In addition, the signifying *process* that is the movement and dialectic between the semiotic and symbolic "will be replaced by a nothingness—the 'lack' that brings about the unitary *being* of the subject." (1974, 131) The subject's being is founded on this lack and the drives are lost:

> Desire will be seen as an always already accomplished subjugation of the subject to lack: it will serve to demonstrate only the development of the signifier, never the heterogeneous process that questions the psychosomatic orders. From these reflections a certain subject emerges: the subject, precisely, of desire who lives at the expense of his drives, ever in search of a lacking object. (1974, 131–32)

The living body is sacrificed to desire, which is cut off from the body. The body becomes only a sign. Kristeva passionately argues that when language is not mixed with drives, this subjugation to the Law of the Signifier turns the living person into a sign and signifying activity stops. (1974, 132) She claims that the exemplary subject of Lacan's desire is the masochistic neurotic engaging in autocastration and bodily mutilation, or the completely catatonic body of the clinical schizophrenic. (1974, 132)

Here Kristeva may be oversimplifying Lacan's theory of drives. She argues that Lacan "castrates" Freud's theory of drives. But Freud also suggests that drives are not accessible in themselves; they are accessible only through their manifestations. Also, Lacan does insist that psychic inscriptions have their most significant impact before the onset of the Symbolic. Lacan does have a theory of drives that induces presymbolic psychic elements.

Kristeva suggests that lack alone cannot motivate a move away from the maternal body and into language. She argues that material rejection is the result of an excess even if it is also a loss. The separation that is inherent in the body is experienced as pleasurable. She concludes that the logic of separation that is taken over in language is founded on pleasure as well as lack, or lack experienced as pleasure. If there were no pleasure in separation and merely a castration threat, why would anyone leave the safe haven of the maternal body? In her writings of the 1980s, *Tales of Love* and *Black Sun*, Kristeva suggests that the paternal function is not merely the stern, castrating Father of the Law. So, while she agrees with Lacan that the Symbolic is founded on lack, she describes a different relation to the lack and a different sort of paternal function that does not merely threaten castration but also loves.[20] Kristeva doesn't argue that Lacan is wrong about the function of the mirror stage or castration. Rather, she emphasizes that Lacan's account does not analyze what is heterogeneous to the symbolic, the semiotic, which results from these functions on the "other scene." (1977a, 276)

The Semiotic

One of the early uses of "the semiotic" is in Kristeva's 1973 essay on Artaud, "Le sujet en proces," which is reprinted in Polylogue. Here she discusses the "asymbolic, semiotic." (1973a, 77) She names the unnameable, that which is heterogeneous to/within signifying practice:

> To keep an account of this heterogeneity implies that one no longer consider the symbolic function as super-corporeal, super-biological and super-material, but as produced by a dialectic between two orders. Therefore, rather than of 'symbolism,' we will speak of the semiotic as the place of this heterogeneity of sense.[21] (1973a, 76)

It is important, especially when working through Kristeva's earliest writings, to note the distinction between la semiotique, the science of semiotics, and le semiotique, her most famous "discovery," what she calls early on "the semiotic disposition." In her 1971 essay "How Does One Speak to Literature?" Kristeva still refers to this "semiotic" element as the "asymbolized" or "asymbolic." (1971, 112) In this same essay, however, she elaborates on some of the precursors to her notion of the "semiotic," Barthes's notions of the "sublanguage," the "flesh" of writing, "semanteme" and "semioclasm."[22] (1971) In this essay, and in many of her other early essays, when she does use "semiotic" it refers to the science of signifying practice (semanalysis), not its heterogeneous element per se. She first fully develops the notion of the semiotic in Revolution in Poetic Language. There she proposes that both psychoanalysis and linguistics need to account for what is heterogeneous to/within signification, the semiotic.

The semiotic disposition that makes its way into language is the rhythm, intonation, and echolalias of the mother-child symbiosis. (1976, 157) The semiotic disposition is based on the primal mother-child relationship. It is the rhythms and sounds of their bodies together fused into one. For Kristeva, this is not merely an imaginary union. Rather, at this point, it is also a real union. The child is physically dependent on its union with the mother. Their bodies physically "signal" to each other before the onset of language proper, before the mirror stage. Their semiotic relation sets up the onset of language proper.

Semiotic Evidence

In her early work (1966–69) Kristeva sets out to prove scientifically that the semiotic exists.[23] She performed several studies on children in order to analyze their language acquisition. She claims that children learn melody and music before they learn syntax. In fact, melody enables them to learn syntax. Kristeva argues, for example, that it is well known that the end of a sentence is indicated by a lowering of the voice. A child learning language first imitates these intonations before it learns the rules of syntax. (1974b, 172) Not only is music prior to syntax in language acquisition, but it is also prior to the mirror stage. (1974b, 168) Prior to its constitution as a subject, let alone a speaking subject, the infant makes "music" as a direct release of drive. It expels sounds in order to release tension, either pain or pleasure, in order to survive. (1977a, 282) One such sound is laughter.

Kristeva maintains that the first laugh is the result of space. It is a coming together of all archaic perceptions, sights, sounds, tastes. (1977a, 283) She argues that the noises that the infant makes in response to muscle spasms, holdovers from its intrauterine experience, turn into laughter. At this point, the laughter has no object. Eventually the mother's face becomes the focus of the laughter. The infant smiles and Kristeva calls this the first sublimation. What was once muscle spasm becomes focused, sublimated, in a smile (another muscle movement). In addition to smiling, infants move other muscles. Infants cry as well as laugh. The infant's cry might be another holdover from its intrauterine experience. But the cry, which seems to be a response to stimulus and not just a random muscle spasm, cannot be as easily interpreted as sublimation as the smile can. While eventually the child's cry, like the child's smile, might be an early sublimation, it is very difficult to determine when the transition takes place. When does the infant's cry become associated with an object?

In these early sublimations the infant experiences a semiotic space, without interior or exterior, which Kristeva calls the "semiotic *chora*." This experience of space is prior to the mirror stage and its preliminary imaginary: "The imaginary takes over from childhood laughter: it is a joy without words. Chronologically and logically long before the mirror stage . . . the semiotic disposition makes its start as riant spaciousness." (1977a, 283)

Following Lacan, Kristeva suggests that the space of the mother-child symbiosis is a space of need prior to desire. This semiotic space of need is still close to the surface in early language use. Kristeva points to traces of the semiotic disposition by looking back through two aspects of early childhood language. She analyzes the child's use of both place names and demonstratives. She argues that laughter, the first sublimation, becomes the denotation of the mother. Laughter becomes a place name: "As if the laughter that makes up space had become, with the help of maturation and repression, a 'place name.'" (1977a, 287) She also argues that children's use of demonstratives, especially to designate places, is related to the mother. (1977a, 287) For the child, every space is the place of the mother. (1977a, 289) "That" and "this" "refer" to the mother.

Kristeva argues that the use of demonstratives indicates a move from the semiotic modality of need to the symbolic modality of desire. The mother's body becomes the word. The fact that the same demonstrative allows for many subject positions as well as object denotations—"that is mother," "this is me," "that is a chair"—points to an archaic and essential *transubstantiation* in language. Kristeva says that certain religious themes, most notably "the words of Christ ('This is my body') where *this* designates both the bread and the body of Christ," call into play this move from body to symbol:

> Might transubstantiation then be an indelible thematization of the fold to be found between two spaces (the real space of need, nutrition and survival: bread; and the symbolic space of designation: the signifying body itself)? Such a fold would then be produced in the archaeology of demonstratives (the archaic designation of the mother, the breaking-off of our need for her) as well as in every practice that is at the limits of corporeal identity, that is an identity of meaning and presence. (1979, 233; see also 1977a, 291)

For Kristeva the early use of demonstratives points to a move from the space of semiotic and need to the space of Symbolic and desire. Along with the child's primal objectless laughter and the first use of place names to "designate" place as the place of the mother, the use of demonstratives to designate "that" as the body of the mother suggests that there is a semiotic disposition that chronologically and logically precedes the mirror stage.

Once again Kristeva employs her double strategy for bringing the body back into the structure of language. She argues both that the logic of language is already operating within this semiotic disposition and that the semiotic disposition makes its way into language. Laughter is a presymbolic symbol of sorts, while place names and demonstratives are semiotic holdovers that make their way into language. In both cases the semiotic is associated with the maternal body. As Kristeva takes us deeper into the maternal body behind the mirror stage and brings the maternal body back into the mirror, she takes us deeper behind the lines of the traditional psychoanalytic fortress. She takes us to a place of love before the onset of desire, a place where the Real, Imaginary, and Symbolic are not yet or no longer distinct.

Accounting for Lacan's I.R.S.

For Kristeva, love ties together the Symbolic, the Imaginary, and the Real. (1983, 7) She replaces Lacan's Hegelian imaginary struggle for recognition, which plays dialectically between time and space, with a return to the imaginary space that supports the narcissistic structure, what she calls the "imaginary father."

For Lacan, the subject can see itself only as the image reflected in the mirror. This becomes the model for subsequent relations and self-definition. The self is reflected in the Other. This results in a primary frustration that becomes the ultimate driving force behind human life. The real body that stands on this side of the mirror experiences a fragmented body and fragmented desires. It does not experience a mastery over its body—it is just a little baby. The image of the body in the mirror, on the other hand, is whole and perfect. The child imagines that it can master that perfect body; after all, it is its own body. When the child realizes that this other is alien and beyond its control and yet constitutive of its own identity, a struggle begins. Lacan's diagnosis of this phenomenon is that the child's desire is the desire of the Other:

> The subject originally locates and recognizes desire through the intermediary not only of his own image, but of the body of his fellow being. . . . [I]t is in so far as he recognizes his desire in the body of the other that the exchange takes place. It is insofar as his desire has gone over to the other side that he assimilates himself to the body of the other and recognizes himself as a body. (1954, 147)

On this level of images the subject is in a precarious position in relation to the other. The tension that Lacan describes is the tension between Hegel's master and slave. Ultimately, it is a dialectical struggle for recognition. Before the subject enters language and a symbol can stand in for its desire, "desire is seen solely in the other." (1954, 170) This specular relation, where the subject can see itself only through the other, leads to an absolute rivalry with the other. The subject wants to annihilate the other so that it might exist. (1954, 170–73)

Once the subject sees its image in the mirror or the body of another, it realizes that it is separated from the rest of the world and from its mother, to whom it had an intimate and satisfying attachment, until now. Following the mirror stage, the mother takes the place of the mirror image as Other. The child is beginning to see her as another being. If she is another being, then it is alienated from her in a way in which it wasn't before in the imaginary unity. The child realizes that the mother can go away and that it has no control over her. At this point, since the child cannot communicate its desire and does not yet have access to symbolic substitutes,

its only options for satisfaction are either to extinguish its desire or annihilate the object who controls the satisfaction of its desire.

For Lacan, a description of this relationship comes directly (through
Kojeve) from Hegel's account of the master/slave dialectic. (1954, 146–47,
222–23) The master/slave dialectic, insofar as what is at stake is recognition, or the desire of the other (that is, to be the object of the other's
desire), moves beyond the Imaginary into the Symbolic. It parallels Lacan's account of the oedipal situation. At the stage of the imaginary relation to the other, since the object/other appears as irremediably separated
from the subject, the other seems to destroy the subject. The other shows
how the subject is split, alienated from itself. And it shows how the subject
is alienated from the world. The subject can never regain the primitive
imaginary dyad where the whole world revolved around the satisfaction
of its needs. The subject "will never truly be able to find reconciliation,
his adhesion to the world, his perfect complementarity on the level of
desire. It is the nature of desire to be radically torn." (1955, 166)

On the imaginary level, the tension between the subject and object is
unresolvable. If the object is unified and autonomous, it cannot be had
by the subject. That means that the subject's desires remain unsatisfied.
The subject remains fragmented. As long as the object is whole the subject
cannot be. On the other side, if the subject is whole, the object cannot be.
Without the Symbolic there is merely this imaginary oscillation, which
is what makes human perception interesting. (1955, 166) So, like Hegel's
master/slave relationship, the mirror stage is a fight to the death where
desire cannot be satisfied except by moving on to another way of conceiving the relationship. The subject becomes self-conscious; for Lacan the
subject takes an ego. But first it must go through the oedipal situation and
acquire language.

Kristeva distinguishes her imaginary from Lacan's by suggesting that
while his imaginary is "blocked" by a representation in the mirror stage,
hers goes beyond the mere representatives of affect to its source in drives.
(1988) Certainly it is difficult to translate Kristeva's theory into the terms
of Lacan's Imaginary, Real, and Symbolic; indeed, it is difficult to define
these terms within either Kristeva's or Lacan's theories apart form each
other.

In an interview in *Critical Texts* Kristeva claims that it is impossible to
translate from one theory to another because it compromises the "specificity of each author." Kristeva wants to remain autonomous from Lacan.[24]
Yet she attempts a comparison between her notions of semiotic and symbolic and Lacan's notions of the Real, the Imaginary, and the Symbolic:

> But it does seems to me that the semiotic—if one really wants to find
> correspondences with Lacanian ideas—corresponds to phenomena that for
> Lacan are in both the real and the imaginary. For him the real is a hole, a

void, but I think that in a number of experiences with which psychoanalysis is concerned . . . the appearance of the real is not necessarily void. It is accompanied by a number of physical inscriptions that are of the order of the semiotic. Thus perhaps the notion of the semiotic allows us to speak of the real without simply saying that it's an emptiness or a blank; it allows us to try to further elaborate it. In any case, it is on the level of the imaginary that the semiotic functions best—that is, the fictional construction. (1986a, 7)

As Kristeva makes it out, her semiotic operates between Lacan's Real and his Imaginary. Her semiotic is, in some sense, the Real that makes its way into the Symbolic through the Imaginary. In her essay devoted to Lacan's texts, "Within the Microcosm of the 'Talking Cure,'" Kristeva distinguishes Lacan's notion of *lalangue* ("the so-called mother-tongue," or the "real from which linguistics takes its object") from her notion of the semiotic by claiming that for Lacan even *lalangue* operates within a structure in which meaning is "homogeneous with the realm of signification." (1983a, 35) In other words, Lacan's theory—even with its notion of *lalangue*—does not allow for nonmeaning or what is heterogeneous to meaning within the realm of signification. Kristeva criticizes Lacan for presupposing an "always already there of language" that prevents what is heterogeneous to meaning—the semiotic—from entering signification.[25] Her semiotic *chora*, on the other hand, "gives a different status to 'signifying' marks." (1983a, 37)

Kristeva has a more complex definition of the Symbolic than Lacan's. She uses *le symbolique* in two senses. *Le symbolique* can refer to the Symbolic order or the symbolic element within the Symbolic order. She often makes the distinction explicit by using *l'ordre symbolique* or *la dimension symbolique* in contrast to *le symbolique* or *symbolique*. We are more likely to see the specific use of symbolic in *Revolution in Poetic Language* than in her later works, where she usually talks about the Symbolic order.

Kristeva identifies both semiotic and symbolic elements within the Symbolic order. She argues that Lacan reduces the Symbolic order to its symbolic elements; he defines the Symbolic order in terms of the symbolic function. For Kristeva, however, to enter signification is not to merely enter the realm of the symbolic element. Rather, it is to enter the Symbolic order that is constituted by heterogeneous elements. To enter the Symbolic order is to take up a position, which is possible only through the symbolic function. Yet not all signification involves taking up a position; or, at least, there is more to signification than taking up a position. Kristeva has a more sophisticated definition of the Symbolic than Lacan's. For her the symbolic function—the ability to take a position or make a judgment—is just one aspect of signification. She suggests, however, that for Lacan signification is synonymous with the symbolic function.

The Symbolic

The break into, and boundary of, the Symbolic is what Kristeva calls the "thetic phase." The thetic phase in the signifying process operates as a break, a threshold. It is the point at which the subject takes up a position, an identification. The thetic is necessary for any symbolic or social functioning. It is, however, the semiotic—the drives and their articulation—that gives rise to the thetic break. This is the process (the semiotic disposition) that leads up to the mirror stage. There is a "breaking," or what Kristeva calls a "rejection," already within the body that becomes, at a certain threshold, the thetic break. The thetic break is the result of the mirror stage where the child recognizes itself as a separate subject through the other of its image. In fact, the mirror stage is characterized by the thetic break. At this point the thetic break *positions* the child as a subject ready to enter language:

> The thetic phase marks a threshold between two heterogeneous realms: the semiotic and the symbolic. The second includes part of the first and their scission is thereafter marked by the break between signifier and signified. *Symbolic* would seem an appropriate term for this always split unification that is produced as a rupture and is impossible without it. (1974, 49)

The thetic unity is divided into signifier and signified, symbolic and real, which are connected through the Imaginary. This was evident in the mirror stage where it is the Imaginary that moves the child from its presymbolic identification with its mother to an identification with the other in the mirror. Kristeva also emphasizes another division in the thetic unity: the division between the two heterogeneous elements that it negotiates, the division between semiotic and symbolic.

She describes two types of "events," which she says can be viewed as the social counterparts to the thetic: sacrifice and art.[26] (1974, 74–85) Kristeva's interpretation of sacrifice is noteworthy here because it provides a clear example of the relationship between the semiotic and the thetic. The sacrifice replaces presymbolic violence with a positioned violence, a violence focused against a victim. What may have been random or instinctual violence is replaced by a localized violence in order to establish the social. In other words, society does not eliminate pre-social violence. Rather, it merely refocuses it into more socially acceptable forms. Sacrifice, which focuses violence, becomes the precondition for society. This is true not only of religious ritual sacrifice but of sacrifice and violence on all levels of the society. Sacrifice, insofar as it confines violence to a single place or position, is thetic. The victim's body is sacrificed for the sake of the Symbolic:

> Far from unleashing violence, sacrifice shows how representing that violence is enough to stop it and to concatenate an order. Conversely, it indicates that all order is based on representation: what is violent is the irruption of the symbol, killing substance to make it signify. . . . [S]acrifice reminds us that the symbolic emerges out of material continuity through a violent unmotivated leap. . . . (1974, 75, 78)

The body, ultimately the semiotic maternal body, is sacrificed through the violence of the Symbolic. Pre-social violence becomes violence aimed at the semiotic body.[27]

Sacrifice gives an example of how the thetic provides a joint between the semiotic and the symbolic.[28] It provides some insight into the relationship between these two heterogeneous elements that make up signification. Sacred sacrifice does not celebrate all violence, only positioned violence. The thetic, which institutes and prefigures the Symbolic, does not prohibit drive discharge or *jouissance*. Rather, it regulates it. It prohibits *jouissance* at the same time that it permits it. (1974, 78) In sacrifice the semiotic violence motivates its thetic focus, which gives rise to symbolization. The semiotic functions as the negative or surplus of the signifying system. (1975, 133) It functions as the precondition to any signification. Although the instinctual semiotic, prior to meaning, is "mobile" and "amorphous," it is also "already regulated" by material laws. (1974, 49) After the thetic phase the "*logic*" of the semiotic is taken over by the symbolic. (1974, 49)

There is no symbolic function without the subject situated through the thetic phase; and this subject is the result of the "heterogeneous contradiction between two irreconcilable elements—separate but inseparable from the *process* in which they assume asymmetrical functions." (1974, 82) On the other hand, the semiotic breaks the thetic only insofar as it *enters* it. In *Revolution in Poetic Language*, Kristeva talks about poetic mimesis as an *effraction* (breaking and entering) of the thetic. (1984, 247) Without entering the thetic, the semiotic cannot break it. (1974, 81) The semiotic in signifying practice needs laws, boundaries, and stases, in order to go beyond and transform them. (1974, 101) The semiotic uses the law against itself.[29] Although the dialectic between them frustrates both and maintains a constant tension, the semiotic needs the symbolic as much as the symbolic needs the semiotic. Together, in constant dialectical alternation, they make up signifying practice.

Negativity

For Kristeva, it is "negativity" that insures the movement back and forth between these two different levels of signification. She imports Hegel's concept of negativity, mixes it up with Freud's drives, and eventually comes up with what she calls "rejection." In the section of *Revolution* entitled "Negativity: Rejection," appropriately, Kristeva begins by discussing what negativity is not. First, it is important to note that negativity is not negation. It is not just saying "no." In fact, negation, or just saying "no," does not insure the movement between the semiotic and the symbolic. Saying "no" to the symbolic merely strengthens it. This is because negation is a thetic act. It is a judgment; and as a judgment it is already thetic and symbolic. Negation merely serves to unify the subject. (1974, 124)

This view of negation is in keeping with Freud's view of negation in "On Negation," where he asserts that there is no "no" in the Unconscious. (1925a, 239) Freud argues that negation is a sign of repression, or, actually, the first sign of the lifting of repression. (1925, 235–36) Repressed material can make its way into consciousness only if it is negated. "No" means "yes." Freud suggests that this is the way that consciousness maintains its unity in the face of threatening unconscious thoughts. It lets them in by negating them. So negation serves to unify the subject.

Negativity is a different matter. It is not static like a negation. Rather, it is a process. Kristeva calls it the fourth term in the (Hegelian) dialectic. She maintains that although the notion of negativity appears in Hegel's logic, it is repressed. Hegel's account erases rupture. The synthesis always, and in the end, emphasizes unity over crisis. For Hegel, negativity always collapses into unity and the unstable process that produces that unity is covered up. (1974, 130) For Hegel, negativity takes place within the One. For Freud, on the other hand, negativity or expulsion takes place on the other scene. (1974, 158) This other scene, of course, is the scene of drives. Kristeva claims that Freud replaces Hegel's law of becoming (which moves forward even as it moves backward and always leads to Absolute *Being-for-Itself*) with the law of repetition (which moves backward even as it moves forward and always leads to absolute *Being-in-Itself*). (1974, 147) This law of repetition becomes what Freud calls the "death drive," the drive toward stability and ultimately inorganicity—absolute Being-in-Itself. The death drive, however, never leads us to a stable point because as long as we are alive it merely repeats, goes backward. In any case, it seems that Hegel's and Freud's accounts of negativity lead in opposite directions. They point to opposite poles of the heterogeneous spectrum of signifying practice. So Kristeva suggests that we add them together in order to produce a truly materialist dialectic.

Negativity is the movement of heterogeneous matter, drives. It is the "material process of repeated instinctual scissions that operate according to objective laws" of society and nature and eventually produce symbolic unification. (1974, 159) "Negativity," says Kristeva, designates "the *process that exceeds the signifying subject, binding him to the laws of objective struggles in nature and society.*" (1974, 119) Because negativity sounds too much like negation, and that is not what she means, Kristeva decides to call this movement "rejection." (1974, 119) Rejection is a specific kind of negativity that functions as the logical and material operator of signification. Rejection is the separation of matter, one of the preconditions for symbolization. (1974, 117)

Kristeva maintains that without material rejection we cannot explain the transition from the presymbolic to the Symbolic. We cannot explain what motivates the move through the mirror stage to the Symbolic. Lacan, of course, gives the castration threat as the motive. But in order to experience this threat in the first place, the child must take a position as a subject in the mirror stage. It must recognize that it *is* its image but that it *is not* its image. It must "see" the gap between its body and its image, the other.

Kristeva persuasively argues that this move is already thetic and symbolic. The mirror stage already requires a negation of the other in order for the child to identify as a subject/self. Negation is already a judgment. A judgment is made only from a position. It is already thetic. In other words, in Lacan's account, we seem to be moving in circles: the child takes a position as subject so that he can negate his image in order to take a position as subject. Criticizing Lacan, Kristeva says that "to say 'no' is already to formulate syntactically oriented propositions that are more or less grammatical." (1974, 122) Rather than prefiguring either the symbolic function or the Symbolic order, the mirror stage is already symbolic.

How, then, do we get to this symbolic in the first place? If the mirror stage is already symbolic then we certainly cannot use it as an explanation for the onset of the Symbolic. Kristeva argues that the only way to explain the transition is to acknowledge the material element that is heterogeneous to the symbolic. Rejection is not unique to the symbolic function or the Symbolic order.[30] Rather, it operates first in the semiotic body. Kristeva suggests several ways in which the logic of signification is already in operation within the body. For example, she argues that maternal regulation prefigures paternal prohibition. (I analyze this argument later in this chapter.) She also argues that the patterns and structures of the logic of signification operate on a material bodily level before they operate on a symbolic level. Specifically, patterns of negation and identification are already working within the material body. (I take up patterns of negation here and patterns of identification in chapter 3.) Kristeva also suggests that material rejection sets up a logic of excess that eventually gives rise to speech. (I explain the importance of her hypothesis of excess in the next section.) Finally, she uses Freud's Fort/Da game as evidence that negativity operates on a material level in order to set up its operation on a symbolic level.

She reinterprets Freud's Fort/Da game and Lacan's use of it. When the child's mother is absent, the child invents a game where it throws a reel out of its cot and says something that Freud interprets as the German word for "gone" (*fort*). Then the child pulls in the reel and says something that Freud interprets as the German word for "here" (*da*). Freud claims that the reel stands in for the child's mother; through language the child can control its mother's absence. Lacan claims that "in this phonematic opposition [*Fort/Da*], the child transcends, brings on to the symbolic plane, the phenomenon of presence and absence. He renders himself master of the thing, precisely insofar as he destroys it." (1954, 173; 1977, 103–104) The child masters the object, and thereby its desire for the object, by substituting a symbol (destroying the object and putting the symbol in its place) that it can control. The child substitutes a symbol for the missing object.

While Lacan sees a negativity in the Fort/Da that functions through metonymy that marks the beginnings of symbolization, Kristeva sees a negativity that is still primarily gestural and kinetic: the bodily act of throwing and retrieving the reel.[31] (1974, 170) Eléanor Kuykendall claims that Kristeva's account of the Fort/Da is adverbial and not performative. (1989, 181) This, however, is precisely Kristeva's criticism of Lacan's account of the Fort/Da situation. Kristeva emphasizes the performance of physically throwing the reel. For her this bodily act is as important to the onset of signification as the "*fort*" and the "*da*." Negativity is primarily material, even gestural, in the case of the Fort/Da game. Kristeva argues that the negativity necessary for the onset of subjectivity is already operating in the body.

Negativity as Excess

Negativity moves through both the symbolic function and the Symbolic order because it moves through the corporeal. It operates in living matter prior to the Symbolic. (1974, 123) And it does not act merely as lack but also as excess. If the Symbolic is founded merely on a lack, then there is all the more reason for avoiding it altogether, for taking refuge in neurosis and psychosis. In Kristeva's account, however, material negativity is founded on excess. Anality is the primary example. When there is too much matter, some must be expelled. In anality, rejection precedes the Symbolic. (1974, 151) Moreover, in anality separation and rejection are pleasurable:

> In all these forms [oral, muscular, urethral, and anal], of which the anal is the last to be repressed and hence the most important, energy surges and discharges eroticize the glottic, urethral, and anal sphincters as well as the kinetic system. These drives move through the sphincters and arouse pleasure at the very moment substances belonging to the body are separated and rejected from the body. This acute pleasure therefore coincides with a loss, a separation from the body, and the isolating of objects outside it . . .

a separation which is not a lack, but a discharge, and which, although privative, arouses pleasure. (1974, 151)

The motive for separation is pleasure even in privation. The separation comes not from lack, but from excess. There is too much so some must be discharged. It is important to note that it is not only anality, but also orality that causes pleasure. This will be an added motivation for speaking.

Kristeva points out that this primary drive pleasure threatens the Symbolic and this is why it is repressed; if it wasn't, there would be no symbolic unity. (1974, 152) The logic of the drives and repetition challenges the unity of the Symbolic. This logic threatens to uncover the process that leads to the appearance of unity and thereby exposes that unity as merely one moment in the process. The unity of reason or consciousness cannot admit that it is part of a process that alternates between unity and the fragmentation and repetition of drives. (1974, 148) To admit this, of course, is to admit that it is not unified.

Rejection does not operate solely according to the logic of repetition. Rather than merely repeat the same identity, it creates something new. As such it is not only the demise of the symbolic function but also its renewal. (1974, 172) In the dialectical oscillation between the semiotic and the symbolic, rejection comes both before and after the Symbolic order. This is why signification is a process and not a static structure. Rejection is not only discharge but also build up. This is how rejection leads to stases, plateaus where excitation is posited and only then discharged. Eventually this oscillation between rejection and stasis jolts the material being (the body) into the thetic and into the Symbolic, where the body is represented by a sign. As the stases between bodily drives and signification, the thetic is prefigured by instinctual stases. Kristeva outlines this "logic of renewal": "rejection$_1$—stasis$_1$—rejection$_2$—stasis$_2$—(etc.)—Thesis—rejection$_n$—stasis$_n$." (1974, 172)

Eventually material rejection reaches a threshold where it produces thetic heterogeneity. It produces a new level. (1974, 174) On this new level rejection becomes desire: "for identification with the other or the suppression of the other are locked within family structure; it is in the family that relations of rejection become intersubjective: they become relations of desire." (1974, 174) Kristeva claims that the logic of the psyche is already operating, possibly malfunctioning, before Lacan's metonymy of desire is in full operation.

At the level of desire, the logic of renewal is the same as it is in the body but its manifestations are different. Although this logic is an oscillation, it is an unstable oscillation which produces something new at each stasis. Without these stases this logic would be merely a repetition of the same things over and over. There would be no change. This is the difference between the logic of repetition and the logic of renewal (which is an oscillation between rejection and stasis). Both rejection and stasis are necessary. Just as when the signifying process tries to cover over the semiotic space that gives rise to it and fetishizes its products, so too, when the signifying process tries to directly reflect the semiotic and forecloses the thetic, heterogeneity is lost.

These two heterogeneous elements oscillate dialectically in a logic of renewal, one produced and destroyed by the other. Material (bio-social) rejection causes the human animal to give way to the speaking being. Through the jolts and starts of material rejection, the expulsions of the semiotic body become the negativity that allow the would-be speaking being to metonymically replace its privation and excess with a signifier. Material rejection *becomes* the paternal function that prohibits the very primary pleasures that gave rise to it in the first place. In addition to the material rejection inherent in the infant's body, the infant encounters an external prohibition that is prior to the paternal prohibition. The infant encounters the maternal prohibition within the "space" of the mother.

The Law before the Law

The space of the mother is what Kristeva calls the "semiotic *chora*." It is the place of the maternal law before the Law. Kristeva defines the semiotic *chora* as "a nonexpressive totality formed by the drives and their stases in a motility that is as full of movement as it is regulated." (1974, 25) The semiotic *chora* is the place of negativity, the place where the subject is both generated and negated. (1974, 28) Kristeva says that her use of *chora* comes from Plato's *Timeaus* where he uses *chora* to designate an unnameable maternal receptacle. (1974, 26 fn 12) In a long footnote in "Le Sujet en Proces," Kristeva describes the *chora*:

> ... the *chora* is a womb or a nurse in which elements are without identity and without reason. The *chora* is a *place* of a *chaos* which *is* and which *becomes*, preliminary to the constitution of the first measurable body ... the *chora* plays with the body of the mother—of woman—, but in the signifying process.[32] (1973a, 57)

This *chora*, this distant place, is not without regulation and therefore it is the prototype for both the place of enunciation (the subject) and the place of denotation (the object). (1977a, 285) The maternal body is the organizing principle of the semiotic *chora*, because the *chora* is the space in which the mother's body regulates the oral and anal drives. (1974, 27)

Before it enters the Symbolic and encounters the No/Name of the Father, the infant has already lived with maternal regulation, the mother's "no." The mother regulates the material processes of the infant's body. She oversees what goes into, and what comes out of, the infant's body. She alters the relationship between her own body and the infant's accordingly. The child first "learns" lessons of social regulation in relation to the mother's breast; the mother gives and takes away the breast. In this space of maternal regulation, the space of the *chora*, the infant "experiences" a regulation that is more unconscious than conscious. This maternal regulation sets up a pattern that becomes reduplicated in the infant's psyche. It is this pattern of maternal regulation that sets up the possibility of the infant's recognition of the paternal "no" or the Name of the Father as it operates in the oedipal situation. The maternal function, with its law before the law, *prefigures* the paternal function.

Kristeva insists that the paternal prohibition is already operating within the maternal function; material rejection is inherent in the maternal function. The paternal prohibition cannot be complete because it is the mother who enacts the primary regulations, the law before the law, over the child's body. The bodily relation that ensures the child's survival also sets up the child's entrance into the Symbolic and Lacan's metonymy of desire. Unlike Lacan, Kristeva rejoices both because the paternal prohibition is prefigured by, and dependent on, maternal regulation and because the paternal prohibition will never completely succeed since the semiotic makes its way into signification. She rejoices because the semiotic *chora* is both the space that supports the Symbolic and an essential element of signification.

II

THE ABJECT MOTHER

Eia mater, fons amoris
"Hail mother, source of love"[1]

The Controversy of the *Chora*

Probably nothing is more controversial among feminist critics than Kristeva's notion of the semiotic *chora*. Because of her association of the semiotic *chora* with a law before the law, a distant space, the maternal body, the feminine, and woman, some critics have accused Kristeva of essentialism. For example, Domna Stanton and Nancy Fraser argue that through her association of the semiotic *chora* with the feminine and the maternal, Kristeva reduces the feminine to the maternal and thereby essentializes the feminine. Judith Butler and Ann Rosalind Jones both argue that Kristeva makes maternity compulsory for women. Elizabeth Grosz argues that Kristeva's description of maternity as a biological process without a subject essentializes the notion of maternity. Judith Butler takes up a similar line when she claims that Kristeva's maternal principle is universal and homogeneous rather than heterogeneous. (1989, 114–17) In one of the most sustained arguments against Kristeva's notion of maternity, Butler maintains that Kristeva's principle of multiplicity—the semiotic *chora*—operates as a principle of identity, as a univocal signifier. She concludes that Kristeva reifies maternity.

Although there are passages that can be read out of the context of Kristeva's larger project that justify some of these criticisms, I think there are other interesting and useful ways to read Kristeva. Part of what makes Kristeva's semiotic *chora* difficult to read is that it is not homogeneous or univocal. Rather, its meaning and function shift throughout her writings. The fact that the semiotic maternal *chora* is interpreted in such completely contradictory ways by Kristeva's critics might be proof of this. Kristeva claims that she is concerned with discourses in which identity breaks down. She is concerned with discourses that call up a crisis in identity. For her the discourse of maternity is such a discourse. It is a discourse that, possibly more than any other, points to a subject-in-process. I take up Kristeva's diagnosis of the discourse of maternity here in order to develop and extend the new discourse of maternity that she begins in "Stabat Mater" and to set up her suggestion that a misdirected abjection is partially responsible for women's oppression.

Kristeva's discussion of the pregnant maternal body is the central focus (around the time of her own pregnancy that led to the birth of her son in 1976) in two essays, "Motherhood According to Giovanni Bellini" (1975a) and "Stabat Mater." (1976a) For Kristeva the pregnant woman or mother is an incarnation of the split subject. The pregnant maternal body is a split body. (1976a, 234–35; 1975a, 297) Ewa Ziarek argues that for Kristeva the maternal body is a site of an "infolding of otherness," and Alison Ainley calls her notion of motherhood a "double." It is precisely this otherness, this doubleness, that the prevalent discourses of maternity in the West cover over. Kristeva argues that the only available discourses on maternity are those of religion, science, and possibly a certain feminism, all of which cover over the semiotic side of the maternal body. These discourses leave out the pain and *jouissance* of the mother because they operate on a level that challenges the Symbolic with its fundamental notions of autonomy and law.

Kristeva is suspicious of a certain feminism's account of motherhood, particularly existential feminism, which she claims rejects motherhood altogether.[2] She argues that this feminist rejection does not look below the inadequate and distorted discourses of motherhood available in phallocentric culture. (1976a, 234, 260) She is equally suspicious of scientific accounts of motherhood. In addition to biological accounts of motherhood as reproduction, we have psychoanalytic accounts of motherhood. For Freud, the child is the woman's satisfaction. The god-child, strangely enough, is Freud's fantasy. And what of the mother? What of her satisfaction? Kristeva suggests that Freud's account of motherhood as either an attempt to satisfy penis-envy (baby = penis) or a reactivated anal drive (baby = feces) is merely a masculine fantasy. With regard to the complexities of maternal experience, claims Kristeva, "Freud offers only a massive nothing, which, for those who might care to analyze it, is punctuated with this or that remark on the part of Freud's mother, proving to him in the kitchen that his own body is anything but immortal and will crumble away like dough; or the sour photograph of Marthe Freud, the wife, a whole mute story. . . ." (1976a, 255)

The Virgin Mother

Kristeva argues that the traditional religious accounts of motherhood, particularly the myth of the Virgin Mary, can no longer explain, interpret, give meaning to, motherhood. What she describes as the "cult of the Virgin" has been used by Western patriarchy in order to cover up the unsettling aspects of maternity and the mother-child relationship. (1976a) The cult of the Virgin controls maternity and mothers by doing violence to them. Like sacrifice, the cult of the Virgin contains the violence of semiotic drives by turning violence against them. The Virgin's only pleasure is her child who is not hers alone but everyone's, while her silent sorrow is hers alone. Kristeva maintains that the image of the Virgin covers over the tension between the maternal and the Symbolic.

In the biblical stories, the Virgin is impregnated by the Word, the Name of the Father, God. This, argues Kristeva, is a way of insuring paternity and fighting off the remnants of matrilinear society. After all, it is the Name of the Father that guarantees paternity and inheritance. On the one hand, the cult of the Virgin is the reconciliation of matrilinearism and the unconscious needs of the primary identification with the mother. On the other hand, "the requirements of a new society based on exchange and before long on increased production" require "the contribution of the superego and rely on the Symbolic paternal agency." (1976a, 259) This symbolic paternal agency both guarantees and is founded on the exchange and control of women and children through the Name of the Father. (Cf. Lacan 1977, 207; Kristeva 1980c.)

The mother is a threat to the Symbolic order in two immediate ways. Her *jouissance* threatens to make her a subject rather than the Other against which man becomes a subject. In addition, she not only represents but *is* a strange fold between culture and nature that cannot be fully incorporated by the Symbolic:

> . . . no signifier can uplift it [the maternal body] without leaving a remainder, for the signifier is always meaning, communication, or structure, whereas a woman as mother would be, instead, a strange fold that changes culture into nature, speaking into biology. Although it concerns every woman's body, the heterogeneity that cannot be subsumed in the signifier nevertheless explodes violently with pregnancy (the threshold of culture and nature) and the child's arrival. . . . (1976a, 259)

The Symbolic order, however, attempts a complete incorporation of the mother with her strange fold and her outlaw *jouissance* through the cult of the Virgin. First, the Virgin birth does away with the "primal scene" and the mother's *jouissance* that might accompany it. The Virgin's is an immaculate conception. For Kristeva this fantasy of the immaculate conception is a protection against a fantasy that is too much for the child to bear: "that of being supernumerary, excluded from the act of pleasure [the primal scene] that is the origin of its existence." (1987, 42) Rather than be excluded from the mother's *jouissance*, the child excludes the mother's *jouissance* from the fantasy of the Virgin birth.

This is all the more striking with Kristeva's claim that "Virgin" is a mistranslation of "the Semitic term that indicates the socio-legal status of a young unmarried woman." (1976a, 236–37) The *jouissance* of the young unmarried woman is a *jouissance* that is not confined within the social sanctions of marriage. It is an outlaw *jouissance* that does not come under paternal control, the remnants of a matrilinear society where the resulting child can take the name of only the mother. The *jouissance* of this young unmarried woman and her "bastard" child present a threat to the paternal function of the Symbolic order. The image of the Virgin, however, controls this threat. The Virgin has no *jouissance*; and her body is marked with the Name of the Father. There is no mistake about paternity here in spite of the fact that in the Christian story Joseph becomes Mary's husband.

The power of the mother in a matrilinear society, the power of the child's primary relationship/identification with the mother, and the power of the mother as the authority over the child's body are all condensed into the symbol of the Virgin mother. The mother's power is brought under paternal control. It is domesticated:

> It is as if paternity were necessary in order to relive the archaic impact of the maternal body on man; in order to complete the investigation of a ravishing maternal *jouissance* but also of its terrorizing aggressivity; in order somehow to admit the threat that the male feels as much from the possessive maternal body as from his separation from it—a threat that he immediately returns to that body. . . . (1975a, 263)

Man returns the semiotic threat to the maternal body through the cult of the Virgin. The maternal body is allowed joy in only pain. Her body has only ear, milk, and tears. (1976a, 248–49) The sexed body is replaced by the "ear of understanding," the Virgin Mary of the Catholic Church. (1976a, 257) In this way, the Virgin covers over the maternal fold between the biological and cultural, both the bodily connection between mother and child and the separation of child from mother that gives way to its entry into the Symbolic order. The Virgin's maternity, and her relation to her child, is purely spiritual. Otherwise, the god-child is contaminated.

Kristeva suggests that the silent ear, milk, and tears "are metaphors of nonspeech, of a 'semiotics' that linguistic communication does not account for." (1976a, 249) The Virgin mother becomes the representative of a "return of the repressed" semiotic. (1976a, 249) Although the myth of the Virgin can control the maternal semiotic, it cannot contain the semiotic. Kristeva argues that Christianity, with its Virgin birth, both unravels and protects the paternal function. (1987, 40) Like sacrifice, the violence of the semiotic returns within the very ritual that attempts to repress it. The maternal semiotic is focused in the symbol of the Virgin and its threat to the Symbolic order is thereby controlled.

Kristeva argues that, until recently, in many cultures the symbol of the Virgin has been effective in subsuming the feminine into the maternal and subduing any semiotic threats from either. She explains this, and the fact that so many women have wished to identify with this tortured Virgin, by suggesting that the Virginal maternal is a way of dealing with "feminine paranoia." (1976a, 257) Paranoiacs, for Freud, are fixated at the stage of narcissism. This is a stage of presymbolic primary identification.[3] It is the idealization of the relationship that binds us to the archaic mother. (1976a, 234) The symbol of the Virgin provides a substitute for feminine paranoia—the primary relationship/identification with the mother—and allows women to enter the Symbolic order without sacrificing their mothers.

An identification with the Virgin is an identification with the mother and the Symbolic at the same time. It is an identification with the perfect, immortal, holy Mother. But it is also an identification with the Word that marks and defines her. She is, after all, a symbolic mother. By identifying with the Virgin, women can identify with the mother within the Symbolic order.[4]

In spite of Kristeva's nostalgia for the Holy mother of the Catholic church, she argues that a woman's identification with the Virgin is masochistic. It sacrifices an identification with the semiotic maternal body for an identification with the symbolic mother, a paternal mother. In the myth, the Virgin's is not a real motherhood. She does not have the mother's ambiguous relationship to the child. She is not supposed to know what the mother knows—that the child is not a god, but that it is real. For in the case of the Virgin, the child is God and the Virgin's relation to the child is always a relation to an Other; and it is not a relationship with just any other, but with The Other, The Transcendental, God. Even from the beginning there is not the undecidability between mother and child that makes/allows the mother's primary narcissism—her identification not with a separate other, but with herself. This is precisely the way in which the cult of the Virgin controls the semiotic in order to maintain the Symbolic. The Virgin doesn't provide a symbolic substitute for primary narcissism. Rather, the myth of the Virgin denies the very possibility of such an identification.

The mother is sacrificed to the Virgin. So it is no wonder that the Virgin can no longer provide the necessary support against feminine paranoia. The myth of the Virgin is crumbling and it no longer provides a solution, "or else provides one that is felt as too coercive by twentieth-century women."[5] (1976a, 262) Kristeva suggests that we need a new discourse of maternity. At the end of "Stabat Mater" she can only hint that this new discourse is a new ethics of music and love. Kristeva suggests that what we need is an ear for listening to motherhood. (1976a, 263) Does the understanding ear of the analyst replace the understanding ear of the Virgin? Does Kristeva, the analyst, take the place of the Virgin Mother?

One of the central claims that Kristeva makes in "Stabat Mater" is that in childbirth a mother identifies with her own mother. Kristeva as mother, then, identifies with her own mother, not just her own mother but also the Virgin Mother. "Stabat Mater" can be read as Kristeva's own identification with the Virgin. In the right column of the essay she analyzes the function of the Catholic discourse of the Virgin Mary. In the left column she describes her *own* experience of childbirth. Kristeva's identification with the Virgin goes beyond the parallel nature of her discourse. Interestingly, there is no father in her description of her own childbirth; there is only the son and the mother.

Through her poetic account of her own childbirth Kristeva reintroduces what has been repressed in the Catholic discourse of maternity: the semiotic body. **"Let a body venture at last out of its shelter,"** says Kristeva in her left column, **"take a chance with meaning under a veil of words. WORD FLESH."** Kristeva's left column is the flesh become word. The fleshed mother with her *jouissance*, her "sexual-intellectual-physical passion, of death," replaces the Mother-God. We no longer need goddesses, says Kristeva, when we have mothers' love and music. Her left column is some of this mother's music. (1976, 262–63)

The split column of "Stabat Mater" depicts what is left out of the discourse of the Virgin. The split column brings to the surface of the text the mother's sex, two columns joined together out of which the child is born, which is subterranean in the Catholic representation of motherhood. In an interview with Rosalind Coward, Kristeva says that with the two columns and the two kinds of typeface she wanted to give the impression of a scar or wound. (1984b, 24) She claims that the theoretician is "posited precisely on the place of this scar" because of the painful transference between the theorist and her object. Kristeva's boldfaced column speaks this pain. It sings not only what has been repressed in religious and scientific discourses on maternity but also what has been repressed in theory in general. For Kristeva the repressed is an encounter with the maternal semiotic. The repressed is an encounter/identification with the mother. This repression leaves a scar.

Kristeva's identification of the two columns—which suggest the mother's sex—with a scar suggests castration, what she might call in *Black Sun* "feminine castration." Cut off from its driving force, the maternal semiotic, any discourse on maternity, including Kristeva's, is castrated. Kristeva, the melancholy theorist longing for the lost mother, positions herself in the place of this painful scar. She identifies with castration, the castration of a mother who has lost her mother; she identifies with the bittersweet reunion of the lost mother through a childbirth that necessarily means losing the child. The image of this split text as wound or scar multiplies interpretations.

For example, it is possible to read the scar in "Stabat Mater" through Kristeva's analysis of feminine castration in *Black Sun*. There she argues that women find it difficult, if not impossible, to give up what she calls the maternal "Thing." (I will elaborate on this "Thing" below.) For now I will call this "Thing" the maternal body. Women, says Kristeva, risk losing all psychic stability when faced with the loss of the maternal "Thing." This loss of a woman's very identity is what Kristeva calls "feminine castration." A woman risks losing herself when she loses her mother. And, for Kristeva, it is through childbirth that a woman identifies with her mother on this semiotic level of the "Thing." This reunion is bittersweet because it reminds the new mother of what she has lost. Insofar as the reunion is not ever fully symbolic, it does not allow the new mother to sublimate her loss. In other words, childbirth is not the cure for feminine melancholia.[6] In this reading, the scar in "Stabat Mater" represents what Cixous might call the new mother's "lack lack." The lack of lack of the maternal Thing" is a reunion with it. It is a reunion through lack. It is the lack lack of Kristeva's "feminine castration."[7]

The scar in "Stabat Mater" can also be read as the loss of the child. Through the split columns of the mother's sex comes the child. It is necessary for the mother to lose her child in childbirth in order to have her child. Also, as Kristeva describes it, it is necessary for the new mother to lose her child in order to rediscover her own mother. This reading takes us back to Freud's thesis that the child is the woman's penis-substitute. In Freud's scenario, childbirth would be a strange sort of feminine castration. Once again the new mother loses in order to gain, this time a penis-substitute. But, even Kristeva believes that the penis-child equation is the fantasy of a hysterical male.

The scar in "Stabat Mater" can also be reread in terms of Jane Gallop's argument in The Daughter's Seduction that Kristeva dephallicizes the phallic position by assuming the position of the phallic mother. (1982, 119) Gallop uses two columns in her chapter on Kristeva in order to mimic what she sees as a conflict between a conservative and a dissident maternal in Kristeva's essay. Gallop argues that Kristeva presumes to speak from the place of the mother—a place that she defines as both double and foreign—at the same time that she maintains that it is impossible to speak from this position because it is antithetical to symbols. It is important to remember, however, that for Kristeva language is heterogeneous; it is composed of both symbols and semiotic drives that are antithetical to symbols. Gallop claims that Kristeva takes up the privileged position of phallic mother at the same time that she exposes the fallacy of the phallic mother. That is to say that Kristeva exposes the Virgin Mary as a fraud at the same time that she usurps the phallic position of the Virgin.

In terms of Gallop's reading of "Stabat Mater," Kristeva's scar can represent the castration of the phallic mother. It is a kind of autocastration. She exposes herself, the human scientist, as fraud even as she exposes the Virgin as fraud. Rather than occupy the phallic position from which she

has evacuated the Virgin Mary, Kristeva claims to occupy the position of
the scar that results from that evacuation. Once again in terms of traditional psychoanalytic theory the scar can be read as the result of the
castration of the phallic mother. This castration is necessary for the child
to be weaned. Also, for Freud, exposure of the phallic mother's lack is
necessary in order to initiate sexual difference. Everything changes when
the child realizes that the mother "does not have one."

Kristeva provides another analysis of the child's relation to its mother
and her scar, a relation that gives rise to sexual difference. She describes
the child's relation to the mother's sex as an abject relation that facilitates
the child's separation from the maternal body. The child does not see the
mother's sex as threatening, as scar, because she "does not have one."
Rather, on Kristeva's analysis, the child sees the mother's sex as threatening because it is the canal out of which it came. For the child at this stage,
its mother's sex represents its birth canal. And, insofar as the child was
once on the other side of that canal, its autonomy is threatened. It is
important to remember that for Kristeva the mother is "alone of her sex."
To say that the mother's sex is reduced to the birth canal for the child is
not to say that women's sex is reduced to the birth canal. If fact, Kristeva
suggests that it is this confusion that leads to the abjection of all women
rather than the necessary abjection of the mother. (I come back to this
argument in chapter 6.) The abject mother's sex threatens the child in a
way that women's sex should not. The abject mother's threat can be read
as a castration threat of sorts, an inverted castration. The child fears the
lack of separation. It fears being sucked back into the mother through her
sex. Once again it is the lack of lack that the child fears. But this castration
and the resulting scar are hidden under the robes of the Virgin Mary.

The Splitting Mother

The cult of the Virgin covers up the semiotic maternal body, especially
what Kristeva calls the "abject" maternal body. Kristeva introduces the
notion of abjection in *Powers of Horror.* (1980a) The abject is disgusting.
It makes you want to vomit. Abjection

> . . . is an extremely strong feeling which is at once somatic and symbolic,
> and which is above all a revolt of the person against an external menace
> from which one wants to keep oneself at a distance, but of which one has
> the impression that it is not only an external menace but that it may menace
> us from inside. So it is a desire for separation, for becoming autonomous
> and also the feeling of an impossibility of doing so. . . . (1980b, 135–36)

The abject is something repulsive that both attracts and repels. It holds
you there in spite of your disgust. It fascinates. Rotting flesh can be abject,

defilement or pollution that requires exclusion or even taboo. Crime can be abject, transgression of the law that requires exclusion or even death. Moral infractions can be abject, a threatening otherness that Christianity calls "sin." (1980a, 17) In Kristeva's account it is not a "lack of cleanliness or health that causes abjection but what disturbs identity, system, order." (1980a,4)

The abject is what is on the border, what doesn't respect borders. It is "ambiguous," "in-between," "composite." (1980a, 4) In her litany on abjection, Kristeva proclaims that it is "a terror that dissembles, a hatred that smiles, a passion that uses the body for barter instead of inflaming it, a debtor who sells you up, a friend who stabs you. . . ." (1980a, 4) It is neither one nor the other. It is undecidable. The abject is not a "quality in itself." Rather, it is a relationship to a boundary and represents what has been "jettisoned out of that boundary, its other side, a margin." (1980a, 69) The abject is what threatens identity. It is neither good nor evil, subject nor object, ego nor unconscious, but something that threatens the distinctions themselves. The abject is not an object that corresponds to an ego; rather, it is what is excluded by the superego: "To each ego its object, to each superego its abject." (1980a, 2) Although every society is founded on the abject—constructing boundaries and jettisoning the antisocial— every society may have its own abject. In all cases, the abject threatens the unity/identity of both society and the subject. It calls into question the boundaries upon which they are constructed.

Even jettisoned, the abject can still threaten the social, the Symbolic order. The Symbolic can maintain itself only by maintaining its borders; and the abject points to the fragility of those borders. The Symbolic is the order of borders, discrimination, and difference. (1980a, 69) Reality is parceled into words and categories. Society is parceled into classes, castes, professional and family roles, etc. The abject threat comes from what has been prohibited by the Symbolic order, what has been prohibited so that the Symbolic order can be. The prohibition that founds, and yet undermines, society is the prohibition against the maternal body, whether it is the oedipal prohibition against incest formulated by Freud, the prohibition against the mother's desire or *jouissance* formulated by Lacan, or the prohibition against the semiotic *chora* formulated by Kristeva. All of these prohibitions are directed against the maternal body. (1980a, 14) It is what is off limits.

On the level of personal archeology, abjection shows up as the struggle to separate from the maternal body. This body, "having been the mother, will turn into an abject. Repelling, rejecting; repelling itself, rejecting itself. Ab-jecting." (1980a, 13) The child tries to separate but feels that separation is impossible. The mother is made abject in order to facilitate the separation from her. At this point the mother is not-yet-object and the child is not-yet-subject. The abject takes the place of the Other that will be occupied by the mother once the mirror stage is traversed. The child cannot tell if the abject is itself (the alter-ego deceives) or its other (the mother's body is still immediate). The Other, says Kristeva, dwells in the abject as the child's alter-ego. Or, the mother's other, the child, dwells in her as alter-ego; in either case, the abject is in between the self and the other. (1980a, 10, 54) The mother cannot tell whether this other in her *is* her or not; and either alternative seems equally impossible. The child in this abject relation to its mother is not yet separated from her but is no longer identical with her.

"Abjection is therefore a kind of *narcissistic crisis.*" (1980a, 14) It is the "realization" that the primary identification with the mother is a "seeming," a fake. It is the beginning of separation prior to the mirror stage. For Kristeva, it is the separation before the beginning. This abjection that calls the child's primary narcissism to account is founded in birth itself:

> Abjection preserves what existed in the archaism of pre-objectal relationship, in the immemorial violence with which a body becomes separated from another body in order to be—maintaining that night in which the outline of the signified thing vanishes and where only the imponderable affect is carried out. . . . This means once more that the heterogeneous flow, which portions the abject and sends back abjection, already dwells in a human animal that has been highly altered. . . . *Significance is indeed inherent in the human body.* (1980a, 10; my emphasis)

Human life, human society, is founded on the abject separation of one body from another at birth. This separation, like subsequent ones, is labored but necessary. This primary separation, which founds and prefigures symbolic separation, is prior even to the maternal authority that separates the infant's body into drives and satisfactions. The prototypical abject experience, then, is the experience of birth itself. It is at the birth of the child, and not before, that the identity of the human subject is most visibly called into question. Before the umbilical cord is cut, who can decide whether there is one or two?

The abject is pre-identity, presubject, preobject. It is undecidable between subject and object, the unruly border, birth. For Kristeva, this not-yet-subject/not-yet-object is associated with the archaic mother: "defilement is the translinguistic spoor of the most archaic boundaries of the self's clean and proper body. In that sense, if it is a jettisoned object, it is so from the mother." (1980a, 73) The most archaic boundaries of the clean and proper self, of course, are those regulated by the maternal authority, in particular anal and oral drives. Food, not yet the body, is taken in through the mouth. Feces, no longer the body, is expelled through the anus. The boundaries between body and not-body are controlled by the mother. And both the subject and society, which depend on the Symbolic order, depend on the repression of this maternal authority, which represents the threat from beyond the borders of the Symbolic. (1980a, 70) The Symbolic that sets up a parceling order represses the parceling order already set up by the maternal authority over the infant's body. (1980a, 72)

The Symbolic order maintains its borders through ritual. Kristeva argues that by means of a system of ritual exclusions the Symbolic looks back toward the archaic experience of maternal authority and makes of it a partial-object. The ritual does not turn the preobjectal abject into an object; rather, it treats the abject as a type of partial-object. These rituals are more reenactments than symbolizations. As such, they never really secure the borders of the Symbolic. Rather, these rituals "illustrate the boundary between semiotic authority and symbolic law." (1980a, 73) They point to the weak spots in the Symbolic. Just as waste is expelled from the healthy body, the abject is expelled from healthy society. There comes a point where the body itself becomes waste, the corpse, and society becomes barbaric, genocide. (Cf. Lacan 1955, 232.) Our rituals, violent in themselves, are flimsy protections against disintegration.

For Kristeva, in the abject subject the maternal body becomes a phobic "object." Unless the subject can confront the abject mother, which requires the help of the father, discourse will not be tenable. (1980a, 6) (See the next chapter.) Although the experience of abjection short-circuits the Symbolic, it does so differently than either neurosis or psychosis. In fact, Kristeva suggests that abjection operates outside of the dialectic of negativity that is central to the theory of the Unconscious upon which Freud's analysis of both neurosis and psychosis is based. She explains that abjection, specifically phobia, is based on exclusion rather than denial. Freud, she argues, put forward a theory of "*denial* as a means of figuring out neurosis, that of *rejection* (*repudiation*) as a means of situating psychosis." The neurotic denies the object or substitutes a fetishized object. The psychotic repudiates the desire altogether, Lacan's "repudiation of the Name of the Father." (1980a, 7) Kristeva argues that the theory of the Unconscious that informs this analysis is based on the hypothesis that the contents of the Unconscious are repressed and, although they do not have access to consciousness, they affect the subject's speech, body, or both. In contrast to neurosis or psychosis, abjection does not display repression, or at least not a repression that is dependent upon the dialectic of negativity. The abject does not negate. Rather, the abject excludes:

> The "unconscious" contents remain here *excluded* but in a strange fashion: not radically enough to allow for a secure differentiation between subject and object, and yet clearly enough for a defensive *position* to be established—one that implies a refusal but also a sublimating elaboration. As if the fundamental opposition were between I and Other or, in more archaic fashion, between Inside and Outside. As if such an opposition subsumed

the one between Conscious and Unconscious, elaborated on the basis of neurosis. (1980a, 7)

The phobic is "borderline." On the edge of psychosis, but not mad. (1980a, 6) Whereas the neurotic has displaced or denied the Other in order to maintain its ego, and the psychotic has foreclosed the Other and therefore the possibility of an ego, the phobic has confused the Other with itself and upholds its "ego" within the Other. (1980a, 15) In some sense, the abject "subject" is too precocious. It realizes that it can be constituted as a subject only by virtue of the Other—that its identity rests on separation—even before it undergoes this process. Still on the level of drives, the abject sublimates the "object" before it is an object proper. The abject sublimates it by taking its place, or, more properly, by taking the place of the undecidable:

> The abject might then appear as the most *fragile* (from a synchronic point of view), the most *archaic* (from a diachronic one) sublimation of an "object" still inseparable from drives. The abject is that pseudo-object that is made up *before* but appears only *within* the gaps of secondary repression. *The abject would thus be the "object" of primal repression.* (1980a, 12)

In this passage Kristeva points out that the abject appears in the structure/logic of the subject as its most fragile relation to the object; and it appears in the history/chronology of the subject as the earliest relation to the object. Although it is "constituted" before, the abject shows up only within secondary repression, language. Through language, it points to the "object," abject, that has been repressed in primal repression. Kristeva defines primal repression as the "ability of the speaking being, always already haunted by the Other, to divide, reject, repeat." But as she points out, in the primal repression the speaking being divides without one subject or object having been constituted yet (or no longer). (1980a, 12)

"Why [this preobjectal splitting]?" asks Kristeva. "Perhaps because of maternal anguish, unable to be satiated within the encompassing symbolic," she answers. (1980a, 12) At this point, the only explanation that she gives for this answer is that the mother has difficulty acknowledging, or being acknowledged by, the Symbolic order. So she is hesitant to turn over her child to it. The conflict is the result of "the problem that she has with the Phallus that her father or her husband stands for." (1980a, 13) Within the economy of this Phallus, only the child authenticates her, and so why should she let it go? Within the economy of the Phallus, and the only available discourse on motherhood, the mother's is always a masochistic joy. She can take joy in the abject—violent and painful—birth of her child.

As for the child, it is left in awkward position between birth and birth (between its birth and the realization of its birth), repulsed by, and yet

mourning for, this maternal anguish.[8] If the mother's desire exists outside
of paternal discourse, if paternal discourse cannot account for it (the discourse of the Virgin, or psychoanalysis, or even a certain feminism), then
in order for the child to become its mother's desire, it too must fall out.[9]
If, within the paternal discourse, the mother's desire has no object, then
in order for the child to become its mother's desire, it must take of the
place of no-object, the abject. To put it in terms of Lacan's metaphor: if
within paternal discourse, especially psychoanalysis, woman is always
and only man's Other, then at most she can only make believe that she is
the Phallus. (See 1974c, 141–144.) That is, she can only pretend to be the
object of man's desire, his gratification, the Phallus. Or, her only gratification, a masochistic jouissance, is to gratify another, to be the Phallus. In
these terms, then, the child must be the object of the phallus's desire, the
hole, the hole out of which it came, "the adored and abhorred [abject]
maternal sex." (Cf. 1983, 79, 369.) The child identifies with the murky
space between the inside and outside of the mother's body.

On the level of personal archeology, abjection becomes a kind of perverse protection in the face of primal repression. The not-yet-subject with
its not-yet, or no-longer, object maintains "itself" as the abject. Abjection
is a way of denying the primal narcissistic identification with the mother,
almost. The child becomes the abject in order to avoid both separation
from, and identification with, the maternal body—both equally painful,
both equally impossible. If the abject "is a jettisoned object, it is so from
the mother." The child is this jettisoned object, the waste violently expelled from the mother's body. The "subject" discovers itself as the impossible separation/identity of the maternal body. It hates that body but only
because it can't be free of it. That body, the body without borders, the
body out of which this abject subject came, is impossible. (1980a, 6) It is
a horrifying, devouring body.[10] (Cf. 1980a, 39.) It is a body that evokes
rage and fear.

Kristeva says in an interview that the maternal body enrages because it
carries the child: "if there is a sort of rage against mothers it is not only
because they take care of the child, it's because they carry it in their
bodies." (1980b, 138) This rage is not just directed against the outside of
the maternal body that nourishes and weans; it is also directed against
the inside of the maternal body, and especially the inside that becomes
outside, the child among other things. This rage and fear are affects that
mediate between primary narcissism and the words that haven't yet been
acquired. They protect the "subject" against a complete collapse into primary narcissism; yet, at the same time, they show the crisis caused by the
loss of union with the maternal body.

Obviously, the identification with the border, or more precisely, with
what breaks the border (between the inside and outside of the body), is
going to have grave consequences for the oedipal situation, in more ways

than one. The child, the male child, feels rage against his mother because her carrying him in her womb compromises his identity. How can he become a man when "he" was once a woman? He was once part, now the expelled waste, of a woman's body. Even more curiously, how can he become a man and love a woman, that abject and threatening hole "represented" by his mother?

In *Powers of Horror* Kristeva describes how the child, there always the male child, must split his mother in order to take up his socially prescribed sexual identity. The mother is split in two: the abject and the sublime. (1980a, 157) Making the mother abject allows the child to separate from her and become autonomous. But if the mother is only abject, then she becomes the phobic object and the child himself becomes abject. In this case, the oedipal situation would be thrown out of alignment, on the border of disappearing altogether. If the mother remains abject, she never becomes the object, and certainly not the object of love. The phobic substitutes the sign, in a denial of sexual difference, for the absent object. (1980a, 45) Within the heterosexual narrative, the mother must also be made sublime so that masculine sexuality can take her, a woman, as an object of love. If she is only sublime, the child will not separate from her. He will have no subject or object identity whatsoever, no primary repression and thus no secondary repression. In other words, the Other will have been completely foreclosed, never set up, and the child will be psychotic. He will still be unable to love a woman, or anyone else. For the psychotic, there is no one else, no object, no other(s). The sublime and abject must come together under the auspices of the paternal in order to produce the object of love.[11] The child can overcome the abject mother only through a paternal agency. (1975a, 263) Although this paternal agency brings with it the need to symbolize, it is not Lacan's authoritarian father. (1980a, 118, 44; 1981, 314) Rather, for Kristeva, it is the loving father who helps the child overcome abjection (see the next chapter).

The Maternal "Thing"

So, the son splits the mother, has his cake, and eats it too; but what about the daughter? Whereas the son splits the mother in order to unify himself, if the daughter splits the mother, she splits herself. In addition, feminine sexual identity does not have to divide the mother. Rather, within the heterosexual narrative, her sexual identity requires that she abandon her mother as love object for the father. (1980b, 137) Now it would seem that within feminine sexuality the mother need only be abject. But when the female makes her mother abject in order to reject her, she also makes herself abject, rejects herself, and not just temporarily. Kristeva maintains that when women do embrace the abject or even make themselves abject, it is in order to please a man, perhaps a pervert turned on by abjection. (1980a, 54; 1980b, 136) Feminine perversion is very rare. Kristeva says that this is because of the difficulty women have in "combat" with their mothers. (1980b, 136–37)

In an interview Kristeva identifies two relations that a woman can have with her mother. One possibility is that she doesn't ever "get rid" of her mother. Rather, she carries with her "this living corpse," the mother's body that no longer nourishes. (1980b, 137) Kristeva claims that usually women close their eyes to this corpse. They forget about it. And they certainly don't eroticize it. (1980b, 137) The other alternative is that a woman forms a defense against the mother. As a defense, some women devote themselves to the Symbolic order. Kristeva identifies feminism as one such defense. Presumably, politics, art, and science are others. Kristeva warns that if a woman enters this "combat" with her mother without any such defense, it can lead to "fairly serious forms of psychosis." (1980b, 137)

In *Black Sun* Kristeva describes feminine sexuality as something akin to an extreme form of abjection. It is not merely the case that the maternal body must be abjected so that the child will not abject herself. Now the maternal body must be killed so that the child will not kill herself. "Matricide" says Kristeva, "is our vital necessity." (1987, 27) It is necessary that the child leave the maternal body. The child must agree to lose the mother in order to be able to imagine her or name her. The negation that this process involves is not the negation of the mother. Rather, it is the negation of the *loss* of the mother that signals proper entry into language. Kristeva suggests that the speaking being seems to be saying: "I have lost an essential object that happens to be, in the final analysis, my mother. . . . But no, I have found her again in signs, or rather since I consent to lose her I have not lost her (that is the negation), I can recover her in language." (1987, 43)

At the moment of loss this "essential object" is not yet an object. In order for the child to have any relation to an *object*, it must first lose the maternal body. But until it does lose the maternal body, it cannot love any *object*. This leads Kristeva to make a distinction between *thing* (*chose*) and *object* (*objet*). Unlike Lacan, Kristeva maintains that this Thing has meaning before it becomes an Object operating within signification proper:

> . . . the continuum of the body, which is in the process of becoming "one's own and proper body," is articulated as an organized discontinuity, exercising a precocious and primary mastery, flexible yet powerful, over the erotogenic zones, blended with the preobject, the maternal Thing. What appears on the psychological level as omnipotence *is the power of semiotic rhythms, which convey an intense presence of meaning in a presubject still incapable of signification.* (1987, 62)

At this stage the child is just catching on to the desire of the other. The key is to invest this meaning in signification; it is a transition from primary to secondary processes. For Kristeva, it is through imagination that the meaning of the Thing can become the signification of the Object. She argues that through the presymbolic imaginary operating before the mirror stage the child can transfer the meaning and affect of the maternal Thing into language. By doing so the child makes the Thing into an object that it can then love. If the child cannot lose the Thing in order to take an object, it is stuck at the level of depression.

Kristeva defines the Thing "as the real that does not lend itself to signification, the center of attraction and repulsion, seat of sexuality from which the object of desire will become separated." (1987, 13) Somehow the Thing must become an Object and the child's erotic relation to this Thing must become desire. "Matricide" is successful only if the child can eroticize the loss either by taking a mother substitute as love object or by eroticizing the *other* and finding substitutes. (1987, 28)

Kristeva argues that feminine sexuality is more likely to be a depressive sexuality because it is more difficult for women to commit the necessary matricide. (1987, 28–29) Because of a woman's bodily identification with the maternal body it is difficult for her to kill the maternal body without also killing herself. For women, matricide does not ward off suicide. For women, matricide is a form of suicide. A woman cannot properly mourn the lost object. She cannot get rid of the maternal body. Kristeva woefully claims that she carries the maternal Thing with her locked like a corpse in the crypt of her psyche.

The loss of the object seems beyond remedy. In what Kristeva calls "feminine castration" woman has much more at stake than man—in spite of the fact that as Cixous claims she lacks lack. For the woman there is more at stake than bodily integrity or gratification of desire. For her it is a question of losing herself. It is a question of losing desire itself. It is a question of *becoming* Lack.

Kristeva suggests that for a woman her Phallus is her psyche. And the castration threat is a threat against her psyche. In order for her psyche to live, a woman must find a way to turn the maternal Thing into an erotic object. She must find a way to turn the maternal body into desire without killing herself. Kristeva says that analysis (among other things) can turn the Thing into an object of desire:

> By revealing the sexual (homosexual) secret of the depressive course of action that causes the melancholy person to *live with death*, analysis gives back its place to desire within the patient's psychic territory (the death drive is not the death wish). It thus marks off a psychic territory that becomes able to integrate *loss* as signifiable as well erogenetic. The separation henceforth appears no longer as the threat of disintegration but as a step-

ping stone toward some other—conflictive, bearing Eros and Thanatos, open
to both meaning and nonmeaning. (1987, 83)

She suggests that part of the reason why feminine sexuality is melancholy is because within our heterosexist culture a woman cannot have a
mother-substitute as an object of desire in the way that a man can. In
other words, feminine sexuality is melancholy because it is fundamentally
homosexual and must be kept a secret within a heterosexist culture. It is
possible, however, that if the dependence on the maternal body can be
separated from the dependence on the mother, then the necessary "matricide" can take place and a woman can lose the maternal body and still
love her mother. This means that she can lose the maternal body as maternal container or maternal Thing and love her mother's body, her own
body, as the body of a woman. Unlike Freud, who maintains that in order
to develop normally females must change their love objects and erogenous
zones by *denying* their original love objects and erogenous zones, Kristeva
suggests that females must admit, even (re)*embrace*, those original loves
and pleasures.

For all children the "battle" to become autonomous is a "battle" with
the mother. For all children primal repression is a repression of the semiotic identification with the mother's body. In the traditional psychoanalytic account primal repression is replaced and strengthened by a
secondary repression, language. Language, in the end, comes through the
Law of the Father, which guarantees that the primary prototype of the
object, the mother, is signifiable even while she is desiring. Kristeva suggests that if we look closely at this thesis—that the mother is the first
object—we see that "no sooner sketched out, such a thesis is exploded by
its contradictions and flimsiness." (1980a, 32) For behind this mother-
object is the mother's semiotic body, filled with drives and preobjects.
Behind this mother-object is the anti-oedipus, semiotic negativity, the
logic of renewal, which takes us beyond Oedipus and the unitary subject.

Although both Freud and Lacan acknowledge that the primary dyad is
made up of mother and child, they emphasize the function of the Father
and his Phallus. The oedipal situation revolves around him and the big
stick with which he enforces the Law. He initiates the speaking being into
language. In this scenario, especially Lacan's version of it, the third term
(the father), or, more precisely, the fourth term (the Symbolic), is not
merely a satellite that circles the primary dyad. Rather, it is their sun that
burns through the milky way that connects mother and child and at the
same time provides life and light to the speaking being. If this sun is
eclipsed, the speaking being gives way to something subhuman, even
animal.

Kristeva takes us back to the milky way of the primary dyad. She analyzes the pulses and jolts of this primary universe made up of only mother

and child. In Kristeva's scenario the father remains a third term that merely echoes with words the sounds already moving through this distant galaxy. The mother-child dyad provides a foundation for all social relations. It provides the basis for an ethics of love that operates outside of the Law of the Father. The mother's experience of pregnancy and birth provides a model for Kristeva's "herethics."

Herethics—Loving the Other as / in Oneself[12]

Kristeva re-asks Freud's question about feminine sexuality, "What does the woman want?" by asking, "What does the mother want?" She answers that the mother's desire is indeterminate; it is a desire for the Phallus of the imaginary father that could be her father or her child's father. In either case, it is a desire for the paternal Phallus that, within this Lacanian framework, represents gratification. What does any desire want? Gratification from an Other. This is the lesson that the child learns even on the semiotic level. But what if the mother wants to be loved like a child herself? What if the mother creates a new kind of love that doesn't require the third party to stand in between both holding apart and bringing together? A love outside of the Law?

Late in *Tales of Love*, in a piece written prior to the rest, "Stabat Mater," Kristeva imagines this outlaw love. She imagines the mother's love for the child, which is a love for herself but also the willingness to give herself up, as the basis of a new ethics, "herethics." (1983, 262–63) To imagine herethics, Kristeva suggests that it is necessary to listen to the mother and her music. She claims that Motherhood needs the support of a mother's mother (even in the person of a father, or imaginary father). (1983, 227) The mother's oscillating union-disunion with her child recalls her own union with her mother. When we listen to Kristeva, the mother, we see that her mother is present in her own motherhood:

> Recovered childhood, dreamed peace restored, in sparks, flash of cells, instant of laughter, smiles in the blackness of dreams, at night, opaque joy that roots me in her bed, my mother's, and projects him, a son, a butterfly soaking up dew from her hand, there, nearby, in the night. Alone: she, I, and he. (1983, 247)

The love that founds herethics is a daughter's love through identification with her mother. A mother's love is her reunion with her own mother, not only as a third party, but also as herself. The child's transferential identification with the imaginary father, then, is an identification with its mother's reunion with her mother. It is this union that satisfies, makes one complete.

What does a mother want, especially in childbirth? She wants her mother. "The Paradox: Mother or Primary Narcissism," the subtitle of "Stabat Mater," points to the mother as the site of the primary identification, what Kristeva calls the "imaginary father." If the mother loves an Other, it is her own mother. And she loves her mother not only as an Other, but also as herself, now a mother. This love, which is narcissism, within patriarchal analysis "the inability to love," is the basis of Kristeva's herethics.

Herethics is an ethics that is founded on the relationship between the mother and child during pregnancy and birth.[13] This ethics sets up one's obligations to the other as obligations to the self and obligations to the species. It is founded on the ambiguity in pregnancy and birth between subject and object positions. Pregnancy, says Kristeva, is an "institutionalized psychosis": Am I me or it? (1986, 297) The other cannot be separated from the self. The other is within the self. It is not in its place—the place of the other. Rather, it is in the place of the subject. This inability to separate self from other is a symptom of psychosis, the fundamental "psychosis" upon which any relationship is built. Pregnancy, says Kristeva, is the only place where this psychosis is socially acceptable.[14]

How can we account for this other that resides in the maternal body without destroying the identity of the mother? And if our mothers have no identity, are we born out of a void? The mother's identity is questionable and as such it points to the questionable identity of the subject itself. After all, is not the mother a subject too? Kristeva argues that to suppose that the mother is the master of her gestation preserves her identity. In this case, she is the master of a process that is prior to the social contract of the group, a process that is presymbolic and therefore without identity; she risks losing her identity again at the same time as she wards off its loss. We assure ourselves that "mamma is there" and that her presence in, and identity through, the process guarantees that everything is representable. (1983, 238) Of course this covers over "mamma's" questionable identity in this process. "In a double-barreled move," claims Kristeva, "psychotic tendencies are acknowledged, but at the same time they are settled, quieted, and bestowed upon the mother in order to maintain the ultimate guarantee: symbolic coherence." (1983, 238)

Maternity is a bridge between nature and culture, the drives and the Symbolic order. The mother's body is the "pivot of sociality," "at once the guarantee and a threat to its stability." (1986, 297) The mother's body guarantees the continuation of the species; and yet her questionable identity threatens symbolic unity. Maternity is impossible for the Symbolic order. Kristeva defines the maternal as "the ambivalent principle that is bound to the species, on the one hand, and on the other stems from an identity catastrophe that causes the Name to topple over into the unnameable that one imagines as femininity, nonlanguage, or body." (1983, 235)

This is because the mother cannot be on the side of the drives or we are born out of something nonsocial and nonsymbolic. Yet, she cannot straddle the drives and the Symbolic for the same reason. And she cannot be completely within the Symbolic or we lose the child. The Symbolic can deal with the mother only as myth and fantasy (the Virgin mother, the denigrated woman), covering over this psychotic process and undecidable identity.

The mother knows better. While the child's relationship to the mother may eventually set up the place of the Other (through the primary maternal authority over the body, which leads to the mirror stage and castration in the oedipal situation) as the place of desire, thereby insuring symbolization, the mother's relationship to the child is another story. Kristeva suggests that the child may be the mother's first experience of an other. After all, in our culture, woman is the Other, and if there is no Other of the Other, then woman has no Other. For woman it is the One and not the Other, says Kristeva, that is taken for granted. So the birth of the child "constitutes an *access* (excess) toward the Other." (1983, 279) The mother experiences her being as a being for an other. Kristeva argues that this is a woman's only access to the Other and, therefore, to love. (1980, 10; 1983, 279)

The mother's experience of the child as other is not a relation to the Phallus. The mother's experience of the child as other is not a relation to unfulfillable desire:

> For a mother . . . [t]he other is inevitable, she seems to say, turn it into a God if you wish, it is nevertheless natural, for such an other has come out of myself. . . . The "just the same" of motherly peace of mind, more persistent than philosophical doubt, gnaws, on account of its basic disbelief, at the Symbolic's allmightiness. It bypasses perverse negation ("I know, but just the same") and constitutes the basis of the social bond in its generality, in the sense of "resembling others and eventually the species." (1983, 262)

The mother's other is a natural other. It is not the unreachable Other, the Phallus. "Turn it into a God if you wish," but it is not transcendent; it is real. The mother has bodily proof of this. For the mother this relationship with the other is not a struggle for recognition.[15] It is not a battle— either me or you, subject or object. The child really is/was part of the mother's flesh. And her own flesh exists for the sake of the child, because, at the limit, it does not and cannot "exist for itself." This other is not yet autonomous; it depends on the subject. As such, it threatens the "allmightiness" of the Symbolic, which requires an autonomous and inaccessible Other. Within Lacanian theory, it is this inaccessibility that opens the gap between signifier and signified and produces the Symbolic. The mother, however, gains access to what is off-limits. She "knows" better. She knows that there is no transcendent Other, no Phallus. The other is the flesh of her flesh, natural, loved. She knows that the Other is not transcendent; rather, it is within.

Whereas the perverse negation, the fetishism, necessary to maintain the Symbolic ("I know that the word is not the thing, but just the same"; "I know that the other is not me, but just the same") constitutes the social bond through force, the mother's "just the same" is its reverse. (Cf. 1980a, 37.) The mother negates the Symbolic order even while insuring its generation. She realizes that the other is the same, that the gap is not absolute. In the face of the Symbolic and its transcendental signifier, she says, "just the same, I know." The mother's "just the same" constitutes the social bond through love, not force. This "just the same" threatens to do away with difference and "it can crush everything the other (the child) has that is specifically irreducible." (1983, 263) In other words, it threatens to do away with the Symbolic order. It threatens psychosis. This is why even if the Symbolic order denies the existence of the mother, she cannot, for the sake of her child, deny the existence of the Symbolic. She must wean the child. She must instigate the breakup of their primary symbiosis. She must be silent about what she "knows" because she knows better.[16] (1983, 260)

The child must separate from its mother in order to be an autonomous being. It cannot remain dependent on her. It is the mother's love and her love for her own mother, a narcissistic love from generation to generation, that supports the move into the Symbolic order. It is this love that fills language with meaning. Is it possible that primary narcissism is repressed because it is a reunion with the mother's love that is founded on, yet mistaken for, a union with the mother's body? In the traditional psychoanalytic story, primary identification with the mother is repressed due to the paternal law against incest. Could the Father of the Law be wrong? Perhaps primary identification is not with the mother's body but with the mother's love. Could it be some primordial transference from body to love that constitutes the first identity? This maternal love is not (yet) the metonymic desire for the Phallus; rather, it is what Kristeva calls the metaphor of love. In terms of the phallocentric discourse this love is narcissism without a properly alien Other. Alterity is within. Yet without this narcissism, Kristeva's "primary narcissism," the mother's "narcissism," discourse is empty, meaningless, mourning the loss of love.

III

THE IMAGINARY FATHER[1]

Jacqueline Rose calls Kristeva's imaginary father a "race back into the arms of the law." (1986, 151) After her emphasis on the maternal function with its semiotic *chora* it does seem strange that in *Tales of Love* Kristeva stresses a return to the paternal function. Critics who embraced her semiotic *chora* were suspicious of this return to the father. Critics who dismissed Kristeva as essentialist because of her semiotic *chora* were not surprised by this strong father to counterbalance the strong mother; it was her adherence to a Lacanian paternal function that they found problematic in the first place.[2] In fact it is the maternal/paternal dualism with its emphasis on the paternal that turns many feminists away from all psychoanalytic theory.

From *within* the discourse of psychoanalytic theory, however, Kristeva challenges many of the notions that have made feminists—including some of those who criticize her work—nervous. Kristeva's notion of the imaginary father undermines the maternal/paternal dualism. It challenges the priority given to the paternal function in traditional psychoanalytic theory. The imaginary father undermines the authority of Lacan's stern Father of the Law. Kristeva's imaginary father is not a "race back into the arms of the law"; rather, it is a race back to the outstretched arms before the Law.

Kristeva develops her notion of the imaginary father in order to explain how a human being becomes a speaking being. She maintains that the stern oedipal Father with his castration threats is not enough to compel the child to leave the safe haven of the maternal body. She develops an account of the narcissistic structure that includes an imaginary agent of love that allows the child to negotiate the passage between the maternal body and the Symbolic order.

On the surface of Kristeva's texts, we see an archaic transference from the abject mother to the imaginary father, which, like Lacanian theory, requires sacrificing the mother for the sake of the father. (1983, 41) Reading "against the grain" of Kristeva's texts it is possible to see an archaic transference that does not sacrifice the mother to the father. It is possible to see an archaic transference from the mother's body to the mother's

desire through the mother's love. The semiotic body is abjected if necessary, but only for the sake of what motivates the bond in the first place:
maternal love.

Reading against the grain of her writing, Kristeva's texts take us deeper
into the maternal body. In her earlier writings she is concerned with
recovering a repressed maternal body that is associated with the child's
relation to its mother's breast. Later she becomes concerned with the
abject maternal body that is associated with the child's relation to its birth
and the mother's "sex." And more recently she is concerned with the
imaginary father, which I read as a screen for the mother's love, associated,
as it is, with the child's relationship to its conception and the mother's
womb. The imaginary father provides the support necessary to allow the
child to move into the Symbolic order. This is a move from the mother's
body to the mother's desire through the mother's love.

I will push to its limits the crisis in the paternal function that Kristeva
sets up, not so that we are thrown into psychotic discourse, but in order
to open up the possibility, as Kristeva does, of multiple discourses and
alternative meanings, including meaning within psychotic discourse. Applying Kristeva's own strategy to her writings, I emphasize the ruptures
and crises in her texts rather than their stability and traditional orthodoxy.
I analyze Kristeva's own condensations and displacements in those very
moments when she seems to fall back into traditional Freudian theory,
especially in the fantasy of the imaginary father. Reading the condensations and displacements in Kristeva's texts, I argue that her insistence that
it is called a "father" is a holdover from traditional psychoanalytic theory
that is betrayed by the way that this father functions in her discourse. Out
of Kristeva's texts I create a reading of the relationship between the maternal and paternal functions that intensifies what I see as her challenge
to traditional psychoanalytic conceptions of the oedipal story with its
threatening Father.

Narcissism

In Kristeva's story Oedipus is really Narcissus turned lover. By retelling
the tale of Narcissus, Kristeva creates a new psychic structure that will
house the oedipal triad. What Kristeva calls the "narcissistic structure"
provides a new way to conceive of the oedipal situation as well as a new
way to use it in the analytic situation. In Tales of Love she looks for the
primary psychic structure that sets up both the experience of abjection
and the mirror stage. She looks for a structure that at the same time offsets
both the horror of the abject mother and the gap between the child's
perfect unified image and its imperfect fragmented body in the mirror
stage. This structure, which enables the child to negotiate between the

maternal body and the Symbolic order, is the "narcissistic structure." As always Kristeva constructs her narcissistic structure within a Freudian framework. And as always she reinterprets Freud and creates a new narcissism.

Freud first identifies narcissism as a homosexual object-choice through which a man loves another man, who resembles him, in the way in which his mother loved him. (1910) Freud next describes narcissism as a stage in an infant's development that comes between autoeroticism and object-love. In this stage, the infant cathects himself as a whole. This stage is correlative to the onset of the ego.(1911, 1912) Later Freud argues that narcissism is related to ego cathexis and is inversely proportional to object-cathexis. (1914) Here Freud suggests that narcissism is not just a stage through which the infant passes. Rather, at this point, Freud sees narcissism as an ongoing structure of the ego. This is the hypothesis that Kristeva takes up.

In the end Freud posits two types of narcissism: primary and secondary. Primary narcissism is an objectless stage in which the infant comprises all of its universe. Secondary narcissism, on the other hand, is a withdrawal of the ego from the world of objects even after the ego has been constituted and taken love objects. While primary narcissism is a developmental stage, secondary narcissism is an "abnormal" regression to this preobjectal stage. (1921, 1923)

Freud's analysis of narcissism is problematic not only because (like most of his theories) it evolves and changes but also because it is difficult to conceive of a primary identification that is not an identification with some kind of object and that does not presuppose some kind of ego—however primitive—doing the identifying. In the myth of Narcissus, for example, Narcissus identifies with his image, which he mistakenly takes for an other. Narcissus, although deluded, recognizes an object in his image. And even if Narcissus wrongly identifies his object, it is still his object. But what is an objectless identification? Even if it is an identification with an undifferentiated self that is not yet an ego, it must be at least a partial ego identifying with a partial object. Otherwise, what is the meaning of identification? How is this primary narcissism different from autoeroticism? And if primary narcissism is an objectless self-enclosed state into which the infant is born, how does the infant ever move out of this state?

Kristeva takes Freud's suggestions block by block and builds what she calls the "narcissistic structure." By rearranging and unfolding Freud's theories, she makes their tensions support a psychic space that guarantees all subsequent identifications. Following one Freud but not another, Kristeva rejects the notion that primary narcissism is a developmental stage. Rather, she maintains that "neither screen nor state, primary narcissism is already a structure." (1983, 374) Insofar as it is a type of identification,

and beyond an undifferentiated autoeroticism, it is intrasymbolic. It is
the structure that sets up the very possibility of symbolization. As such,
Kristeva maintains that it is prior to the oedipal ego that begins to take
shape with the mirror stage. (1983, 22, 27, 44, 374) In other words, primary narcissism is a structure that pre-exists and sets up the identification in the mirror stage. While an identification with the mirror image
may be the result of the narcissistic structure, it is not the primary identification. The narcissistic identification in the mirror stage is merely the
reduplication of earlier narcissistic identifications. These earliest narcissistic identifications are the result of mimesis in the mother-child dyad.
(1983, 22) This mimesis, however, is not an imitation. And because it is
not an imitation it does not presuppose an already constructed ego in
relation with an already constructed object. It is not one being imitating
another, the child imitating its object. Rather, it is a reduplication of a
pattern.

Kristeva explains, following Freud, that the archaic identification with
the mother's breast is a preobjectal identification. The infant *becomes* the
breast through its incorporation. Kristeva maintains that this breast is not
an object for the infant but a "model," a "pattern." (1983, 25) The infant's
identification with this model or pattern of/through incorporation is not
the *imitation* of an object or a pattern. Rather, Kristeva describes this
identification as a *reduplication* of the pattern. This suggests that this
archaic identification, a strange identification indeed, is biological, or, at
any rate, semiotic. It is intrasymbolic only in a very primitive sense. It is
as if here again Kristeva follows her logic of rejection backwards through
the first semiotic negations, now to discover the first semiotic identifications. This archaic semiotic identification with the mother's breast, which
is merely a reduplication, becomes the first in a series of reduplications.
It prefigures and sets in motion the logic of object identifications in all
object relations, including both discourse and love. (1983, 25)

Kristeva compares the infant's incorporation of the breast to the subsequent incorporation of "the speech of the other." (1983, 26) She explains
that through incorporating the speech of the other the infant incorporates
the pattern of language and thereby identifies with the other. In fact, it is
the incorporation of the patterns of language through the speech of the
other that enables the infant to communicate and thus commune with
others. And through the ability to "assimilate, repeat, and reproduce"
words, the infant becomes like the other: a subject. (1983, 26)

The operator within this structure—the logic of reduplication, put in
motion by the first identifications with the mother's body—sets up the
logic of the psyche: repetition. The logic of reduplication itself becomes
a pattern reduplicated by the psyche. Like Kristeva's earlier notion of the
logic of material rejection (with which she explains how we separate
ourselves from others), the logic of reduplication reproduces itself differ-

ently on different levels. Patterns are reduplicated on level after level until thresholds are crossed, the semiotic gives way to the Symbolic, biology becomes culture; but like fractals in geometry, the patterns are recognizable. What the logic of reduplication provides, which the logic of rejection did not, is a theory of identification. With her theory of narcissism, Kristeva can explain not only how we break away in order to become individuals but also how we come together in order to commune and love. In fact, she uses her notion of primary narcissism to reconceive the process of becoming a subject as a process that does not involve a break motivated by a threat that cuts off the possibility of love without fear.

Even before the first rejections, the structure of narcissism provides the first separation between pre-ego and preobject in the form of identification. Narcissistic structuration, maintains Kristeva, is "the earliest juncture (chronologically and logically) whose spoors we might detect in the unconscious." (1983, 44) Narcissistic reduplication creates the space between the not-yet-subject and the not-yet-object so that they can become subjects and objects. This space is what gives rise to the Symbolic order. Narcissism protects and causes this space, this "emptiness." (1983, 24) The "elementary separation" intrinsic to reduplication guarantees borders. And, borders are necessary for any distinctions between objects or symbols. Kristeva's Narcissus, or more precisely her reading of Freud's Narcissus, is an "infinitely distant boundary marker." (1983, 125) This boundary narcissism is the product of imagination. Kristeva's Narcissus imagines a love that is stable while receding always out of reach.

Kristeva maintains that it is imagination that comes to life in this space opened up by reduplication. This is why, although it is "intrasymbolic," elementary reduplication is not a symbolic relation. Rather, it is an imaginary relation. This is also why Kristeva argues that the gap in Lacan's mirror stage is not a symbolic structure but an imaginary structure that sets up the Symbolic. She maintains that the "gaping hole" in Lacan's mirror stage, the space between the mirror and the infant, is guaranteed by the structure of narcissism through the separation in reduplication that comes *before* the mirror stage. The child's identifications are neither symbolic nor asymbolic, psychotic. Rather, they are narcissistic—before and through the mirror stage. Against Lacan, Kristeva argues that the narcissistic child does not merely need the Symbolic in order to replace the missing Real; it also needs the imaginary, imaginary love:

> The child, with all due respect to Lacan, not only *needs* the real and the symbolic. It signifies itself as child, in other words as the subject that it is, and neither as a psychotic nor as an adult, precisely in that zone where *emptiness and narcissism*, the one upholding the other, constitute the zero degree of imagination.[3] (1983, 24)

The child begins to distinguish the Real from its symbolic substitutes through narcissistic imagination.[4] Even though the narcissistic structure guarantees symbolization, it does so through a preoedipal, preobjectal, identification. Here once again Kristeva sets herself apart from Lacan. She maintains that the narcissist cathects a preoedipal preobject rather than the paternal Phallus. (1983, 125) This cathexis precedes the oedipal identification with the paternal Phallus. Against Lacan, Kristeva argues that need is not lost to desire. Rather, the semiotic need is a pattern that sets up the possibility of desire, not only chronologically but also logically. In other words, there is an intrasymbolic structure that precedes the metonymy of desire. "The whole symbolic matrix sheltering emptiness is thus set in place in an elaboration that precedes the Oedipus complex." (1983, 27) For Kristeva, this narcissistic "elaboration" supports a semiotic reduplication that she describes as a type of transference.

The fundamental transference, which sets up the ego ideal and thereby the metonymy of desire, is from the mother to what Kristeva calls the "imaginary father." I will come back to the "imaginary father," but first more on primary narcissism as transference. This transference, like all others, "transfers me to the place of the Other." (1983, 37) This is how the child's having the mother's breast becomes the child's being the mother's breast. Through the transference enabled by the structure of primary narcissism, the child is transferred to the place of the mother, to the place of the breast. The Other in this transaction is neither an object nor a "pure signifier." Rather, Kristeva breaks with Lacan when she claims that the Other is "the very space of metaphorical shifting," the space protected by the structure of narcissism. (1983, 38) The structure of primary narcissism sets up the possibility of *metaphorical* shifting, which in turn sets up the possibility of *metonymical* shifting. (1983, 30) This metaphorical shifting is another form of transference.

Before I explain why Kristeva describes metaphorical shifting as a transference, I will say more about her notion of metaphor. In *Tales of Love* she urges us to think of "modern theories of metaphor that decipher within it an indefinite jamming of semantic features one into the other, a meaning being acted out; and, on the other, the drifting of heterogeneity within a heterogeneous psychic apparatus, going from drives and sensations to signifier and conversely." (1983, 37) Later she suggests that "metaphor becomes antithetical, as if to blur all reference, and ends up as synesthesia, as if to open up the Word to the passion of the body itself, as it is." (1983, 277–78) Metaphor is where the drives burst into language; and the passion of the body itself has no object. This passion is preoedipal, preobjectal, and presymbolic. It is prior to a distinction between subject and object. Kristeva calls metaphor "the economy that modifies language when subject and object of the utterance act muddle their borders." (1983, 268) It makes sense that if metaphor is language that does not refer to an object, then it expresses the objectless identification.

Metaphor is the reduplication in language of the primary transference that takes place through the structure of primary narcissism. The pattern that is reduplicated is the pattern of displacement. Both the primary transference (as well as transference in general) and metaphor are patterns of displacement. (1983, 27) The subject of utterance puts itself in the place of signs. The transference that once took place with an other now takes place with language itself. The result is the metaphor, particularly the synesthetic metaphor, where the subject's bodily passions are put into the place of language. This is the transferential displacement that Kristeva claims is at the heart of metaphor. (1983, 275)

She argues that the metaphorical "object" is prior, both chronologically and logically, to the metonymic object. She maintains that in order to avoid tyranny in analysis we must postulate the formation of the unified subject within an "objectality in the process of being established rather than in the absolute of the reference to the Phallus." (1983, 30) Lacan, however, locates the feature that unifies the subject "solely within the field of the signifier and of desire; he clearly if not drastically separated it from narcissism as well as from drive heterogeneity and its archaic hold on the maternal vessel." (1983, 38)

Separating the onset of the subject from the drives and narcissistic reduplication makes the process static rather than dynamic. The process is static insofar as it is anchored to the Phallus. This is why Kristeva argues that there are *various* ways in which the subject develops (although never completely). She suggests that there are advantages to untethering the onset of the subject from the Phallus. Above all, it allows the imagination of both analysand and analyst to intervene in the Symbolic. It prevents the tyranny of the Symbolic and tyranny in analysis:

> [I]ts "unary feature," which by having it choose an adored part of the loved one, already locates it within the symbolic code of which this feature is a part. Nevertheless, situating this unifying guideline within an objectality in the process of being established rather than in the absolute of the reference to the Phallus as such has several advantages. It makes the transference relation dynamic, involves to the utmost the interpretive intervention of the analyst, and calls attention to countertransference as identification, this time of the analyst with the patient, along with the entire aura of imaginary formations germane to the analyst that all this entails. Without those conditions doesn't analysis run the risk of becoming set within the tyranny of idealization, precisely? Of the Phallus or of the superego? A word to wise Lacanians should be enough! (1983, 30; cf. 31, 125)

Paradoxically if it is true that the Lacanian analyst is a slave to the Word or the Phallus, then a word should be enough to make the wise analyst realize that discourse is not absolutely dictated by the law of the Phallus or signifier. But which word will be enough? Or, perhaps any word will do insofar as it opens onto the Imaginary. In any case, Kristeva suggests that *wise* Lacanians will heed her warning that it is the realm of the Imaginary and not the Symbolic that psychoanalysis should address. The Imaginary allows the semiotic bodily drives to fuse with symbols in language. It is by attending to this Imaginary—which is not reducible to the word—that the analyst can touch the semiotic body, bring drives to language and make it meaningful. The word to wise Lacanians, then, is that the word is not enough.

If the "unary feature" of the subject is a metaphor, then it is objectless, an objectality-in-process. In which case, the analyst is not dealing with a subject in relation to the Phallus but with a presubject in a relation of reduplication to a preobject. All of this takes place *before* the Law of the Father and not because of a foreclosure of the Law. In other words, it is not because the Law has been foreclosed that the subject has difficulty with the Law. Rather, it is because the sequence of reduplication, of metaphor, of imagination, has broken down before the Law is even set up. Kristeva claims that the breakdown that gives rise to psychosis is a breakdown of the narcissistic structure. What is needed is not the Law or the stern Father and his threatening Phallus. Rather, what is needed is the loving father, what Kristeva calls the "imaginary father," which goes beyond/behind the Lacanian mirror stage, castration, and Father of the Law.

In an interview with Rosalind Coward, Kristeva claims that one of the ways that she goes beyond Lacanian theory is to "make more detailed the archaic stages preceding the mirror stage because I think that the grasping of the image by the child is a result of a whole process. And this process can be called *imaginary*, but not in the specular sense of the word, because it passes through voice, taste, skin and so on, all the senses yet doesn't necessarily mobilise sight." (1984b, 22) Kristeva says that Lacan's "specular fascination is a belated phenomenon in the genesis of the Ego." (1983, 40) Whereas Lacan takes up merely the visible, Kristeva takes up the invisible. She takes us behind the specular image in Lacan's mirror.

What we find before the mirror stage are the maternal and drive that lie behind Lacan's signifier and desire. (1983, 38) In addition to the logic of negation and rejection before the mirror stage that I discussed in the last two chapters, Kristeva describes a primary identification that is before the mirror stage. She claims that Lacan's identification of idealization solely within the field of the signifier and desire cuts off the drives. In addition, it undermines the importance of the maternal function. More than that, it makes it impossible to treat borderline patients for whom, according to Lacan, the law of signification is foreclosed. For Kristeva, on the other hand, idealization does not operate merely within the law of signification. Signification is also the result of affect and drive, which operate before the metonymy of desire.

The difference between identifying idealization—what takes place in the mirror stage—with desire or with affect and drive force is that desire "emphasizes *lack*, whereas *affect*, while acknowledging the latter, gives greater importance to the movement toward the other and to mutual *attraction*." (1983, 155) Just as she describes primary rejection and privation as excess rather than lack, so too she describes primary identification as an excess toward the other, love, rather than lack. For Kristeva it is the difference between founding the social relation on a Hegelian notion of desire, which requires lack and struggle, or founding the social relation on a Freudian notion of eros or identification. And Kristeva concludes that love is the only hope for the social relation. (1980a, 142) Perhaps her word to wise Lacanians is "love."

The Loving Father

In *Tales of Love* Kristeva sets her loving father against Lacan's stern authoritarian father. By *Black Sun* they seem to be two faces of the same father, or at least collaborators. Here, the loving imaginary father must not only support the paternal function and the move to the Symbolic but also be able to take the place of the stern oedipal Father. (1987, 23) In *Tales of Love* she develops her notion of the imaginary father out of Freud's "father in individual prehistory" from *Group Psychology and the Analysis of the Ego.* (1921) Her interpretation of Freud's father becomes her "loving father." She chides Lacan for not seeing this loving father in Freud.

Kristeva argues that, for Freud, primary identification is with this "father in individual prehistory." As it turns out, this father is not really a father, or not only a father. Rather, the "father in individual prehistory," Kristeva's "imaginary father," is a combination of the mother and the father. It has no sexual difference. (1983, 26) It has the characteristics of both masculine and feminine. (1983, 40) Kristeva calls it the "father-mother conglomerate." (1983, 40) The identification with this conglomerate is the vortex of primary identification within what Kristeva calls the "narcissistic structure." This identification is the originary identification that sets up all subsequent identifications, including the ego's identification with itself. (1983, 33)

In "*La Vierge de Freud*" Kristeva provides evidence for interpreting Freud's fantasy of a "prehistory" as a fantasy of a maternal semiotic meaning. (1987a, 26) Here, she argues that in Freud's text on Leonardo da Vinci we can read a "prehistoric," "unforgettable," "imaginary," "maternal function." The maternal that Kristeva extracts from Freud's interpretation of the Catholic Virgin Mary is a maternal function that foreshadows the Symbolic and meaning in the realm of the Imaginary. She describes Freud's interpretation of the Virgin as a type of condensation in which he ultimately negates the maternal value of meaning, the semiotic, even while he exposes it. The maternal function that she describes in *"La Vierge de Freud"* performs a function that bears an uncanny resemblance to the function that she attributes to the imaginary father in *Tales of Love* and *Black Sun*. This "maternal function" is "a function which, already susceptible to meaning, reveals the archaic in signs and permits not only the elaboration but also the sublimation of introjective and projective fixations with 'the originary.'" (1987a, 26) Here Kristeva reads Freud's fantasy of a prehistoric maternal as a maternal function already full of meaning, an imaginary formation somewhere between "the archaic and the symbolic," an imaginary mother. (1987a, 26)

In *Tales of Love* the identification with the prehistoric father-mother conglomerate is an identification with an "imaginary father." This identification with the imaginary father is a transference between the semiotic body and an ideal other who lacks nothing. It is called a father in spite of the fact that it is also a mother because, following Lacan, Kristeva identifies the Symbolic with the Father. She explains this curiosity by arguing that even though the child's first affections are directed toward the mother, these archaic "object" relations are already "symbolic" and therefore associated with the father. This is to say that the logic of the Symbolic is already within the maternal body. Although it seems strange, this combination is called a father because it is a metonymic relationship-in-the-works.

Here, Kristeva's position with regard to the Phallus in *Tales of Love* is a bit confusing. Later in the text she suggests that there are advantages to a nonphallocentric explanation of primary identification. She suggests that there are fathers other than the Father of the Law and yet she maintains a strict identification between the Father of the Law (Law of the Father) and the Symbolic. It seems that if she wants to multiply fathers rather than reinforce the Father of the Law, she should give up the connection between the Father and the Symbolic.

What Kristeva is suggesting is that the infant identifies, through an immediate transference that is preoedipal, with the gap between the mother and her desire that founds the oedipal move and motivates the child's entrance into the Symbolic order. There is an archaic transference to the site of the symbolic in a preobjectal state. Here the father is not yet the Father of the Law of the Symbolic. Rather, he is a presymbolic imaginary father who stands in as a support for the place of the mother's desire. The imaginary father is a metaphorical function that gives way to the metonymic paternal function; love gives way to desire.

Kristeva claims that the imaginary father allows an identification with the mother's desire for the Phallus. In other words, the identification with the imaginary father allows an identification with the paternal function as it *already exists in* the mother. And this identification with the imaginary father also allows the child to *"ab-jet"* its mother's body and thereby separate from her. But the separation from the mother's body is not tragic because it is supported by the imaginary father, which is the mother's love itself.

In my reading, the mother's love enacts the transference from the mother's body to the mother's desire. The mother's love provides the needed support for the transference to the site of maternal desire. The transference to the imaginary father leads to a transference to the site of the mother's desire. The mother's desire is her desire for the Father, her desire to be satisfied, her implication in the paternal function. Insofar as the mother is a speaking being, the Other is already within her. That is, she is always already implicated in signifying systems. The mother-father conglomerate, then, is the combination of the mother and her desire. It is a father within the mother, a "maternal father."[5]

I suggest that Kristeva's imaginary father can be read as a metaphorical or *imaginary* reunion with the maternal body that takes the place of the real union with, dependence on, the maternal body. Kristeva asks us to follow her back beyond images of the nourishing semiotic maternal body, and the abject image of birth, to the first possible image of a life: conception. The fantasy of the imaginary father as the conglomeration of mother and father can be read as a *fantasy* of reunion with the mother's body, which takes the place of the real union that must be lost so that the child can enter language. And the child's identification with the conglomerate mother-father can be read as an identification with its conception. On my reading, the identification with the imaginary father, the father in individual prehistory, is an identification with a fantasy of one's own conception. It is a transference to the site of the *jouissance* of the primal scene.

Let us run through the story again. Through the immediate transference onto the imaginary father, the child undergoes a transference to the site of maternal desire, which Kristeva claims is the desire for the Phallus. It is an identification with the father whom the child imagines took part in the primal scene. But it is an identification with this imaginary father only insofar as he represents the Phallus that satisfies the mother's desire. The child is identifying with the imaginary father entering the mother; it is identifying with a reunion with the mother. It is identifying with her *jouissance*, her satisfaction. Through its identification with the imaginary father, the child, in its imaginary, can re-place itself back inside its mother. It can re-place itself in the mother's womb. This imaginary identification

with the mother's body provides the support needed to lose the real identification with the mother's body and the move to an identification with
her desire, which is a move into the Symbolic order.

Kristeva's analysis of the child's fantasy of the primal scene in *In the
Beginning Was Love* suggests this reading. There she says, in another
context, that the child identifies with the father as a protection against a
fantasy too much for the child to bear: "that of being supernumerary,
excluded from the act of pleasure that is the origin of its existence."
(1987a, 42) Perhaps the fantasy of the imaginary father enables the child
to insert itself into the primal scene. Through the figure of the father, the
child can rejoice in a (re)union with the mother. Through this fantasy, the
child can rejoice in the beginnings of its existence, an existence founded
on (imagined) pleasure rather than lack. Kristeva suggests that imagined
pleasure may be more of an incentive to leave the maternal body than the
oedipal Father's threats of castration. As she asks, with such stern threats
and no loving support, why wouldn't we all just avoid the pain and refuse
to leave the maternal body, which of course would end in psychosis?

Kristeva's diagnosis of Giovanni Bellini also presents the fantasy of a
father-mother conglomerate in the primal scene. Here the fantasy is a
primary identification with "the very space where father and mother meet
. . . a space of fundamental unrepresentability toward which all glances
nonetheless converge; a primal scene where genitality dissolves sexual
identification beyond their given difference." (1980b, 249) This fantasy,
which I am reading as the fantasy of the imaginary father, is a fantasy that
embraces alterity and difference in an imaginary wholeness. It is not that
one becomes the other, or that both disappear. Rather, the combination
provides complete satisfaction, which fills any gap between them. Alterity
becomes a pleasurable excess rather than painful gap.

Kristeva provides further analysis that supports reading the imaginary
father as a fantasy of wholeness. She maintains that adults seek love in
the form of the couple in order to experience a sense of wholeness, which
she identifies with a reunion with the mother. She argues that adult love
in the form of the couple, homosexual or heterosexual, is a recreation of
the imaginary father, who once again turns out to be the mother:

> The child, male or female, hallucinates its merging with a nourishing-
> mother-and-ideal-father, in short a conglomeration that already condenses
> two into one. . . . One soon notices, however, in the last instance (that is, if
> the couple truly becomes one, if it lasts), that each of the protagonists, he
> and she, has married, through the other, his or her mother. (1983, 222–23)

In Kristeva's scenario, the husband is the phallic mother for the woman,
while the wife is the mother that allows the man to remain a child. Certainly in the traditional story of oedipal resolution the man finds his
mother in his wife while the woman finds her father in her husband.

Kristeva, moving through Lacan's twists in the oedipal story, argues that the woman finds her mother in her husband. She finally becomes the Phallus (satisfaction) for her mother in the person of her (nourishing) husband. Her oedipal wish, to be the mother's Phallus, is, like the man's, satisfied in marriage. The woman, like the man, needs to couple in order to re-find the lost mother. The mother is the "pedestal" of the couple because the couple provides a reunion with the mother.

Although Kristeva insists that this analysis applies to homosexual couples as well as heterosexual couples, she doesn't explain how. It seems, however, that it may be much easier for a woman to find her mother in a homosexual relation with another woman's body. The primary identification that supports the archaic regression would be more straightforward. (Cf. 1983, 226.) Kristeva, however, has been criticized because she relegates homosexuality, especially female homosexuality, to the borders of intelligibility, psychosis. For example, Judith Butler argues that because Kristeva accepts the structuralist assumption that society is founded on heterosexual exchanges of women, she maintains that homosexuality is capable only of psychotic sexual expression. (1989) It seems to me, however, that Kristeva is more concerned with a preoedipal relation to the mother, which for women requires a kind of homosexuality. Also, in spite of those aspects of her writings that privilege heterosexuality and take up a traditional psychoanalytic framework, Kristeva does explicitly claim that every individual has his or her own sexuality. She wants to move away from the dualism between heterosexuality and homosexuality. (1984b, 24) I come back to Kristeva's apparent homophobia in chapter 5.

The Crisis in the Paternal Function

Once again it seems that the fantasy of a conglomerate mother-father, a fantasy of wholeness, is a fantasy of the reunion with the mother. Kristeva postulates the loving imaginary father as the archaic disposition of the paternal function preceding the Symbolic, the mirror stage, and the oedipal Father. (1983, 22) She challenges traditional psychoanalytic conceptions of the paternal function. She suggests that there are various paternal functions, not just Lacan's paternal Phallus that lays down the Law. (1983, 46) As Kristeva sets it out, the imaginary father is not only a forefather to Lacan's Father of the Law but also a rival. (1983, 46) In *Tales of Love* she says:

> Maintaining against the winds and high tides of our modern civilization the requirement of a stern Father who, through his Name, brings about separation, judgment, and identity, constitutes a necessity, a more or less pious wish. But we can only note that jarring such sternness, far from

leaving us orphaned or inexorably psychotic, reveals multiple and varied destinies for paternity—notably archaic, imaginary paternity. Those destinies could or can be manifested by the clan as a whole, by the priest, or by the therapist. In all cases, however, we are dealing with a function that guarantees the subject's entry into a disposition, a fragile one to be sure, of an ulterior, unavoidable oedipal destiny, but one that can also be playful and sublimational. (1983, 46)

In *Tales of Love* Kristeva chooses the loving father over Lacan's stern Father. In *Black Sun* she imagines a father who is both stern and loving, and for the infant, primarily loving.

Kristeva's claim to the loving father seems to be her claim to an inheritance that may have been given to Lacan but is rightfully hers. As I have suggested, her claim to the loving father ideal is a claim to the loving mother. She takes her stand, separated from the mother but loved by the father (Freud?), in order to rival Lacan. Through this identification with the father, a father who loves like a mother, she can become the "imaginary" son, the rightful heir of psychoanalysis. Otherwise, she remains the abject mother outside of the Law and nothing but a threat to it. Her position as abject mother calls into question her position as an analyst. As the abject mother, she cannot stand in for the Father of the Law, Lacan's stern Father, and thereby engender the necessary transference to put the analysand back on track. She cannot be the place of that stern Third Party for whose sake the analytic relationship (like all others) exists. She postulates a loving Third who gives herself up to the countertransference and loves the analysand like her child. (See 1987a.) Which is to say, she loves her own mother through the analysand who "is" her child. So, through analysis, Kristeva seeks an identification with her mother. And this identification, the mother's with the mother, is the site to which the analysand transfers, the site of primary identification that Kristeva calls the "imaginary father." The analyst, then, becomes the loving mother and not (merely) the stern Father.

Kristeva qualifies the search for a primary identification itself by claiming that she is not trying to discover whether "daddy or mummy" is the primary object. Rather, she is looking for a way to treat her patients. She is looking for an identification that can provide, through the psychoanalytic transference, a sense of completion and wholeness that combines the maternal gratifications and the paternal prohibitions. (1983, 29) She invents the imaginary father who loves like a mother.

For Kristeva, the identification with the imaginary father sets up the emptiness within the narcissistic structure. The child finds itself between the mother and the imaginary father as that which is not the object of its mother's desire. The postulation of the imaginary father allows the child to imagine that the mother desires an other, "not I." This "not I" sets up the space that eventually will be filled in by the Father of the Law, the

Symbolic. Now, it seems that Kristeva has only a small bone to pick with Lacan over what she might call the "reduplication" of fathers that stand behind his one Father of the Law.

But, Kristeva argues that the loving and not the stern Father is necessary in order to serve at least two functions that protect the narcissistic space properly required to begin the process of becoming a symbolic subject. The loving imaginary father is needed to offset devouring by the abject mother. Also, the loving father is needed to provide an imaginary secular replacement for a dead Christian god. Without the loving father we are abandoned by god and possibly devoured by abjection as well.

In *Black Sun* Kristeva calls the melancholic a "radical atheist." (1987, 5) The empty discourse of the melancholia is a eulogy to the dead god, or at least to a god who has abandoned his children. Working within a Christian imaginary, Kristeva seems to suggest that God is the Word and as such still exists. God is also Love and as such he is dead. And without Love the Word is empty. Kristeva, herself mourning the loss of God the Loving Father, creates his secular substitute in the loving imaginary father. The function of a God who is the Word and yet whose Name cannot be spoken is taken over by the imaginary father, what Kristeva also calls the "cult of the irrepresentable." (1983, 313)

The irrepresentable that makes representation possible is represented, strangely enough, by the imaginary father. Without the loving father, psychoanalysis, like religion, makes for masochism and/or paranoia. (1983, 311) We live in fear and under the constant surveillance of the stern Father: superego or God. This stern Father cannot coax us away from our maternal shelter even if that shelter threatens to devour us. This is why we need the loving father as a support against abjection. Without "him," we are "extraterrestrials suffering for want of love." (1983, 382–83) For Kristeva, it is not a crisis in the Law that has led to this suffering; rather, it is a lack of love:

> There has been too much stress on the crisis in paternity as cause of psychotic discontent. Beyond the often fierce but artificial and incredible tyranny of the Law and the Superego, the crisis in the paternal function that led to the deficiency of psychic space is in fact an erosion of the loving father. It is for want of paternal love that Narcissi, burdened with emptiness, are suffering; eager to be others, or women, they want to be loved. (1983, 378)

Kristeva sees the crisis in paternity as the lack of love and not the lack of Law. The contemporary analyst doesn't have to repair the analysand's relation to the Law or the Symbolic but provide imaginary love to support that relation. Kristeva argues that if there were only the symbolic or oedipal Father, then there would be no way to offset the abject mother. Without the loving father, there is no way for the child to separate itself from

the body of its abject mother. Kristeva suggests that the negation seen in
borderline cases is not the repudiation of the Name of Father but the
inability to escape the abject mother. (1983, 50)

If the discourse of the borderline person seems empty, this does not
necessarily mean that the Law of the Father has been foreclosed. Rather,
the Third Party to whom the discourse should be addressed, the Third
Party in/for whom the discourse becomes meaningful, is not necessarily
the Father of the Law. The Father of the Law may well be in place; and
this is evidenced by the possibility of the discourse and the transference
in the analytic situation. (1983, 50) But, the discourse seems empty without the support of the primary identification with the loving imaginary
father. "He" is the missing Third. It is only in the context of "his" love
that the Symbolic has meaning:

> What was interpreted as a "problematic repression," or even as a "lack of
> repression" in such [borderline] patients appears to be another position of
> repression. . . . To say that this indicates a "repudiation of the Name of the
> Father" is too sweeping and inaccurate. . . . [A]ffect representatives pass
> through the censorship of repression and appear within discourse as empty,
> without signification . . . for want of that elementary archaic Third party
> who would have been its addressee and, by receiving it, could have authen-
> ticated it. If all that remains is an Oedipal Father, a Symbolic Father, no
> struggle against the "abject," no becoming autonomous with respect to the
> phallic mother, could be inscribed in the body of language. (1983, 50)

Following my earlier reading, this archaic Third allows a reunion with
the mother in a different guise and thereby facilitates the separation from
the mother's body and a playful and sublimational entry into the Symbolic order. Without this loving archaic Third for whom we speak, we
enter language with mourning and melancholy. We long for the lost maternal "Thing" from whom we necessarily separate in order to enter the
Symbolic. If there is a loving imaginary father, who is really the mother's
love in disguise, then our reunion with the mother comes through giving
her up. In order to begin the process of becoming a subject we must abject
the mother in order to separate from her. But without the support of the
imaginary father—the mother's love—we will be devoured by abjection
rather than become autonomous. We become abject, in-between, emptiness. We become the borderline between drives and symbols.

The borderline speaks of desire but the discourse is empty. Kristeva
says that the borderline discourse is laden with drives that pass through
repressive censorship because the words do not signify. This is why the
discourse is experienced as empty even though it is full of drives and
affect representations. The structure of the metonymy of desire is in place
but the narcissistic structure of what Kristeva calls the "metaphor of love"
is broken. The break is not within the Symbolic proper, but earlier. The

Symbolic is set up on emptiness, an emptiness unprotected by the Imaginary. For Kristeva it is an archaic transferential imaginary identification that moves the would-be-subject away from the mother and into the Symbolic order. This imaginary Third, the imaginary father, is the missing addressee in and for whom the translation of drives into language has meaning. (1983, 50)

Kristeva maintains that the Imaginary is the ability to transfer meaning where it is lost. (1987, 103) The imaginary father transfers meaning to the lost maternal body. "He" reconciles the child to the loss of the maternal "Thing." (1987, 13) Kristeva argues that we must agree to lose the mother in order to imagine and name her. (1987, 41) She says that the "link between pleasure and symbolic dignity . . . is insured by an imaginary father, as he leads his child from primary to secondary identification." (1987, 92–93) Imaginary pleasure is associated with the maternal body while symbolic dignity is associated with the paternal. (1986, 231; 1987a, 26)

In order for the child to move away from the maternal container, it must encounter the Third party, the Other. This Other, the Third in the oedipal situation, is nothing other than the "Meaning of discourse." (1983, 13) The child, then, must encounter the meaning of discourse as the Other for/in "whom" it must speak, love, exist. Within the Lacanian framework, insofar as the Other is also the desire for the Phallus—the unfulfillable desire for satisfaction that keeps us talking—it is the mother's desire. The imaginary father is the maternal desire for the Phallus. (1983, 40) It is the Other already within the mother. The Other exists within the mother, not only in the real sense during pregnancy, but also in the imaginary and symbolic senses. The mother is, after all, primarily a speaking being.

The mother loves the child through the Third so that the child feels loved. Early in *Tales of Love* Kristeva maintains that the mother must love her child for the sake of a third party. (1983, 34) If she doesn't love it for the sake of a third party, then she loves only herself. She is the classic narcissist, incapable of love. In other words, if she loves the child without any "diversion" toward an other, she is clinging to the child, hysterically demanding its love. (1983, 34) She is loving the child as herself and is not, therefore, loving any other. The child believes that it is not loved since its mother loved no *other*. (1983, 34)

Love, for Kristeva, is neither biology nor desire. Rather, it is the domain of the imaginary that moves between biology and desire, the maternal body and the Symbolic order. Love is not a "narcissistic merger with the maternal container but the emergence of a metaphorical object—in other words the very splitting that establishes the psyche and, let us call this splitting 'primal repression,' bends the drive toward the symbolic of an other." (1983, 31) The mother's love, rather than calling the child back to the maternal body, moves it toward the maternal desire, "toward the sym-

bolic of an other." It is the mother's love that supports the move to the
Symbolic through "loving idealization," the function of the imaginary
"father." (1983, 33–34) The mother's love is the imaginary Third. As early
as "The Father, Love, and Banishment," Kristeva suggests that the mother's
love is the "facsimile of the third person." Here, Kristeva argues that not
until Freud did motherhood:

> . . . by means of a language that "musicates through letters," resume within
> discourse the rhythms, intonations, and echolalias of the mother-infant
> symbiosis—intense, pre-Oedipal, predating the father—and this in the third
> person. Having a child, could a woman, then, speak another love? Love as
> object banished from paternal Death, facsimile of the third person, prob-
> ably. . . . (1980b, 157)

In an interview with Rosalind Coward, Kristeva claims that it is not
necessary to call the terms of the oedipal situation "mother" and "father."
She says that we could just as well call them "X" and "Y." In addition,
she suggests that the sharp distinction between these two is breaking
down. "There are contaminations between them." "This," says Kristeva,
"is due to the crisis of the paternal function and the rendering of my 'X'
and 'Y' ambiguous." (1984, 23) Kristeva endorses this ambiguiazation of
identity. In another interview she says that women can take the role of
the Third and fulfill the paternal function.[6] (1980a, 139) By reading the
condensations and displacements in Kristeva's writings, the Third appears within the maternal function; the physical envelope of the mother
is separated from both the mother's love and the mother's desire. Of
course, the analyst is also a facsimile of the Third Party regardless of
sexual differences. Kristeva breaks open the paternal function and the
identification between the necessary Third and paternal Law.

On my reading, the movement between the abjected maternal body and
the imaginary father or mother's love—which provides an incentive for
the child to replace its demands on the mother's body with desires in
language—suggests three terms prior to the oedipal triangle of traditional
psychoanalysis. On the "presymbolic" imaginary level that Kristeva describes, the narcissistic "subject" is the result of a transferential identification with the imaginary father, the seed of the Ego ideal, which supports
a separation from the abject mother.

For Kristeva, an archaic oedipal triangle is set up within the maternal
body. The parties to this oedipal triangle are the narcissistic subject, the
abject mother, and the imaginary father. The narcissistic subject, the child,
is, or discovers itself, in relation to the mother's body, specifically the
mother's breast. Recall that originally the child identifies with the
mother's breast. But in its attempts to separate, to wean, it abjects the
breast and the mother. At this point it identifies with the indeterminacy
of the mother's sex and its birth through the canal that brings the insides

of the body out. The child, once an attachment on the mother's breast, struggles with the distinction between the mother's body and its products. The child sees itself as one of those products, a waste product, an abject preobject, expelled from the mother's body in birth. From here the imaginary father or identification with conception comes to the rescue. The child moves further into the mother's body, back into the womb, back into the primal scene filled with the *jouissance* that fills language and life with meaning.

Within the maternal body, the three terms of the oedipal structure are the maternal breast, the maternal sex, and the maternal womb. Kristeva sets up the oedipal structure within the maternal body in order to provide a setup for the oedipal structure proper. All of this is within her greater project to reinscribe the body in language by reinscribing the symbolic logic already within the body. The structures and logics of the Symbolic are already operating within the body, particularly the maternal body. Even the oedipal structure can be prefigured here.

In traditional psychoanalysis, on the other hand, in a reductionistic reading, on one level, the ego is formed by pitting reality against the id. On another level, it becomes the battle between the father and the mother where, if the process is normal, the father wins out and the desire for the mother is at best sublimated and at worst denied. I suggest that within Kristeva's texts, the paternal function is preceded and superseded by the maternal function. The imaginary father is more important than the traditional Father of the Law. And "he" is merely a disguise for the mother's love. Even the oedipal movement from the imaginary father to the stern oedipal Father turns out to be a move from the mother's love to the mother's desire.

In order to talk about the move from the mother's body, what Kristeva calls the "maternal container," to the mother's love or desire requires that Kristeva, in some significant sense, separate the maternal body from motherhood.[7] It is important to recognize why Kristeva separates maternal bodies from women's bodies. She attempts to formulate a new discourse of motherhood that allows for an account of what she sees as the necessary abjection of the maternal body without also abjecting women.

In traditional discourses on maternity women's bodies are reduced to the maternal body. Kristeva tries to provide an antidote to this oppressive representation of women and motherhood. She suggests that there is much more to motherhood than the nourishing maternal body and the bodily relation to the child. The maternal function is a complex of body, love, and desire. It operates through the Real, Imaginary, and Symbolic.

For Kristeva the maternal body is implicated in all three realms, Real, Imaginary, and Symbolic. Still, she seems to emphasize the connection between the maternal body and the Real by associating the Imaginary with the paternal in the character of her imaginary father. Here I am puzzled by Kristeva's seeming identification of the father with the Imaginary and the mother with the Real. If the imaginary father allows the child to identify with its conception, then does the child also identify with the father's semen? In other words, does the child see itself as a product not only of the mother's body but also of the father's body? If this is the case, then we have not only an abject mother, but also an abject father. Recall that the experience of abjection comes primarily from a confusion of the borders between the child's body and the mother's. Obviously this confusion doesn't require great powers of imagination. If the child, however, has the power to imagine itself as part of its own conception, does it not have the power to imagine itself a secretion, a waste product, of the father's body, which in turn would require some kind of abjection in order to begin, at least, to try to set up borders between bodies? Moreover, this fantasy would make a powerful accomplice to the child's abjection of its self.

Kristeva's account of the immaculate conception in the Christian imaginary suggests this reading. Recall that in *In the Beginning Was Love* Kristeva explains that the child identifies with the imaginary father, in order to avoid the fantasy of being left out of its own conception. Yet this imaginary father along with his symbolic counterpart, the Father of the Law, leaves out the real father, specifically the father's bodily contributions to the child. The Virgin is impregnated by the Word and not by a product of a body. Perhaps the fantasy that is too much for the child to bear is that it is also a waste product of the father's body. If this is the case, how can an identification with the father serve as the counterweight to abjection? While the fantasy of a disembodied father works to offset the abject maternal body, lurking in the background is an even more disturbing abject fantasy, the fantasy that the child is merely the waste product of the father's body.

This may explain Freudian psychoanalysis's perverse fascination with the penis/Phallus. As an abject become sublime, the penis/Phallus is not an object proper. Rather, it is the undecidable that has become exalted to a beyond-the-object through perversion. The pervert becomes fascinated with the repulsive and disgusting forces of the abject and eroticizes them, idolizes them. In this way the pervert fortifies himself against the threat from this abject. Of course, the threat is also always present. The abject is threatening even as it is fascinating. As Kristeva points out in *Tales of Love*, perversion provides only fragile films with which to cover one's loss of unity:

> The other discovers a wounded, pierced, bleeding Self that attempts to stave off its losses, or overcome its losses, through eroticizing its parts or its rage. Perversion—from voyeurism and exhibitionism to the eroticization of waste and sadomasochism—then proposes its screen of *abjects*, fragile films, nei-

ther subjects nor objects, where what is signified is fear, the horror of being one for an *other*. (1983, 340)

The pervert discovers a split self, split off from any other and split within itself. In order to stave off the loss of the (m)other and thereby the loss of himself, he eroticizes a part of himself and substitutes it for the lost Thing (the not-yet-object, his union with his mother).[8] So his thing stands in for the Thing that he lost and becomes an eroticized Thing-beyond, the symbol of his gratified longing for his lost Thing-mother. But this eroticized Thing-beyond becomes only a fragile film, a flimsy screen, a sham even, for the lost Thing-mother. Does this story sound familiar? Could it be the story of traditional psychoanalysis?

Lacan maintains that his Phallus has nothing to do with Freud's "thing-ummy." It is beyond that, beyond any object. Yet, it is a sham. It is the signifier *par excellance* that destroys the possibility of a signified. Once the sham is exposed, all we see behind this Phallus is Lacan's "gaping hole." Whose hole is this, this hole that prohibits our wholeness? Could the abject mother and the abjection of birth be a screen of sorts for an abject father? After all, the child emerges whole from the mother's body through its private pathway. But the "child" emerges from the father's body a truly not-yet, a "potential" being. The literally not-yet "child" has a fragile existence, moving along the border between animate and inanimate. It emerges from the father's body into the mother's not through its own private pathway, but as a waste product, through a waste hole. Unlike the child when it emerges from the mother's body, this not-yet is not accompanied by supports for its own individual existence. Rather, it is accompanied by threats to its own existence, competitors, and death.

Turning back once again to the Christian imaginary, we can read the Holy Mother not only as a defense against the mother's outlaw desire but also as a defense against the father's abject body. The penis/Phallus is what is absent from the immaculate conception. Both Freud's penis and Lacan's Phallus are absent in immaculate conception. Obviously, the real penis is absent. Also, the Phallus that stands for gratification, specifically sexual gratification, is absent too. On the other hand, both the Christian imaginary and the imaginary of Lacanian psychoanalysis turn the penis/Phallus into the Word. Of course, Lacanian analysis goes one step further to expose this fantasy as a sham by exposing the "gaping hole" behind the Word. Lacan's "gaping hole," however, is a flimsy screen, a fragile film, set up in the place of the hole of the abject father.

The loving mother provides the necessary support against the fantasy of the abject father. Even as the connection to the mother can be over-whelming and without borders, it provides a necessary support against a fantasy that calls forth the contingency of being. The mother's loving care, the mother's knowledge that the child is real, protects the child from falling over the border of animate into inanimate, necessity into accident. Without the mother's love, the child can only abject itself as one waste product of its father's body, a not-yet that becomes a being through sheer chance, a not-yet surrounded by death. Without the mother's love, perversion becomes one defense against death.[9] The abject and hollowed penis/ Phallus is set up as a beyond-the-object around which all objects proper are constructed. This transcendental signifier stands in for the Thing. Insofar as it is not a thing of this world, the Phallus wards off death. The imaginary father, then, as a loving father, must confront the abject father. Otherwise, multiplying fathers merely multiplies fragile films over abjection. Kristeva's imaginary father needs to be reread as the outlaw love of the mother.

IV

REVOLUTIONARY LANGUAGE
RENDERED SPEECHLESS

Semanalysis

Over twenty years ago, Julia Kristeva began her project to make a new science that she called "semanalysis." Although greatly influenced by Russian formalism and French structuralism, Kristeva was dissatisfied with their treatment of the speaking subject and the history and process of language itself. She begins her breakthrough text, *Revolution in Poetic Language*, by stating:

> Our philosophies of language, embodiments of the Idea, are nothing more than the thoughts of archivists, archaeologists, and necrophiliacs. Fascinated by the remains of a process which is partly discursive, they substitute this fetish for what actually produced it. . . . These static thoughts, products of a leisurely cogitation removed from historical turmoil, persist in seeking the truth of language by formalizing utterances that hang in midair, and the truth of the subject by listening to the narrative of a sleeping body—a body in repose, withdrawn from its socio-historical imbrication, removed from direct experience. . . . (1974, 13)

Kristeva spends much of her early writing criticizing contemporary theories of language (and literature)—from Saussure and Chomsky to C. S. Peirce and Husserl—and setting the groundwork for her semanalysis.[1] In general, she maintains that contemporary language theory, structural linguistics in particular, has attempted to drain the speaking subject off of language. She claims that since Saussure and the beginnings of the *science* of linguistics, the truth and meaning of language were dissociated from the speaking subject. (1974a, 24) Kristeva, on the contrary, continues to believe that any theory of meaning must necessarily be a theory of the subject. (1973, 27) In fact, she argues that any theory of meaning presupposes a theory of the subject, even those theories that attempt to drain it off. (1975, 124)

For example, Kristeva argues that in Saussurian structuralism one can find the subject in the gap between the signifier and the signified. (1975, 128) While Saussure may be correct to point out that the relationship between the signifier and the signified is arbitrary, it is the speaking subject who makes the connection between them. This is also why for Kristeva, Chomsky's generative grammar reinstates the subject. In this case, she objects that it is the Cartesian subject that is reinstated. The Cartesian subject, the Husserlian transcendental ego, and the subject of Chomsky's generative grammar are unified subjects without histories. (1975) The transcendental ego or unitary subject, however, are only moments, albeit very important ones, in the signifying process. For Kristeva, there is more to the subject than the judging transcendental ego.

Kristeva maintains that the unitary subject, transcendental or otherwise, who posits meaning is the result of a process that is prior to meaning. Any language theory that presupposes a unitary subject cannot account for this pre-meaning element in the subject. There is part of language that cannot be accounted for, that part that doesn't mean: nonsense, tones, rhythms. Kristeva suggests that ultimately these theories cannot account for transgression and pleasure. (1973) She proposes that it is Freud who points to this process prior to meaning. (1968, 83). In his analysis of dreams, he concludes that the dream product is the result of such a process; the dream's meaning is the result of unconscious "thoughts" that are prior to meaning. Kristeva suggests that there is a scene behind the scene described by contemporary linguistics, Freud's "other scene."

Semanalysis, then, is a combination of psychoanalysis and semiology. (1973, 28) Through Kristeva's semanalysis, psychoanalysis benefits (with the help of Lacan) from linguistics and linguistics benefits from psychoanalysis.[2] Unlike structural linguistics, semanalysis does not conceive of meaning as a sign system but as a signifying process. "Within this process," says Kristeva, "one might see the release and subsequent articulation of the drives as constrained by the social code yet not reducible to the language system." (1973, 28) The science of semanalysis addresses this element that is beyond, heterogeneous to, language. It is, however, this "other" element prior to meaning that challenges the very possibility of science. Science, after all, tries to discover meaning; even Freud tried to give meaning to that "other scene." Semanalysis, in order to avoid the necrophilia of other theories of language, must always question its own presuppositions and uncover, record, and deny its own ideological gestures. Kristeva says that "[n]o form of semiotics . . . can exist other than as a critique of semiotics. As the place where the sciences die, semiotics is both the knowledge of this death and the revival, with this knowledge, of the 'scientific'; less (or more) than a science, it marks instead the aggressivity and disillusionment that takes place within scientific discourse itself."[3] (1968, 78)

In her early work, Kristeva suggests that science can be renewed through the renewal of its terms. (1968, 79) She recommends that semanalysis borrow terms and models from the exact sciences, including linguistics, and transform their meaning. At its crucial points, semanalysis can introduce "completely new terminology." (1968, 80) Kristeva calls this process "intertextuality." Initially she introduced the term to refer to Bakhtin's notion that "any text is constructed as a mosaic of quotations; any text is the absorption and transformation of another." (1966, 37) The notion of intertextuality points to the history of the text. As Kristeva develops the notion, it transforms even the meaning of history. Intertextuality points to a specific kind of textual history, a history left out of contemporary language theory.

Intertextuality, or transposition, breaks the stability of the thetic. Movement between signifying systems, the activity of intertextuality, requires continuous rearticulations of the thetic. The unity of both subject and object positions are called into question:

> If one grants that every signifying practice is a field of transpositions of various signifying systems (an inter-textuality), one then understands that its "place" of enunciation and its denoted "object" are never single, complete, and identical to themselves, but always plural, shattered, capable of being tabulated. (1974, 60)

Semanalysis's intentional intertextuality or transposition points up the intertextuality of all signifying systems. All signifying systems are mixtures of sign systems and therefore no one sign system can determine the meaning of any one sign. Semanalysis uses intertextuality in order to transform meanings. It alters the positions of enunciation and denotation, the positions from which the subject speaks as well as what it speaks about. And, by so doing, semanalysis points to a shifting subject position, a subject in transformation, a "subject-in-process/on trial."

The history that contemporary language theory leaves out, but semanalysis develops, is the history of *transformation*. For Kristeva, by recognizing this subject-in-process/on trial, semanalysis can lead to a "historical typology of signifying practices" and possibly arrive at a new perspective on history itself. (1973, 32) Following Philippe Sollers (following Nietzsche), Kristeva calls this new history "monumental history."[4] (1968, 85) This new history stands behind linear cursive history as its foundation. Monumental history is a history of the processes of signifying production. While linear history is the history of products, monumental history is the history of "*types* of signifying production prior to the product." (1968, 85) Semanalysis's new monumental history is a *logic* of transformations.[5] Kristeva suggests that this logic of transformation is not without its own transformative power. It is a way of playing the system against itself. (1973, 31)

In her preface to *Desire in Language* Kristeva says that semanalysis carries "theoretical thought to an intensity of white heat that set[s] categories and concepts ablaze—sparing not even discourse itself." It describes "the signifying phenomena, while analyzing, criticizing, and dissolving 'phenomenon,' 'meaning,' and 'signifier.'" (1980, vii) Semanalysis must point to its own limits. (1973, 30) It can do this only by postulating a subject as "the subject of a heterogeneous process." Kristeva maintains that this is the only way that a theory of language can show what lies "outside of its metalinguistic mode of operation," outside of semanalysis. (1973, 30–31) And the only way to do this is to "transform all critical and traditional conceptual apparatus, since the methods of classical thought privilege in signifying practice the moment of stability, and not of crisis."[6] (1973a, 519) The point of semanalysis, then, is to put itself and all signifying systems into crisis.

Kristeva criticizes structuralism in general, maintaining that it eliminates the drives from the semiotic and retains "only the image of the unconscious as a depository of laws and thus a discourse." The result, warns Kristeva, is that "[s]ince they are considered solely from the point of view of their relationship to language, and deprived of their drive bases, these structural operations depend on the phenomenological reduction, just as they depend on what this reduction is able to make visible: thetic symbolic functioning." (1974, 41)

This leaves post-structuralism in a position to remove these structural operations from their "phenomenological refuge" and define their function in the signifying process. Various tactics have been used in order to do so. (1974, 41) Kristeva prefers semanalysis, which she says tears "the veil of representation to find the material signifying process." (1974, 103) This technique enables us to understand how drive charges make their way in and through language, the subject, and society. (1974, 103)

For Kristeva signification is always heterogeneous, made up of both semiotic material rejection and symbolic stability. If, as Lacan maintains, the Unconscious is structured like a language, she argues that the Unconscious is also always heterogeneous. Her theory of semiotic material rejection has profound implications for a notion of the Unconscious. The Unconscious is not only structured like a language, but it is also structured like what is heterogeneous to language.

Lacan claims that "since Freud the unconscious has been a chain of signifiers that somewhere (on another stage, in another scene, he wrote) is repeated, and insists on interfering in the breaks offered it by the effective discourse and the cogitation that it informs." (1977, 297) Here Lacan is alluding to Freud's description of dream symbols, jokes, and slips of the tongue that make their way into "effective discourse." Lacan's claim that Freud's Unconscious is a chain of signifiers is based primarily on his interpretation of Freud's work on dreams. Dream interpretation, as Freud describes it, is a process of following a chain of signifiers back to the unconscious thoughts that they symbolize. Lacan says that the fact that Freud doesn't come out and say that the Unconscious is structured like a language is merely a "defect of history." (1977, 298) Freud did not have the benefits of modern linguistics, "of which the names of Ferdinand de Saussure and Roman Jakobson will stand for the dawn and its present-day culmination," says Lacan. (1977, 298) It is only this "defect of history" that Lacan suggests separates his Unconscious from Freud's.[7]

Lacan argues that the way in which Freud describes the unconscious "primary processes," particularly in dreams, is the same way that modern linguists describe the most radical operation of language: the effect of metaphor and metonymy, or substitution and combination, or what Freud called "condensation" and "displacement." (1977, 298) Lacan claims that condensation is the linguists' (Jakobson's) notion of metaphor, or the substitution of "word for word." (1977, 158) Displacement is the linguists' metonymy or the combination of words, "word to word." (1977, 156)

Freud identifies displacement and condensation as two of the techniques used in the dream work that allow unconscious repressed material to make its way, in this disguised form, into the dream. These techniques are also at work in jokes and slips of the tongue. Elizabeth Grosz succinctly defines these techniques:

> With condensation, a compression of two or more ideas occurs, so that a composite figure, image or name, drawing on and leaving out features of both, is formed. In this way, a single image in a dream is able to represent many different wishes or thoughts through compression of common feature and elimination of (relevant) differences. In the case of displacement, the significant, unconscious wish is able to transfer its intensity or meaning to an indifferent term, allowing the latter to act as its delegate, thus disguising it. The insignificant idea is able to represent the more significant one without the repressed features of the significant idea breaching the barriers of censorship. (1990, 87)

The major thesis of *Revolution in Poetic Language* is that the speaking subject is heterogeneous, the result of the signifying process with its two heterogeneous elements: the semiotic and the symbolic. The semiotic drive charge makes its way into the material of language (tones, music, rhythms, etc). While for Lacan the material of language points to an Unconscious that is structured like a language, for Kristeva it points to an Unconscious that is heterogeneous to language. (1987, 204–205) It points to the semiotic body that both gives rise to language and destroys it. It points to the maternal music in and beyond language. For Kristeva, the Unconscious is structured like the maternal music in language. Was this Unconscious, Kristeva's Unconscious, beyond both Freud and Lacan because, as she says in *Tales of Love*, neither of them liked music? (1983,

192) Or because of a repression of the primary identification with their mothers? Or, ultimately, because they weren't mothers?

Revolutionary Poetry

Semiotic Dialectic

For Kristeva, it is the recovery of this semiotic disposition in language that calls signifying practice to its crisis; the semiotic in language is revolutionary. Kristeva compares the revolution in language to a political revolution. (1974, 17) Like a political revolution, the semiotic in language causes an upheaval of the Symbolic and the subject. The political revolution is not merely a model or analogue for the linguistic revolution; rather, "the explosions set off by practice-process within the social field and the strictly linguistic field are logically (if not chronologically) contemporaneous, and respond to the same principle of unstoppable break-through; they differ only in their field of application." (1974, 104) In *Revolution in Poetic Language*, Kristeva insists that the "artistic" and the "political" are two modalities of the same process. Revolution in either sphere is brought about through the introduction of the semiotic that points up the process of production, whether it is linguistic or political or both. Kristeva also suggests that a revolution in one sphere is a revolution in the other. I will come back to this suggestion later in this chapter. For now, however, I will concentrate on the revolutionary power of the semiotic itself, especially with regard to language.

The semiotic has this power because it introduces drives into language; the semiotic is the repository of drives in language.[8] For Kristeva, drives are not, as some of her critics suggest, extra-linguistic.[9] Rather, the linguistic is itself heterogeneous. It is composed of symbols and nonsymbols, meaning and nonmeaning. From her earliest writings Kristeva describes biological operations as operations that are subject to signifying and social codes. But biological operations violate those codes at the same time. This violation, which actually takes place within the realm of the code—that is, within signifying systems—allows the subject to both take pleasure in and endanger the code. (1973, 30) There is also a pleasure in endangering the code.

The semiotic is the bio-social element of language that is reciprocally engendered by, and engendering, the Symbolic even while it is transgressing the symbolic. The semiotic in language is the rhythm and music that express drives. Kristeva argues that instinctual rhythm passes through symbolic theses and "meaning is constituted but is then immediately exceeded by what seems outside of meaning: materiality." (1974, 100) Certainly the pleasure found in drive discharge through language is in excess of meaning and representation. The materiality of language itself can discharge drives through the Symbolic but always necessarily in excess of the symbolic. It is not that language represents the drive, which is impossible. Rather, language, specifically poetic and avant-garde language, can *reactivate* drives. And it is precisely because what is going on here is *not* representation that poetic language "pulverizes" signification.

Words are made up of two heterogeneous levels. While on the symbolic level they signify, on the semiotic level they act and activate. Insofar as poetic language points to the heterogeneous process of language itself, it doubly reactivates drives. Poetic language, as I analyze below, "pre-alters" representation even while it exceeds it. (1974, 103) And for Kristeva it is this double-movement that is revolutionary. Even in revolutionary language the semiotic is dependent on the symbolic. So too, the symbolic is dependent on the semiotic. The heterogeneity of language operates in a dialectical oscillation.

Without the symbolic function within the Symbolic order, the semiotic could never be transformed into a practice, and certainly not a revolutionary practice. It is the constraints imposed by the Symbolic that insure that the semiotic does not merely lapse into delirium. (1974, 82) These constraints separate an effective signifying practice from psychosis. In order to be effective the semiotic must combine with the symbolic:

> This combinatory moment, which accompanies the destruction process and makes it a *practice*, is always produced with reference to a moment of stasis, a boundary, a symbolic barrier. Without this temporary resistance, which is viewed as if it were insurmountable, the process would never become a practice and would founder instead in an opaque and unconscious organicity. (1974, 102)

The semiotic is effective at the frontiers of language. It works the limits of language; it is the dialectical oscillation between the semiotic and the symbolic that breaks and redefines the limits of language because a space in itself (like Lacan's Borromean knot), the semiotic *chora* cannot challenge meaning's closure. Only a new way of speaking can do that. (1977a, 280–81) And this new way of speaking comes only through acknowledging that the signifying process is necessarily a heterogeneous process.

There is always something that cannot be said and that is why we keep talking. That something in excess is the remainder of the semiotic *chora* in language. On the one hand, without the symbolic we would have pure unconscious organicity or madness—this is why Kristeva maintains that art accepts the thetic to the extent that it does not become either delirium or nature. (1974, 80) On the other hand, without the semiotic, if it were possible to have speech, we would have empty speech. The oscillation, then, that Kristeva describes is not the movement of a stationary pendulum. Rather, it is a dialectic operated by a tension between two heterogeneous elements that move it in some direction.

Perhaps we could imagine this dialectical oscillation like the movement of a top spinning on a table. This top dances back and forth in one circle after another, moving closer to the edge of the table until one of its circles sends it over the edge onto another surface where it continues its dance until it goes over another edge and so on. In other words, although the movement is an oscillation, it is not stationary. Rather, there is movement onto new levels of signification. Signifying systems eventually change as a result of this dialectical oscillation. In terms of language, syntax and meaning change. The structure, or language itself, changes. In terms of psychoanalysis, the analysand's behavior changes. The structure of the analysand's psyche changes.

The dialectic between the semiotic and symbolic, however, is not a Hegelian dialectic with its continual return to the subject position. Unlike Hegel, Kristeva emphasizes crisis and not reconciliation. If the symbolic negates the semiotic in order to posit the unity of the thetic, then the transgression of the thetic—within a Hegelian dialectic—might be the negation of the negation of the semiotic. But for Kristeva, the transgression of the thetic in poetic language is not the negation of the negation of the semiotic. Rather, the transgression of the thetic is the *reversed reactivation of the contradiction* between the symbolic and the semiotic. It is not the Hegelian *negation of the contradiction*, or synthesis. This reversed reactivation of the contradiction is a *reactivation* because it points up the heterogeneity, the contradiction, between the semiotic and symbolic, which the symbolic negates in order to simulate the unity that taking a position requires. This reactivation of the contradiction is a *reversal* because it uses the thetic against itself. By showing the contradiction that gave rise to the thetic, the reversed reactivation pulverizes the thetic. The reversed reactivation of the contradiction exposes the symbolic sham of positional unity. The dialectic that gives rise to language continues through language in order to exceed language.[10]

Revolutionary Effects

This dialectic between semiotic and symbolic determines what kind of language we have. For Kristeva, language oscillates toward the semiotic in certain kinds of poetry and avant-garde writing. This poetry is characterized by an attention to the materiality of words, their rhythms and tones, which connects them to the repressed semiotic. In her writings around *Revolution in Poetic Language*, Kristeva calls the semiotic disposition in language the "genotext," which she opposes to the "phenotext." The genotext is the text of the drives as they are constrained by social code and yet show up within that code. It is a return of the repressed in language. Genotext is therefore overdetermined and connected to what Freud called primary processes.

Kristeva argues that in addition to the music of poetry, avant-garde writing uses innovative grammars that loosen the linguistic constraints on the repressed semiotic. Revolutionary language speaks the Unconscious. But it does not do so in any ordinary way. As I indicated earlier, poetic language discharges rather than represents drives. In this way, the repressed makes its way into the Symbolic: the unconscious drives become conscious, but they do so in a way that is analogous to the psychoanalytic process and not merely a form of mimesis; poetic language enacts a transference between drives and language rather than an imitation of drives in language.

Poetry is a type of borderline case that calls into question all that is central to representation. In addition to the discharge of drive, poetry "pre-alters" representation. Poetry pre-alters representation by showing the *process* of representation itself. Within this type of poetry, representation cannot appear as a self-sustaining unity, or as a necessary relationship between signifier and signified. Rather, poetry functions to show how signifiers and signifieds are produced. In this way poetry unravels the symbolic and the unity that it requires. For example, the signified cannot be unified if poetry shows that the signified is merely the effect of signifiers that are themselves overdetermined and therefore never stable. Moreover, poetry shows this signified-effect as merely one stage in the whole ongoing process of signification.[11]

Poetry negates the symbolic in order to call it back to the process of signification of which it is part. But poetry's negation is neither symbolic negation nor neurotic negation. Kristeva calls poetic negation "third degree negation." (1974, 164) Poetic negation is the rejection of symbolic negation because while it operates on and within both the symbolic function and the Symbolic order, its force is drive force that is heterogeneous to the symbolic. In addition, poetic negation is the rejection of unconscious "negation." As Freud says, there is no "no" in the Unconscious. Poetic negation, however, is not the no "no" and therefore "yes" of the Unconscious. Poetic negation can have an effect because it is a different kind of negation. And, importantly, because it operates within the Symbolic through the symbolic function, it is not neurotic negation or pure denial. Poetic negation, then, unlike symbolic, unconscious, or neurotic negation, does not use negative symbols, substitution, or denial to compromise the symbolic function. If it used any of these means, it would not be revolutionary.

Poetic negation "recalls, spatially and musically, the dialectical moment of the generating of significance." (1974, 164) It is a third-degree negation constituted by a double-movement through which poetic language reactivities the repressed semiotic by discharging drives through its music and overdetermination and by recalling the dialectical process and repression that enables the symbolic to function. For Kristeva, in poetic language the semiotic recalls its own repression and this is revolutionary. Of course, this process of "recall" also involves the expenditure of repressed unconscious drives.

Poetic language is explicitly involved in the destructuring and structuring of language at the "outer boundaries" of the Symbolic. (1974, 17) Because the authority of the Symbolic requires unity and autonomy, the semiotic disposition in poetry destablizes the Symbolic order so as to recreate a new Symbolic order. For Kristeva this is the nature of all signifiance. Poetry reveals the nature of all signifiance through its *practice*. Kristeva defines a practice as the acceptance of the symbolic Law together with the transgression of the Law for the purpose of renovating it. (1973, 29); (See also 1974, 195–234.) Because poetic language is text as practice, it constructs a "new symbolic device—a new reality corresponding to a new heterogeneous object." (1974, 181) This new heterogeneous reality is the reality of a new heterogeneous subject, what Kristeva calls the "subject-on-trial/in-process." The revolution in poetic language is also a revolution in the subject, for any theory of language is also a theory of the subject.

Poetic language puts the subject on trial through a double operation. Most obviously, insofar as poetic language shatters the unity of the thetic, it also shatters the unity of the subject position. Without a unified thetic, there is no unified *position*. The unified subject becomes one stage in the process of signification. In addition Kristeva suggests that there is a transference that can take place between the reader and the text. (1974, 210) Through this transference the subject identifies with the text. The revolutionary poetic text, however, is never a unified text. It is always in process and points to the process of signifiance itself. The subject, then, through this transference takes the place of the process. Through this transference, the subject is put on trial/in process. At the time of *Revolution in Poetic Language* it was Kristeva's hope that this revolutionary subject could subvert capitalism.

Kristeva argued that the function of revolutionary texts is to produce these revolutionary subjects. (1974, 105) But, like the oscillation between the conservative symbolic and the revolutionary semiotic, Kristeva's writings around *Revolution* oscillate with regard to the revolutionary effects of poetic language. While she argues that the revolutionary text has an effect on the subject that is analogous to political revolution, she suggests that social revolution may have made the 19th-century avant-garde texts useless. (1974, 17, 212) While she argues that in the "contemporary situation" we cannot attack capitalism directly so we do so through texts, she also suggests that 19th-century poetic texts were coopted by the dominant ideology. (1974, 105, 211–12) While she argues that revolutionary texts prepare subjects for social changes that shake the foundation of contemporary society, she suggests that these texts embody a "moral gesture" that is inspired by the concern to socialize what rocks the foundations of sociality. (1974, 191; 1973, 32)

What kind of a *revolution* is this that breaks the Symbolic even while it is coopted by it? In her writings around *Revolution*, Kristeva seems to believe that a revolutionary textual practice is an "acceptance of the symbolic law together with a transgression of the law for the purpose of renovating the law." (1973, 29) Kristeva makes it clear that the semiotic revolution in poetic language always and only takes place within the Symbolic. If it didn't, it would be psychotic babble at best. The semiotic cannot be revolutionary without the symbolic and there can be no symbolic without the semiotic, in spite of the symbolic's attempts at repressing it.

So, is the effect that Kristeva describes revolutionary? A "renovation" or "renewal" of the social code does not seem analogous to a political "revolution." Perhaps the process that she describes is a *reform* of the social code, or an *evolution* of the social code. As she describes this process, however, the sequence is not necessarily a progressive sequence. In fact, by the time we get to *Powers of Horror*, the way in which Kristeva describes the disruptions and reforms in poetic language suggests a very problematic politics.

Revolutionary Horror[12]

In *Powers of Horror* Kristeva gives an example of the revolutionary effect of the repressed maternal in language. According to her, the authority of our religion, morality, politics, and language comes through the repression of horror; behind their authority lurks abject and unspeakable fascistic terror. Our culture is founded on this horror. Kristeva claims that this horror can be said through what she calls the "language of abjection" that has its source in the repressed Unconscious. (1980, 205–206) Part of the horror said through the language of abjection is the crisis in the authority of the Word; the power of the language of abjection is to demystify authority. (1980, 208, 210) Abject literature calls into question language itself, along with the authority of the subject. Kristeva suggests that like revolutionary poetry, the content of abject literature is maternal; it is the semiotic music and rhythm of language. (1980, 155, 157, 206, 208) On one level abjection is what is repressed with the symbolic element of language, and when this repressed shows itself, it undermines the authority of language itself.

But, unlike some of her earlier writings on revolutionary poetry in *Powers of Horror*, the power that Kristeva identifies with abject language is almost purely aesthetic. She suggests that the language of abjection points to the lack of meaning and only through its own beauty does it have meaning:

> Neither Céline, who is such a writer, nor the catastrophic exclamation that constitutes his style, can find outside support to maintain themselves. Their only sustenance lies in the beauty of a gesture that, here, on the page compels language to come nearest to the human enigma, to the place where it kills, thinks, and experiences jouissance all at the same time. (1980, 206)

Kristeva claims that the real content of the language of abjection is style. In this style "any ideology, thesis, interpretation, mania, collectivity, threat, or hope become drowned." (1980, 206) And in *Powers of Horror* she presents the writings of Céline as an example of repressed maternal "horror" expressed through abject literature.

Kristeva's fascination with Céline has disturbed many theorists. Because of her praise of Céline, she has been accused of fascism. Her harshest critics have been Jennifer Stone and Peter Gidal, both of whom claim that Kristeva is fascist and anti-Semitic. While I agree that Kristeva's praise for Céline's anti-Semitic writing is troubling, to argue that she endorses Céline's racism is to oversimplify her position. Kristeva praises Céline's writing because it lays bare a horror that underlies all of culture. In Céline's writings the horror is on the surface, whereas it is hidden in other aspects of culture. I prefer to accept Jacqueline Rose's conclusion:

> Kristeva is able at one and the same time to lay out the horrors of fantasmatic structure which underpin the writings of an author like Céline, while at the same time praising that writing for exposing psychic drama which— with massive social repercussions—is constantly denied, projected onto the other, and then played out by the culture at large. Céline's writing is a symptom. It reveals horror as a matter of power—the power of fascination when we are confronted with the traces of our own psychic violence, the horror when that same violence calls on social institutions for legitimation, and receives it. (1986, 155)

In an interview Kristeva says that the problematic of *Powers of Horror* "was to describe how in different religions and literary elaborations people have tried to defend against these negative impulses, negative drives, through different rituals: for instance catharsis, purification, and so on." (1984b, 26) In the case of Céline, negative and murderous impulses are cathected in his writing. And poetic murders are better than real murders. Kristeva's point is that through style abject language is cathartic because it is antipolitical. That is, it has no affiliations and undermines any claims to affiliation. The appropriate effect of abject language is aesthetic. And this aesthetic experience can somehow be therapeutic for the reader as well as the writer. This experience takes the reader and writer back to a "presymbolic" existence, an immediacy earlier and beyond symbols. It discharges this semiotic violence in language. Kristeva says, "While everything else—its archeology and its exhaustion—is only literature: the sublime point at which the abject collapses in a burst of beauty that overwhelms us—and 'that cancels our existence' (Céline)." (1980, 210; cf. 206)

Kristeva suggests that abject language allows us to experience this earlier maternal sphere in language through the sublime and comic; abject language turns horror into the "sublime" and "comic." (1980, 201, 205) Abject literature laughs at horror. "A laughing apocalypse," says Kristeva, "is an apocalypse without god." (1980, 206) Kristeva's litany sends Nietzschean chills. She chants that "without master, this universe has rhythm; without Other, it is dance and music; without God, it has style." (1980, 179) She even invokes the Dionysian festival as the most striking example of the dissolution of symbolic order into a "dancing, singing, and poetic animality." (1984, 79) Kristeva believes that the Dionysian horror, which both creates and destroys without discrimination, can be tolerated only through the sublime and comic of art. With Nietzsche, she seems to conclude that only aesthetically can life be justified. Nietzsche's insight that "if man [sic] was not also a poet, he could not bear to be a man" shines through each dense page of Kristeva's *Powers of Horror*. Perhaps it is because she is haunted by Nietzsche's tragic insight that she concludes, "suffering, he [man] beguiles himself with the sound of his cross, an acrobat walking a tightrope: should he let himself be walled in alive or make a poem out of it?" (1986, 268)

Kristeva has a vision of the recuperation of a lost maternal force, an instinctual force buried under repressive symbols. In *Powers of Horror* this vision sometimes seems like a romantic yearning for some prelinguistic bodily experience. This tendency in Kristeva's writing is extremely problematic and in most texts Kristeva makes it clear that she is trying to avoid a simple opposition between linguistic and prelinguistic. She always emphasizes that signification is an ongoing process that is only artificially categorized. She insists that there are two heterogeneous elements in this process. Even so, there are still difficulties with how these elements relate to each other.

One of Kristeva's most articulate critics, Judith Butler, takes up some of these difficulties. She argues that Kristeva can postulate the existence of the semiotic *chora* only through a circular movement. (1989, 112–13) She maintains that we attribute meaning only to what is representable in language and therefore we cannot attribute meaning to the semiotic drives before they emerge in language. In addition, we cannot attribute any kind of causality to semiotic drives since we are already operating within the confines of language and we know causes only through their effects. Butler concludes that either drives and representations are coextensive or representations pre-exist drives. (1989, 113) These problems disappear if we do not read the semiotic *chora* as something that is prelinguistic or pre-cultural. Certainly Butler reads the semiotic *chora* as prelinguistic and precultural. In an earlier article, I develped a similar interpretation.[13] Since then, however, I have come to believe, along with Jacqueline Rose and Ewa Ziarek, among others, that not only are those places where Kristeva seems to locate the semiotic *chora* outside of language and history the least useful elements of her theories but also that they go against her overall project.[14] Usually Kristeva is very careful to point out that the semiotic *chora* is not brute biology. Rather, it is the intersection of biology and culture. It is not, therefore, precultural. Neither is it prelinguistic. It is the drives as they become manifest in language. Which is not to say that we can postulate drives as they exist independently of language. Rather, Kristeva realizes that her own postulates always occur within language. Her unique thesis is that language itself, signification itself, culture itself, and meaning itself are heterogeneous. That is, they are composed of, and contain, elements of nonlanguage and nonmeaning. So Kristeva would take issue with Butler's interpretation that meaning is what can be represented. For Kristeva meaning is always made up of both symbolic and semiotic elements. Meaning and representation are not purely symbolic. They are also semiotic. It is difficult to defend an interpretation of Kristeva's writings that places the semiotic outside of language. Certainly, the semiotic is not prelinguistic in any straightforward sense.

Butler also challenges the political efficacy of the semiotic in language. Among other things, she argues that Kristeva naturalizes the semiotic and therefore it is not emancipatory but yet another face of paternal power. If the semiotic, however, is always a cultural phenomena and always a part of language, then it is not natural in the way in which Butler maintains that it is.

The concern with the politics of the semiotic leads me to question Kristeva's own relation to her writing. What is the relation between her own writing and the semiotic? Is her writing abject? Does she intend an aesthetic effect from her work? At times it seems that Kristeva merely uses the rhetoric of revolution for a certain poetic effect. Her revisionist politics of language, which uses rhetoric of revolution for poetic effect, might explain some of the oscillations in her own writings between poetic and dense theoretical language. Since it is not, and does not claim to be, poetic language, does Kristeva's theoretical discourse coopt the semiotic? What is the intended effect of her semanalysis if it cannot discharge drives after the fashion of poetic language? In a move that is not completely reconcilable with her theory of poetic language, she claims that semanalysis speaks the heterogeneous tension in language. In her theory, this is true to greater or lesser degrees of all language. The important question from Kristeva's theory to Kristeva's theory is, "Is semanalysis a practice?"

Does semanalysis accept the Symbolic in order to transgress the symbolic? How is it any more than a symbolic negation of the symbolic, which is in fact merely another affirmation of the symbolic? Another look at what Kristeva proposes as the relationship between the semiotic and symbolic will begin to answer these questions.

With Kristeva it is always impossible to pinpoint an origin: in addition to an oscillation between poetry and dense theory in her own writing, there seems to be an oscillation between assigning the semiotic priority and assigning the symbolic priority.[15] In some places Kristeva says that the semiotic is both logically and chronologically prior to the symbolic, while in other places she maintains that the symbolic is both logically and chronologically prior to the semiotic. She most consistently maintains that the symbolic is prior to the semiotic in a contribution to a collection of essays on Lacan. In her contribution, "Within the Microcosm of 'The Talking Cure,'" Kristeva says "I have posited the logical and chronological priority of the symbolic in any organization of the semiotic (into a structure but also a 'chora,' a receptacle)." (1983a, 34) This is because the semiotic cannot be *articulated* without the symbolic; in this sense, the symbolic is primary.

Although she acknowledges that Lacan's development of "*lalangue*," the mother-tongue, which goes beyond any utterance, is an advance over his claim that the Unconscious is structured like a language, she maintains that even *lalangue* is not heterogeneous to the structure of language for Lacan. (1983a, 34–35) Recall that Kristeva argues that Lacan's "impossible real" and *lalangue* are homogeneous with the structure of language. Ultimately, they are reducible to language. And Kristeva insists that there is an element of the signifying process that is not reducible to language. Still in this piece on Lacan, she makes it extremely clear that this heterogeneous element "can be conceived only through the position, the thesis, of language." (1983a, 36) Also, Kristeva insists that "the position of the semiotic as heterogeneous does not derive from a desire to integrate, within language often accused of being too 'abstract,' a supposed concreteness, a raw corporeality, or an immanent energy." (1983a, 36) Compare this with Kristeva's assertion in *Revolution in Poetic Language* that "[t]he heterogeneous element is a corporeal, physiological, and signifiable excitation which the symbolizing social structure—the family or some other structure—cannot grasp." (1974, 180)

With the exception of a few romantic moments conjured for poetic effect in which Kristeva suggests that the semiotic is the voice of a raw corporeality or an immanent bodily energy, she consistently maintains that the semiotic is part of the signifying process that is itself heterogeneous. There are plenty of passages, however, where she explicitly claims that the semiotic both "logically and chronologically precedes the establishment of the symbolic and its subject." (1974, 41) (See also 1974, 27, 36, 49, 50, 62, 68; 1974b, 172, 168; 1977a, 283; 1987, 5.) This is not to say, however, that the semiotic is *not* part of the signifying process.

Kristeva's description of the semiotic as both "logically and chronologically" prior to either the symbolic function or the Symbolic order is complicated, perhaps a necessary contradiction, a hermeneutic circle. This position seems to inadvertently place the semiotic firmly within the Symbolic. In the dialectic between the semiotic and symbolic that Kristeva describes, the semiotic is *prior* to both the symbolic function and the Symbolic order; the relation between the semiotic and symbolic is temporal. Yet linear time is the time of the Symbolic order, which is provided by the symbolic function. But according to Kristeva the semiotic is outside of time. It is pre-time, the womb out of which time is born. The dialectic that Kristeva describes as an oscillation that continually pushes the symbolic beyond itself is always framed by the symbolic itself. It is possible that what she reads as revolutions in the symbolic function or the Symbolic order can be read as illusions with which the Symbolic perpetuates its own logic against any possibility of revolution. In other words, her revolutionary texts are merely reappropriations of resistance within the Symbolic.

Kristeva admits that the semiotic is "only a *theoretical supposition* justified by the need for description." (1974, 68) This suggests that the semiotic is a symbolic construction that is needed in order to perpetuate symbolic description. Symbolization, says Kristeva, "makes possible the complexity of this semiotic combinatorial system, which only theory can isolate as 'preliminary' in order to specify its functioning." (1974, 68) In other words, only the post-thetic theorist, operating quite firmly within the Symbolic, can identify the complexities of the semiotic function. In fact, in some sense, the semiotic is just a theoretical supposition that allows us to explain how it is that we become speaking beings. Of course, this is possible only because we are already speaking beings. Kristeva still insists, however, that the semiotic is something more than "an abstract object produced for the needs of theory." It is put in place, she says, by a "biological set-up" that is already social and historical. (1974, 68) The semiotic is postulated through the symbolic; yet, and at the same time, it always exceeds it. For Kristeva, signification contains an unrepresentable element. She knows that positioning the unrepresentable outside of signification sets up a metaphysics or theology. (1987, 66)

Even so, insofar as it is the result of contemplation, Kristeva finds the semiotic *chora* disenchanting. (1974, 96) In "The Novel as Polylogue," Kristeva's essay on Philippe Sollers' (her husband) novel *H*, in a moment of what appears to be a frustrated passion, she protests:

> What I am saying to you is that if this heterogeneous body, this risky text
> provide meaning, identity, and *jouissance*, they do so in a completely differ-

ent way than a "Name-of-the-Father." Not that they do not operate under
the shield of a tyrannical, despotic Name-of-the-Father; I understand that,
and we could engage in endless forensic contests. But it is only a question
of power; the important thing is to see what exceeds it. (1974b, 163)

Perhaps Kristeva speaks from the position of a woman frustrated within
the tyranny of the Name-of-the-Father. Perhaps this is what makes her
defensive about her identification with the Father in her early writings.
This is what makes her defend the privilege of her theoretical bent. Can
the critic engage in revolutionary poetry and still be a critic? Is the critic
a poet?

There are poetic moments in Kristeva's texts, most notably "Stabat
Mater" and parts of *Powers of Horror*, where she attempts to tap the semiotic in her own language. Even these are problematic; for Kristeva, while
it may take a woman in order to *theorize* the repressed maternal in language, it is nearly impossible for a woman to be a revolutionary poet
who can renovate this language. The relation of women to language, and
therefore poetic language, is tied to a relation to the maternal. Since men
and women have a different relation to the maternal, they also have a
different relation to language. This difference, which constitutes sexual
difference, also sets up a double-bind for women in relation to language.
It is unclear how the theoretician/poet/analyst Kristeva escapes this bind.
It seems to make Kristeva herself a paradox, an anomaly, or a "man."

The Marginal Women

In the year of the publication of *Revolution*, Kristeva took a trip to
China. Later that year she published some notes from her travel journals,
About Chinese Women. In this early text, we find her most dramatic description of the position of women in monotheist capitalist culture. In
her introduction to *About Chinese Women* Kristeva ruthlessly sketches
Western women's marginal relation to the Symbolic—language, politics,
time, culture.[16] There she argues that monotheism is responsible for patriarchy. Sexual difference is defined in relation to the Law of the Symbolic
order generally, represented by the law of monotheistic religion specifically. The unity of the one Law/God is both sustained and threatened by
bodily desire. This bodily desire is contained within the "other" sex,
woman's sex. In this way, unity can be maintained since everything that
threatens it is contained in something that is assigned a position outside
of the unity. (1974c, 19) Woman becomes the waste, the sacrifice, but also
the "truth" upon which the unity of the Symbolic order is maintained.
Any power, however, that she might have in that capacity is taken from
her when she is represented as waste/"truth" within the Symbolic order.

As Kristeva describes her, woman is put into circulation within the economy of the Symbolic order as fetish, which denies her position as the repressed desire upon which culture is based. The necessary fetish of any "woman" as she is put into the Symbolic order is what Kristeva calls "a crude but enormously effective trap for feminism." (1974c, 37)

This trap springs on a double twist: woman is set up as inarticulate Other and then she is articulated within the Symbolic order. Of course, the trick is that the inarticulate cannot be articulated and retain its status or power. When represented, the unrepresentable woman becomes what she is not. The existence of the unrepresentable upon which representation rests is denied; and the representation of that unrepresentable, woman, is a fetish. Kristeva suggests that this is a trap for feminism because it seems necessary for feminism to claim some identity for woman or women. It seems necessary for feminists to represent women in order to work for the emancipation of women from the oppressive representations of them in patriarchal cultures. But for Kristeva this is to once again fetishize her, or refetishize her, and thereby render her powerless, completely coopted by the Symbolic. This is true, however, only within the logic of monotheistic patriarchy, which sets this trap in the first place.

If, in order to sustain the unity of monotheism, women's only power was not defined as a presymbolic, unrepresentable, threatening power, then representations of woman/women would not coopt her power. It is only because her power is defined as mysterious and unrepresentable that representation is a denial of that power. It is only because of a mystification of women's power and bodies that representation is always a trap for feminism. There are and have been feminists who problematize women's identity even while engaging it. And although it seems like the problematization of women's identity has been a recent phenomenon, as Denise Riley illustrates (1988), it has been part of the history of Western feminisms for centuries.

Kristeva argues that Western culture puts women into a double-bind. Either women can enter the Symbolic—language, politics, time, culture—only by identifying as men, or they can withdraw into their silent bodies as hysterics:

> We cannot gain access to the temporal scene, i.e. to political affairs, except by identifying with the values considered to be masculine (dominance, superego, the endorsed communicative word that institutes stable social exchange). . . . [W]e have been able to serve or overthrow the socio-historic order by playing supermen. . . . Others, more bound to the mothers, more tuned in as well to their unconscious impulses, refuse this role and hold themselves back, sullen, neither speaking nor writing, in a permanent state of expectation punctuated now and then by some kind of outburst: a cry, a refusal, an "hysterical symptom." (1974c, 37)

Although Kristeva suggests that the logic of Western culture condemns women to one of these two fates, she also suggests a way out of this double-bind. First, she says that we must realize that it is necessary to know an ostensibly masculine identifiction in order to be heard within the Symbolic order. But we have to guard against the narcissism of that identification. We have to avoid becoming "virile women," or supermen. On the other hand, we cannot fall back into the silent body. We need to listen to this body from within the Symbolic. From within the Symbolic that demands and guarantees identity, we have to refuse all identity. The end result of this procedure will be "to summon this timeless 'truth'—formless, neither true nor false, echo of our *jouissance*, of our madness, of our pregnancies—into the order of speech and social symbolism." Kristeva argues that we can do this by listening to the "unspoken in speech," and the "incomprehensible," that which "disturbs the status quo." (1974c, 38) She suggests an "impossible dialectic" that endlessly alternates between "time and its 'truth.'" She wonders who is capable of this dialectic: the political analyst, the politician who listens to the Unconscious, or a woman?

This is not the only time that Kristeva mysteriously suggests, always in passing, that the kind of analysis or language that is necessary may take a woman. (1975, 146; 1980, x) Although Kristeva may fancy herself as this woman analyst concerned with politics and history, she doesn't leave room for any others. Throughout her writings she argues that women's relation to language is problematic. And her relation to revolutionary poetic language is impossible. This is because a woman must deny her identification with the mother in order to enter the Symbolic. Recall that in *Black Sun* Kristeva argues that women can never even enter into a proper mourning for the maternal let alone work through this mourning. (1987a, 28–30, 86) In addition, it is necessary to lose the maternal in order to enter language. (1987a, 43) In *Black Sun*, Kristeva concludes that women's speech is depressive speech because feminine sexuality is addicted to the maternal. (1987a, 71) On the other hand, a man can properly mourn for, and lose, the maternal. In fact, a man must overcome this repression of his identification with the mother in order to produce poetic language or art. Although poetic language is threatening in a certain way for a man, for a woman it is dangerous and possibly deadly. By identifying with the maternal, a man breaks through repression. By identifying with the maternal, a woman, however, takes up her place as the repressed. As Kristeva suggests in one passage from *About Chinese Women*, if she tries to bring the maternal into the Symbolic, a woman risks death or psychosis. (1974c, 41)

In *About Chinese Women*, only a few paragraphs after she encourages women to refuse the double-bind and listen to the unspoken maternal in language, Kristeva warns that such activities have led to death or psychosis. As Kristeva sees it this is because women's goal is to escape the confines of the paternal Word; and certainly reinscribing oneself into that Word is no escape. The only possible escapes are suicide and psychosis:

> For a woman, as soon as the father's not calling the dance and language is being torn apart by rhythm, no mother can serve as an axis for the sacred or farce. The girl tries herself: the result is so-called female homosexuality, identification with men, or a tight rein on the least pre-Oedipal pleasure. And if no paternal "legitimation" comes along to dam up the inexhaustible nonsymbolized impulse, she collapses into psychosis or suicide. (1974c, 41)

Here Kristeva names three such women, women who attempted to listen to the maternal in language, Virginia Woolf, Marina Tsvetaeva, and Sylvia Plath, all of whom committed suicide. When writing about these women, Kristeva romanticizes their suicides: Women's suicides are "black lava," "without a cause," "without drama," "without tragedy"; they are the natural result of this process of fighting the mother in order to enter language: "slowly, gently, death settles in" (1974c, 39); they are "non-acts," "a gesture that is imperative on the basis of an elsewhere," "a fullness beyond." (1987a, 73) Kristeva speculates that although these women are victims in our society, elsewhere they may not be. (1974c, 41) At this point, she turns to the China of the Cultural Revolution. She describes the Cultural Revolution as a women's revolution and China as a place were the gap between the sexes is not nearly so wide. Romantically, she argues that women and mothers are respected and powerful there. For Kristeva, foot-binding becomes proof of women's power. She maintains that just as men are circumcised in the monotheistic West, a social and symbolic prohibition that confers "superior political and symbolic knowledge," women undergo foot-binding in China. She argues that these rituals are analogous because they both limit an excessive power in order to constitute the whole. For Kristeva, both men in the West and women in China represent social power (even if they do not have it). (1974c, 83–85)

How is it that Kristeva can argue that circumcision is analogous to foot-binding when girls are in pain for years and crippled for life as a result of their "castration"? Through this suffering and "masochistic pleasure" Chinese women "will have the symbolic premium," but what price do Western men pay for their "symbolic premium"? (1974c, 883–84) Perhaps Kristeva romanticizes the suffering and suicides of women who are her Foremothers in order to ease the guilt of the death of the mother and her own identification with the mother that she argues are necessary in order to write. She does, after all, mention that she "owes her cheekbones to some Asian ancestor"—some Chinese woman with bound-feet? (1974c, 12) And she probably owes more to Virginia Woolf, Marina Tsvetaeva, and Sylvia Plath, to name only a few.[17]

In her texts, Kristeva mentions very few women by name. And when she does, most often they are women who have fallen into psychosis or committed suicide. The revolutionary poets are always men: Artaud, Bataille, Céline, Joyce, Lautremont, Mallarmé, among others. Within the economy of Kristeva's psychoanalytic theory this makes sense. For, as she describes them, the first sounds that a child hears and makes are associated with the maternal body. Those sounds and that body are repressed and reappear in language as the semiotic. But because of their relation to castration, men and women have different relations to the semiotic, and to language in general.

For Kristeva, whereas men can fully enter language because they experience the threat of castration that forces them away from any identification with their mothers, women do not fully enter language because they never experience the castration threat in the same way and therefore do not completely sever their identification with their mothers. If women do not have complete access to language, then they cannot reinscribe/discover the semiotic there. In some ways it seems that for women, accessing the semiotic in language poses the threat of falling back into a preoedipal identification with the mother, which is psychotic; whereas for men, accessing the semiotic in language engenders a postoedipal return of the maternal within the Symbolic. In this way, the semiotic threatens women since it cannot "free" them from a symbolic that they have never fully known; but, it "frees" men from a symbolic that they know all too well. The revolution in poetic language, then, can be carried out only by men.

This is also why only men can laugh at the breakdown of the Symbolic order. Unlike Cixous or Irigaray, Kristeva suggests that women's laughter is not revolutionary. According to Kristeva, rather than threatening the Symbolic, women's laughter threatens women. Once again this has to do with women's and men's different relationships to the maternal. Men can laugh with the maternal in language that challenges the Symbolic. They can laugh at their phallic shield, still securely protected by it. Women, on the other hand, have no protection without the phallic shield provided by the Symbolic order. Their association with the Symbolic is already precarious and therefore not a laughing matter:

> Therefore the rush of these nonsensical, periphrastic, maternal rhythms in her speech, far from soothing her, far from making her laugh, destroys her symbolic armour: makes her ecstatic, nostalgic, or mad. . . . A woman has nothing to laugh about when the paternal order falls. . . . [I]ts dissolution can be her death. (1974c, 30; see also 1983, 77)

Kristeva maintains that women's writing cannot be revolutionary poetry or abject language that laughs at the Symbolic order. Women must take the Symbolic order very seriously in order to challenge it. This might be why Kristeva says we do not see a lot of female laughter. (1977b, 298)

For Kristeva, women in our culture have two alternatives in relation to writing: They can write phallic virility or write a silent underwater body. (1974e, 166) The former makes woman complicit with the Law and requires that she identify with the phallic position, while the latter insures that she will remain an outlaw, outside of politics and history. "Estranged from language," writes Kristeva, "women are visionaries, dancers who suffer as they speak." (1974e, 166) In passages like these Kristeva seems to suggest that women can either wait for men to revolutionize the Symbolic order and discharge the repressed maternal drives in language, or they can be strong enough, or identified strongly enough with the maternal, to rejoice in the discharge of drives in their own language. But this latter option is dangerous and may lead to psychosis or suicide. Some feminists have taken Kristeva to task for these types of claims. While I am sympathetic to some of these criticisms, as usual, Kristeva complicates any attempt to present a straightforward feminist critique of her theories.

In a 1980 interview, Kristeva criticizes "certain feminists in France" who say that language and theory are male and phallic. She argues that to say that that which is imprecise, impulse, primary process, in language is feminine is not sufficient to liberate women. She claims that "if one assigns to woman that phase alone, this in fact amounts to maintaining women in a position of inferiority, and in any case of marginality, to reserving them the place of the childish, of the unsayable, of the hysteric." (1980b, 134) While Kristeva admits that the "valorization of this modality can be subversive," she maintains that it is not enough. This position would probably be more acceptable to American feminists, myself included, who have problems with Kristeva's identification of the feminine and maternal with the "unspoken" in language. In this 1980 interview, Kristeva makes it clear that the goal of what she called earlier "listening" to the unspoken maternal in language cannot be to recover some unrepresentable power of women. Rather, the goal is to undermine constructions of identity and difference that repress the feminine and maternal. In this interview Kristeva begins to sound like Foucault when she says that women's protest is:

> . . . not first of all a social protest, although it is also that. It is a protest which consists in demanding that attention be paid to the subjective particularity which the individual represents, in the social order, of course, but also and above all in relation to what essentially differentiates that individual, which is the individual's sexual difference.[18] (1980b, 133)

In *About Chinese Women* Kristeva remarks that it is a "profound structural mechanism concerning the casting of sexual differences and even of speech in the West" that gives rise to women's double-bind in the face of language. (1974c, 37) Here she suggests that we need to change this structure that casts women as other and difference as opposition. We must work against an identity that binds us to it in a oppressive way.

What are we to make of her earlier claims that we must acknowledge the abyss between the "sexes of the bible" and keep "fighting the war of the sexes" until somehow a new economy of the sexes "works itself out," and that speakers (men) reach the limit of the Symbolic through art while women reach it through giving birth? (1974c, 23; 1975, 240) What of *Powers of Horror*, published in 1980, the same year as this possibly anomalous interview, where she continues to celebrate that only men can have access to the revolutionary "unsignifiable," "unsymbolizable," "feminine body," "maternal body"? Is Kristeva merely *describing* the repression of the feminine and maternal that might be responsible for the oppression of women in the West? If she is, she might have emphasized the contingent and cultural specificity of her claims. Can Kristeva's seriousness, sometimes to the point of dogmatism, and her ambiguities, sometimes to the point of contradictions, be read as her own strategy to undermine the identification of women with the repressed from within some of the theoretical discourses that have perpetuated that identity? Is Kristeva a "superman," a "hysteric," or the rare, possibly the only, revolutionary woman to step out of the double-bind? She is, after all, a legal alien, not a child of the West.

V

REVOLUTIONARY ANALYSIS

*"I told him that during my childhood
my mother's sorrow took up the space of dreams."*
The Lover, Marguerite Duras[1]

Analytic Privilege

Although for Kristeva it is language as art—what she identifies as poetic language, avant-garde writing, and abject literature—that shows the "other scene" and thereby brings the signifying system to crisis, she positions herself in a privileged position in relation to this crisis. Her style becomes noticeably more poetic, yet she maintains that she has intentionally avoided the "strong post-Heideggerian temptation" to write theory as literature. (1980, ix) In her preface to *Desire in Language* Kristeva defends the fact that she writes theory, even metaphysical theory. She claims that such a theoretical stance is "the only guarantee of ethics." (1980, ix) For Kristeva, this turns out to be the analyst's ethical responsibility to try to find ways to alleviate the suffering of her patients.

In addition to defending her stance, Kristeva privileges it.[2] First, in a self-reflective passage in *Revolution in Poetic Language*, Kristeva makes explicit the role of intellectual theory:

> Intellection—the logical explanation of the struggle between two heterogeneities, is the site of the most radical heterogeneity . . . but is, at the same time, the site of the subtlest signifying differentiation . . . subtle differences in rhythm or color, or differences made vocal or semantic in laughter and wordplay—keeps us on the surface of pleasure in a subtle and minute tension. (1974, 179–80)

This subtle differentiation is the goal, and privilege, of Kristeva's semanalysis. Second, although in her earlier writings she is less enthusiastic in her praise, Kristeva privileges psychoanalysis. Ultimately, Kristeva is the analyst. "Analytic discourse," laments Kristeva, "is perhaps the only one capable of addressing this untenable place where our species resides, threatened by madness beneath the emptiness of heaven." (1980, xi)

Finally, and more mysteriously, in a few passing passages and interviews, without explanation, Kristeva almost whispers that perhaps it was also "necessary to be a woman to attempt to take up that exorbitant wager of carrying the rational project to the outer borders of the signifying venture of men. . . ." (1980, x) Kristeva gives more hints later in "From One Identity to an Other" when she claims that although semanalysis inevitably makes an object of that which departs from meaning, it does so by positing itself as nonuniversal, by positing a questionable subject-in-process. "And this," says Kristeva, "requires that the subjects of the theory must be themselves subjects in infinite analysis; this is what Husserl could not imagine, what Céline could not know, but what a woman, among others, can finally admit, aware as she is of the inanity of Being." (1975, 146) The philosopher cannot imagine and the artist cannot know, but the woman who subjects her theory to constant analysis can admit that it is questionable. The woman analyst is wiser than the philosopher because she not only knows that she does not know but she can also imagine what she does not know.

It is the marginalized intellectual analyst who can see, hear, feel, what others cannot. Perhaps this is why Kristeva, so often revelling in her loneliness, cries out that she writes for the marginalized. In a passage that turns sour and haunts her closing remark in *Powers of Horror*, Kristeva names the addressee of her work:

> The semiotics of signifying practices is addressed to all those who, committed to a practice of challenge, innovation or personal experiment, are frequently tempted to abandon their discourse as a way of communicating the logic of that practice, since the dominant forms of discourse (from positivist grammar to sociologism) have no room for it, and to go into voluntary exile in what Mallarmé called an "indicible qui ment", for the ultimate benefit of a practice that shall remain silent. (1973, 32)

What is it that positivist grammar and sociologism have no room for? Semanalysis? What is the silent practice that Kristeva assigns to her reader? Reading? Writing? Could this disillusioned innovator be Kristeva herself? In the terms of her *Tales of Love*, could this be the analyst's countertransference?

Since Kristeva finished her psychoanalytic training in 1979 her work has given increasing priority to psychoanalysis and psychoanalytic theory.[3] She took up psychoanalysis because of her interest in the speaking subject, psychotic speech, and children's language acquisition. She claims that psychoanalysis is the only place where the "wildness" of the speaking being can be heard. (1984c, 275) In some interviews she says that she was not content with mere abstract analysis so she became a practicing analyst. In those interviews she says that she believes that psychoanalysis is the only place where theory and practice come together so absolutely.

(1984c, 275; 1984b, 27; 1986, 219–20) Psychoanalysis is the practice and the metalanguage or theory at the same time. The analyst is constantly applying theory as well as altering it in the analytic situation. It is the discourse in that situation, the practice, that is also (in some sense) its theory.

Kristeva's latest works, since *Powers of Horror*, start out with psychoanalytic theory and move to psychoanalytic readings of literary, philosophical, or religious texts. They often include transcripts from her own psychoanalytic practice. In these latest works Kristeva maintains that psychoanalytic discourse has a privileged function that distinguishes it from literary, philosophical, or religious discourses. Early in her career, she criticized philosophical discourse for its "necrophilia" that denies the process through which human beings become speaking subjects. At the same time she privileged poetic language for its revolutionary effect that points to this process. But, Kristeva argues that psychoanalysis can go beyond poetry's pointing. While poetry can merely temporarily ward off delirium in the face of its constant threat, psychoanalysis can domesticate this delirium and turn its threat into play.

In *Black Sun* Kristeva suggests that literature, religion, and psychoanalysis all deal with the "subject's battle with symbolic collapse." (1987a, 24) In a sense, all of these are ways of releasing the drives into the Symbolic without threatening its collapse. Psychoanalysis is an "elaboration" of the psychic causes of suffering, while literature and religion are "closer to catharsis." (1987a, 24) She stresses that this is not to say that psychoanalysts should not make use of cathartic solutions to their patients' suffering. On the contrary, she insists that analysts need to pay greater attention to "these sublimatory solutions to our crises," and incorporate them into their practices, in order to be "lucid counterdepressants rather than neutralizing antidepressants." (1987a, 25) While antidepressants—Kristeva alludes to antidepressant drugs—treat only the symptoms without working through the causes, counterdepressants work through symptoms in order to treat the cause and realign the psychic structure (so to speak).

In chapter 4 I explained Kristeva's thesis that poetic language discharges drives into language. In her later work she seems to see an advantage to naming these semiotic processes as well as discharging them. Whereas literature "displaces" and "dissolves" these semiotic forces, analysis names them. (1981, 318) Like poetic discourse, analytic discourse is involved in the creation of metaphors that, through the processes of imagination, transfer semiotic forces into language. In addition to this metaphorical process analytic discourse involves interpretation. It is this combination of semiotic discharge and interpretation that gives analytic discourse its privilege. Because analytic discourse both discharges and interprets semiotic forces, it can work not only as a safety valve for repressed drives but also as a tool for altering the place of those drives within the psychic structure. While in her earlier writings Kristeva proposed that merely pointing to the repressed processes could change the very structure of those processes, in her later writings she emphasizes the necessity of *interpreting* the repressed processes. In her later writings she seems to suggest that perhaps psychoanalysis is a better bet for changing the structure of psychic processes.

Unlike poetic discourse, analytic interpretation produces what Kristeva calls a "knowledge effect." (1983, 276) This knowledge effect helps to fasten the analysand to the Symbolic, but in order to allow her to play with it. The knowledge effect gives her the confidence to use her imagination. The knowledge effect created by analytic discourse is much different than the knowledge effect created by philosophical or traditional scientific discourses. Kristeva argues that analytic knowledge effects are always only provisional. And their provisional status points to a process in which they are merely moments. In analytic interpretation, "for the *moment*, this means such-and-such." Unlike philosophical or scientific interpretation, analytic interpretation cannot purport to be absolute. (1983, 276) Analytic interpretation is free "from the authoritarian domination of a *Res externa*, necessarily divine or deifable." (1983, 276–77) The object of analytic interpretation is not real. Rather, it is imaginary. Therefore, the status of "correct" interpretation or analytic "truth" is much closer to narrative fiction than philosophical or scientific truth. (1987, 19)

In the analytic situation, the analysand does tell a story about her life that may appear as a statement of facts or historical reality. But it is not the reality of the story that matters to the analyst. Rather, the analyst treats this "history" as symptoms and listens for the meaning and logic of those symptoms. (1987, 20) In order to do this the analyst must remove the realistic meaning from the analysand's discourse so that the "meaningless/madness of desire may appear." (1981, 312) Unlike philosophical meaning, analytic meaning is both provisional and heterogeneous. Kristeva argues that the analyst's interpretation is privileged because it is the only discourse that hypothesizes a fundamentally split meaning. This fundamental split or heterogeneity is the very condition for meaning. "Psychoanalysis, the only modern interpretative theory to hypothesize the heterogeneous in meaning," says Kristeva, "nevertheless makes that heterogeneity so interdependent with language and thought as to be its very condition, indeed, its driving force." (1981, 312)

The ramifications of this claim for a theory of meaning are extraordinary. First, meaning is never transparent. What appears at first glance to be the meaning is just a surface reflection of a deeper heterogeneous process. Moreover, a necessary element of this process is meaninglessness or nonmeaning. In part, meaning is composed of nonmeaning. Therefore, meaning is neither present nor metaphysical. As much as it *is*, meaning *is not*. It is the instability of this meaning that makes psychoanalysis an ongoing process whose interpretations are always provisional, never absolute.

Analytic meaning operates according to a logic of metaphoricity. Kristeva might say that meaning, like the Other, is "a condensation of semantic features as well as nonrepresentable drive heterogeneity that subtends them, goes beyond them, and slips away." (1983, 38) Kristeva suggests that in meaning just as in metaphor there are two heterogeneous elements condensed into one signifier. Like metaphor, analytic meaning is a condensation of representation and nonrepresentable drives. Analytic interpretation involves reading the nonrepresentable through the representation. The analyst must try to figure out (or create) how the analysand's words are metaphors for drives.

Here, Kristeva disagrees with Lacan's thesis that the Unconscious is structured like language and that it is the discourse of the Other. More precisely, she argues that if the Unconscious is structured like language, it is not the language that Lacan imagines. Kristeva argues that language is not a system of pure signifiers. Rather, language is always made up of heterogeneous elements: semiotic drive force and symbols. The Other, then, is not a pure signifier. It too is made up of these heterogeneous elements. The Other, or the system of language into which we are born, is not the metonymical space that Lacan imagines in which one signifier is associated with, or displaces, another. Rather, for Kristeva the Other is the space of metaphorical shifting in which symbols are substituted for, or condensed with, drive force. (1983, 38) Analytic interpretation is not merely a matter of following a chain of signifiers or representations. Rather, analytic interpretation is a matter of listening to the unrepresentable within signifiers.

For Kristeva, analytic interpretation is "correct" or "true" when it expands what is analyzable. (1981, 309) It does this by linking the analysand's discourse with that heterogeneous element that motivates it. Through imagination and fantasy more of the unrepresentable becomes "discharged in language." This discharge does not correspond to some external reality or truth. In fact, Kristeva claims that in a successful analysis the analysand leaves with "a renewed desire to question all received truths . . . he becomes capable once again of acting like a child, of playing." (1987, 58) Strangely enough, the "true" analytic interpretation has the effect of dismantling "truth" and creating playful fantasies in its place. As Kristeva points out, in analysis the search is not for truth but for "innovative capacities." (1983, 15)

Imagination provides the link between semiotic drive force and symbols. Kristeva is quick to point out that imagination does not translate drives into symbols. The goal of analysis is not to turn the analysand's discourse and meaning into a homogeneous whole. Neither is its goal to turn the speaking subject into a unified subject, an "own proper self." (1983, 380) Analysis does not recuperate drive heterogeneity and close the fundamental split in language. Rather, analysis creates polyvalent identities as false identities, imaginary identities. It creates, as Nietzsche might say, "fictions with which we can live." Rather than dissolve non-meaning, the analysis creates fantasies in which nonmeaning and its emptiness are necessary parts of discourse, parts that the analysand has the right to play with. Kristeva suggests that play can alleviate the analysand's suffering by "turning the crisis into a *work in progress*":

> To the extent that the analyst not only causes truths to emerge but also tries to alleviate the pains of John or Juliet, he is duty bound to help them in building their own proper space. Help them not to suffer from being mere extras in their lives, or splinters of parceled out bodies carried along by the spate of their pleasure. Help them, then, to speak and write themselves in unstable, open, undecidable spaces. . . . It is not a matter of filling John's "crisis"—his emptiness—with meaning, or of assigning a sure place to Juliet's erotic wanderings. But to trigger a discourse where his own "emptiness" and her own "out-of-placeness" become essential elements, indispensable "characters" if you will, of a *work in progress*. (1983, 380)

In a successful analysis the narcissistic structure is adjusted such that the analysand no longer experiences the "crisis" of the nonrepresentable as suffering. Rather, she can continue to create fantasies that name the crisis as necessary crisis in her "work in progress." Kristeva says that the task of the analyst (as well as the theoretician) is not to give a final interpretation, but "to record the *crisis* of modern interpretative systems without smoothing it over, to affirm that this crisis is inherent in all symbolic function itself and to perceive as symptoms all constructions, including totalizing interpretation, which try to deny this crisis." (1981, 318)

If there is no totalizing interpretation and no absolute, then the philosopher may wonder if analytic truth is relative and/or nihilistic. If the analyst creates "truth" and meaning, then aren't truth and meaning reduced to, or relative to, the subjective idiosyncrasies of this "all-mighty" individual? In addition, isn't the analysand turned into a mere object for the analyst? Or, even if the analysand creates "truth" and meaning, isn't it still subjective and relative to her own idiosyncrasies?

In the last section of *In the Beginning Was Love*, "Is Psychoanalysis a Form of Nihilism?" Kristeva argues that psychoanalysis is not a form of nihilism. In fact, she claims that "psychoanalysis is the modest if tenacious antidote to nihilism in its most courageously and insolently scientific and vitalist forms." (1987, 63) First, psychoanalysis does not grant control, or the role of creator, to anyone, including the analyst. The analyst, insofar as she is subject to the Unconscious, is also an analysand.

Moreover, for Kristeva psychoanalysis does not objectify either analysand nor analyst. Rather, since the analytic situation is a dialogue spoken through language, it is a process and not an object. It is a process that operates between two subjects and does not allow one unified subject to exist in isolation. (1987, 60) Kristeva suggests that because of this necessary relationship between two subjects-in-process, and the fact that a subject's desire is known only through an other, psychoanalysis may be the basis for a morality in this nihilistic age:

> Its [analysis's] vital efficacy is inseparable from its ethical dimension, which is commensurate with love: the speaking being opens up to and reposes in the other.
>
> No restrictive, prohibitive, or punitive legislation can possibly restrain my desire for objects, values, life, or death. Only the meaning that my desire may have for an other and hence for me can control its expansion, hence serve as the unique, if tenuous, basis of a morality. (1987, 60–61, 63)

While it is true that human beings are subject to unconscious drives, these drives operate within the social environment of language. Since human beings are linguistic beings, they desire. And within Lacanian theory, desire always comes through an other. For human beings, it is only through a relationship with an other that meaning exists. This is to say that meaning, in its heterogeneity, is both in and beyond the subject, who is always a work in progress. Therefore, psychoanalysis is not nihilistic. In analysis meaning does exist. But that meaning is not the construct of some individual. Rather, meaning is an ongoing process that moves between two subjects engaged through language. Kristeva says that in this precarious exchange between analyst and analysand, "the modern version of liberty is being played out, threatened as much by a single, total and totalitarian Meaning as it is by delirium." (1981, 319) In the analytic relationship, linked through language, we are creating meanings in a process bordered by totalitarianism on one side and delirium on the other. For Kristeva it is only through "love" that we can avoid both extremes.

Revolutionary Love

Kristeva's *Tales of Love* (*Histoires d'amour*) presents a kind of psychoanalytic history of "love." She traces "love" from Plato, through the Middle Ages, to twentieth-century literature, and concludes that Freud was the first to propose that love is the optimum model for the operations of the psyche. (1983, 14) In addition, Kristeva says that Freud was the first to "turn love into a cure." (1983, 381) Psychoanalysis is this cure. For Kristeva, psychoanalysis is love, transference love. In order to begin to fully understand the psychoanalytic cure, she claims that we have to read *Tales of Love* together with *Powers of Horror.* (1984c, 26) *Tales of Love* deals with identity and idealization, while *Powers of Horror* deals with negation and violence. Both of these are part of the analytic cure. Both are part of love. Love, says Kristeva, is a combination of the sublime and abject. (1983, 368) It is a combination of identification with the sublime ideal and detachment from an other, which involves abjection.

Kristeva develops what she reads as Freud's suggestion that love is a "reciprocal identification and detachment . . . one open system connected to another." (1983, 14–15) She does, however, criticize Freud's notion that there is only one, male, libido, because amorous discourse requires an interaction between heterogeneous elements. (1983, 75–76, 80–82) Love requires two, the self and the other, and enables the subject to cross the boundaries of the self and "be" an other. (1983, 4, 6) The subject identifies with an other even while she remains detached from that other. In love, the other can retain its otherness, its alterity, and still provide the lover with an image of herself. (1983, 33) The love that Kristeva describes provides an identification through difference without abolishing or assimilating that difference.

Kristeva claims that the possibility of the amorous identification is the place of primary narcissism. And it is love that makes primary identification possible. She describes the play between identification and love that eventually leads to the subject's self-identification and her identification of/with the object. Preobjectal reduplication, says Kristeva, sets up love (still without an object). (1983, 25) Love provides the support for the subject's separation, self-identification, and identification of the object. So, it is love that sets up the possibility of the subject and the object. "The lover," says Kristeva, "is a narcissist with an *object.*" (1983, 33) This is why in her later works she emphasizes the importance of love to the proper functioning of the psyche. She establishes the analytic relationship as the model of the love relationship.

The love relationship is Freud's transference-countertransference relationship, which exists through language. (1983, 8–14; 1987, 3) Kristeva maintains that transference love requires three terms: the subject, the object (real or imagined), and the Other (the meaning of discourse). (1983, 13) Love, then, is something spoken. (1983, 277) It is through language that we can love each other. This does not mean that we have to speak the same mother-tongue in order to love each other. It means that we *are* through language and that others *are* through language. And our relationship to others is constituted only through language. This, of course, is central to Lacanian psychoanalytic theory. Still, it is crucial in order to understand Kristeva's theory to remember that, for her, language is always heterogeneous; it is made up of semiotic and symbolic elements. So it is through these heterogeneous elements that we can love each other. Love is neither merely semiotic nor merely symbolic. It is always and at the same time both. This is why Kristeva defines the effect of love as:

> a permanent stabilization-destabilization between the Symbolic (pertaining to referential signs and their syntactic articulation) and the *semiotic* (the elemental tendency of libidinal charges toward displacement and condensation, and of their inscription, which depends on the incorporation and introjection of incorporated items; an economy that privileges orality, vocalization, alliteration, rhythmicity, etc.).[4] (1983, 16)

Love—constituted through language—constitutes language in all its heterogeneous fullness. (1983, 277) Kristeva claims that in the amatory discourse of transference love, the Symbolic, Imaginary, and Real (the realm of semiotic drive force) are tied together. (1983, 7) It is love that links these three elements of signifying processes. Without love, the links break down, possibly to the point where the Symbolic is completely cut off from the Imaginary and the Real in psychosis. It is transference love that allows the analysand to sort out the Symbolic, Imaginary, and Real and to reestablish links between them. (1983, 10)

Kristeva exclaims that love is the life of the psyche. Without love, inside analysis or out, she says that "we are living death." (1983, 15) For Kristeva, however, it is only inside analysis that it is socially acceptable to search for human love charged with desire. (1983, 6) In order to satisfy and recharge the desire for love, she claims that the analyst must give in to countertransference and love her patients. The analyst must be able to put herself in the place of the analysand in order to feel her suffering and understand it. Love, transference love, requires a reciprocal identification and detachment. Kristeva says that a word of love from the analyst may be more effective than electroshock therapy. (1987, 48) She sees psychoanalysis as "an infinite quest for rebirths through the experience of love." (1983, 1)

With regard to love, psychoanalysis is privileged. Unlike other love relationships, it is not subject to the possibility of hurtful, even devastating, separation, breakup, or loss. Psychoanalytic love is beyond the "hazards of loves" and can therefore serve as a refuge against love's pain. (1983, 382) Kristeva argues that analysis establishes the permanence of love that allows the analysand to turn the crises of failed and broken primary loves into fantasies with which she can live. Transference love opens new psychic spaces for wounded "extraterrestrials suffering for want of love." Kristeva maintains that we are all ETs, extraterrestrials, suffering for the want of love. (1983, 372–83) Rather than bring us home, psychoanalysis lets us enjoy our extraterrestrial adventure:

> Are we to build a psychic space, a certain mastery of the One, at the very heart of the psychic founderings of anguished, suicidal, and impotent peo-

ple? Or on the contrary are we to follow, impel, favor breakaways, driftings? Are we concerned with rebuilding their own proper space, a "home," for contemporary Narcissi: repair the father, soothe the mother, allow them to build a solid, introspective inside, master of its losses and wanderings, assuming that such a goal is possible? . . . I see psychoanalysis rather as the instrument of a departure from that enclosure, not as its warden. (1983, 379–80)

Kristeva argues that the function of psychoanalysis is to reawaken the imagination in order to wean the analysand from former truths and allow illusions to exist. Given the theory of transference, it would seem that the analysand must identify with the analyst's imaginings. Does the analyst show the analysand how to use her imagination by a sort of example? Is it possible that the meaning that is created through this imagining is the analyst's meaning that can be taken over by the analysand? In Freudian analysis, since there is no "no" in the Unconscious, the analysand's resistance to the analyst's interpretation can be interpreted as a sign of its truth. Kristeva proposes a much less authoritarian analysis. She believes that the analyst can no longer be stern and resist the seductions of the analysand. Rather, the analyst must give something new to the analysand that she can accept. (1984b, 26) The meanings that the analyst creates by listening to the discourse of the analysand, and through her own countertransference, are "true" only if they "trigger associations" in the analysand and expand what is analyzable. (1981, 309) Moreover, her interpretations are "true" only if they work. That is, they are "true" only if they have some effect on the analysand's behavior or affects.

In order to be effective, it seems necessary that the analysand accept the analyst's interpretation. The analysand must identify with the meaning that the analyst assigns to her symptoms. In a lecture, Kristeva described one of her cases, an unorthodox analysis in which she had gone to view paintings by one of her patients. She decided that the key to his symptoms was buried in the "formless and wordless images" of these paintings. So, she reconstructed a meaning for them and articulated it in speech for the patient. She calls this procedure "fantasy grafting." (1988; 1987, 18) In this lecture, she asked "was the meaning I suggested mine or was it his?" She concluded that what is important is that the patient accepted it and that his somatic symptoms disappeared.[5] (1988)

Kristeva suggests that the analyst's interpretative position "builds a strong ethics" because she is called upon to suspend her desire at the same time that she experiences it for the sake of the other. She has an ethical obligation to her patient. Yet, as Kristeva insists, this ethics is neither normative nor guaranteed by transcendence. While the ethics that she imagines operative in psychoanalysis is not a normative ethics, it is "directed" toward helping others and promoting life. (1981, 319) It does not rely on laws and/or punishments. The analyst does not threaten the analysand or deny the reality of her experience. Rather, the analyst legitimates the analysand's experience and "allows the patient to seek out other means, symbolic or imaginary, of working out her suffering." (1987a, 86)

Kristeva maintains that the analyst's fantasy construction passes "through perversion to assure that flow between affect and language, sometimes passing through non-linguistic signs." She calls this dynamic "analytic perversion," or "A-perversion." (1988) In this transference love between analyst and analysand, where there is a reciprocal identification, the analyst takes over the patient's perversion. Analytic perversion is not an act and it is named only in analysis. It is the story of the analysand's perversion as told by the analyst. The analyst necessarily must identify with the patient's perversion through the countertransference. This is to say that it is also the analyst's perversion. After all, the analyst tells the story. She names the perversion. The "moral," says Kristeva, is to:

> . . . let ourselves be dizzied and let us look for meaning where there is no more language. How? By trusting our perversion and by making it appear in discourse, as it is the secret side of our wit and our witticism. This is the imaginary aspect, necessary and unavoidable, of the analytic interpretation. (1988)

The analyst names the perversion that belongs both to her and her patient so that neither will have to act on it. Through her imagination, the analyst speaks to the imagination of her patient so that unnamed images and semiotic drive force can begin to have meanings as they are named. This is not to say that the images are *translated* into symbols. Rather, they are *reconnected* with the already operative symbols from which they had become disconnected.

Along with the personal power dynamic between the analyst and the analysand, I wonder about the personal nature of psychoanalysts' interpretations of their patients' sufferings. I suspect that in some cases a patient's suffering could be caused or significantly intensified by oppressive social structures. But traditionally analysts provide personalized meanings for their patients' suffering; they do not invent *political* interpretations, or fantasies of oppression, in order to give meaning to their patients' suffering.[6] Rather, psychoanalysis only interprets the analysand's relationship to the social structure in terms of personal perversions or psychoanalytic structures that always take us back to some form of the oedipal triangle. In some cases it seems that political fantasies and interpretations or feminist discourse can provide a way of naming frustrated affects and providing interpretations that allow the wounded subject to live, even to fight.

Paul Smith argues that Kristeva's texts have moved from advocating resistance to advocating acceptance—"love your crisis." (1989, 92) At a lecture, when Kellianne O'Brien asked Kristeva if psychoanalysis merely normalizes its patients by coopting their "deviance" and tendencies to resist, Kristeva replied that she does not seek patients. Rather, she pointed out, they come to her looking for help. They are in pain and she has an obligation to help them. (1988) While this is true, and her sense of ethical obligation is noble, it is possible that these wounded subjects could be turned into political activists who would not only be able to live with their crisis but also would try to change the world in order that everyone could better live with the crisis of modern Western culture.[7]

Religion

Kristeva emphasizes that, in part, the crisis of modern Western culture is caused by the breakup of religion. Religion once provided meaning, security, and love. And with its decline we are looking for replacements. Since her psychoanalytic training, she has become interested in religion, particularly Christianity, and how it relieves psychic wounds. Taking off from some of the work of *Tel Quel*, Kristeva has become increasingly interested in the dynamics of religious fantasies and symbols. (1984c, 268) She suggests that religion is based on the exclusion of the abject through certain taboos that serve to reinforce the Symbolic against any threats from the semiotic. (1980) Yet it is through semiotic drive force that religion has its power. For Kristeva, Christian fantasies reflect some of the basic desires of Western people: enduring paternal love and virginal mothers. She claims that these fantasies come close to those of many of her analysand's fantasies. (1987, 39–40) In much of her latest work she has analyzed how religion defers, denies, or temporarily sublimates drives.

In *Powers of Horror*, Kristeva discusses biblical prohibitions on food, waste, and women. (1980) In *Tales of Love*, she discusses Christian love, *agape*, and the cult of the Virgin. (1983) In *In the Beginning Was Love*, Kristeva discusses the relationship between Christian faith and psychoanalysis. (1987) In *Black Sun*, she discusses forgiveness and resurrection in Christianity and psychoanalysis. (1987a) In *Strangers to Ourselves*, she discusses the Old Testament and the role of foreigners and St. Paul and St. Augustine's therapy of exile and pilgrimage. (1989)

Although Kristeva maintains that some of the same forces that lead people to religion also lead people to analysis, and that analysis can be a secular replacement for religion, she emphasizes their differences. Most obviously, analysis does not prepare people for life in another world, but for life in this one. (1987, 27) Also, Kristeva claims that the analyst does not accept theological accounts of redemption and merely analyzes them for their meaning. (1989, 130) Most importantly, analysis reveals desires, whereas religion merely operates through repressed or sublimated desires. Analysis reveals the analysand's unconscious motivations for belief. In the best case, this revelation, analytic "knowledge," leads to an increase in the analysand's freedom to invent stories and decide how to redirect unconscious drives in beneficial ways. Religion does not provide this knowledge effect or the ensuing freedom:

> Once analyzed, I continue to make demands and to feel desires, but in full awareness of cause and effect. Knowledge of my desires is at once my freedom and my safety net. Now I can love and delude myself at my own risk. In this sense analysis is not less than religion but more—more, especially, than Christianity, which hews so closely to its fundamental fantasies. (1987, 52)

Kristeva suggests that religion takes its fantasies more seriously than psychoanalysis. In another context, she somewhat sardonically defines religion as "this phantasmic necessity on the part of speaking beings to provide themselves with a representation (animal, female, male, parental, etc.) in place of what constitutes them as such, in other words, symbolization—the double articulation and syntactic sequence of language, as well as its preconditions or substitutes (thoughts, affects, etc.)." (1979a, 50) She maintains that religion provides a homogeneous meaning that covers over the heterogeneous process through which that meaning develops.

For example, in *About Chinese Women* Kristeva argues that monotheism maintains its unity by maintaining the radical separation of the sexes. (1979c, 141–42) It is upon a radical separation that unity can be built. This process, says Kristeva, corresponds to the process of signification in which symbolic cohesion is built upon radical heterogeneity between semiotic and symbolic elements. But religion does not acknowledge that its unity is built upon heterogeneity. It denies the heterogeneous process through which its meaning is produced. Psychoanalysis, on the other hand, provides a heterogeneous meaning that reflects the process in which it is implicated.

Still, Kristeva claims that unlike philosophical or scientific meaning, religious meaning uses semiotic rather than symbolic elements for overcoming separation. In Lacanian psychoanalytic theory, speech/language provides a substitute for the fusion with the maternal body. Kristeva claims that in religious discourse, however, words do not *substitute* for the lost maternal fusion. Rather, she explains, religious discourse *reestablishes* the fusion with the maternal body in the agency/structure of God. She uses St. Augustine's image of the believer suckling from his nourishing God as "evidence" for her claim. (1987, 24) Kristeva argues that Christianity provides a type of primary identification with the agency/structure God. It is, she says, an immediate transference to the nourishing, loving, protective maternal body become paternal sign. It is the same kind of transference as the transference to the site of imaginary father that she describes in *Tales of Love*. (1987, 25) It is a transference that is still preobjectal.[8]

For Kristeva, psychoanalytic transference is similar to faith in that the analysand must trust and love the analyst. (1987, 52) The goal, however, of transference love is a permanent stabilization/destabilization of the subject, an identification/detachment. "Analysis," says Kristeva, "is a means of transition from trust to separation." (1987, 56) On the other hand, the religious transference—the Christian's identification with God—provides support for the wounded subject suffering from the primary loss; but it does not go any further. It does not analyze the dynamic of the painful loss or imaginary support/identification. It does not use the temporary coherence of the subject established through this identification in order to set up the object as proper other from whom the subject must separate.

The crisis that ensues in the modern age with the breakup of religion and the "death of God" sends us looking for secular replacements for nourishment, love, and protection. Kristeva proposes that psychoanalysis is the most promising replacement. Does psychoanalysis become a secular religion? Does the analyst replace God? Only in the worst cases, answers Kristeva:

> Yet if analysis is more than just therapy but also a certain kind of ethic, then it has nothing in common with lay religion or the initiation rites of a sage. The analysand delves beyond childhood to discover the immemorial origins of his desires; in the course of his analysis he recreates his sense of time, alters his psychic economy, and increases his capacity for working-through and sublimation, for understanding and play. (1987, 57)

Yet in her latest writing Kristeva uses so many religious images to describe the psychoanalytic process that it is hard to avoid thinking of analysis as a "lay religion" or of religion as "lay analysis." It seems that traditional psychoanalysts, including Kristeva, "hew" as closely to their oedipal triad as Christianity does to its Holy Trinity. I suggested earlier that with the breakdown of religion, the analyst takes the place of the loving Father, the Virgin Mother, and the priest. Certainly Kristeva argues that the supports that Christianity has provided for the wounded subject need to be replaced once they falter. (1983, 374–76) She insists, however, that psychoanalysis should not merely recreate the lost Christian subject. (1983, 379–80) Yet does psychoanalysis, as Kristeva describes it, recreate the Christian imaginary?

In *Tales of Love* Kristeva argues that in addition to providing a support against the abject mother, the loving imaginary father replaces the loving God. There she also suggests that we need a secular discourse of motherhood to replace the fantasy of the Virgin Mary. Also, Kristeva describes Christian love that operates through the crucifixion of Christ in terms reminiscent of the psychoanalytic account of the move from need to desire:

> Christian love is an idea that changes my body into a worshiped name. The killing of the body is the path through which the body-Self has access to the Name of the Other who loves me and makes of me a Subject who is immersed (baptized) in the Name of the Other. A triumph of idealization through a sublimatory elaboration of suffering and of the destruction of the body proper. . . . (1983, 146)

As Kristeva describes it, Christian love sounds very much like the psychoanalytic account of the move through the mirror stage into speech. Christian love's "killing" of the body so that the subject can be born into the "Name of the Other," language, echoes the primary transference love that Kristeva describes as the assent to language. Compare the passage on Christian love to the following passage, in which Kristeva describes primary identification:

> . . . a body to be put to death, or at least deferred, for the love of the Other and so that Myself can be. Love is a death sentence that causes me to be. . . . The subject exists because it belongs to the Other, and it is in proceeding from that symbolic belonging that causes him to be subject to love and death that he will be able to set up for himself imaginary objects of desire. (1983, 36)

In the Beginning Was Love describes the analytic process as a type of faith and love. The analysand has faith in the analyst whom she loves. In return, the analyst loves her patients. In describing the relationship between the subject and the Other (the third party, language, the father, the government, etc.), Kristeva maintains that analytic discourse reveals that the Other is "in Me." (1987, 55) There she claims that "analytic discourse speaks of a humanity that is willing to lose in order to know itself as pure loss and thus pay its debts to the Allmighty." (1987, 55–56) These strange metaphors appear in the context of an essay that exposes the psychic dynamics that underlie Christianity. Indeed, they appear in an essay devoted to distinguishing faith and love in analysis from religious faith.

There is, however, an important difference between using psychoanalytic metaphors in order to analyze religion, on the one hand, and using religious metaphors in order to describe analytic processes, on the other. Kristeva does both. While the former provides original and useful insights not only into religion but also the logic of the Western psyche, the latter is perhaps a symptom of Kristeva's nostalgic relationship to Christianity. Certainly, using religious metaphors in order to describe the psyche and analytic processes privileges and recreates the Christian imaginary. In addition, it makes it difficult to escape from the Christian imaginary, which traditionally has been the seed of various forms of racism and sexism.

At points Kristeva's analysis is questionable at best. For example, in *In the Beginning Was Love* Kristeva argues that "more than any other religion, Christianity has unraveled the Symbolic *and* physical importance of the paternal function in human life." (1987, 40) She seems impressed that Christianity reveals the human need for the paternal Third Party in order to learn language. Is it possible that Christianity has something to do with the association between this necessary Third Party and the paternal? There is nothing inherent in human life that requires that this Third Party be a father or paternal. Kristeva makes this clear in an interview when she says that the maternal function is not necessarily the domain of females and the paternal function is not necessarily the domain of males. Recall that she maintains that we could call them "X" and "Y." (1984b, 23) In addition, she points out that Christianity replaces the loving, nourishing *maternal* body with a *paternal* God. And she argues in *Powers of Horror* that monotheism, the Christian heritage, is the result of battles of patriarchies against matriarchies. The Name (language, the Third Party, the Other) becomes paternal property. It is possible that Kristeva reads the causality between Christianity and the paternal function in the wrong direction. Perhaps Christianity does not reveal the *paternal* function, but creates it.

Earlier, in *About Chinese Women*, Kristeva makes another questionable claim about religion. She argues that we need to be suspicious of perverse denials of the Bible:

> Let us recall the fascist or social-fascist homosexual community (and all homosexual communities for whom there is no "other race"), and the fact that it is inevitably flanked by a community of viragos who have forgotten the war of the sexes and identity with the paternal Word or its serpent. The feminist movements are equally capable of a similar perverse denial of biblical teaching. We must recognize this and be on our guard. (1974c, 145)

It is not an accident that the Bible and its paternal Word have contributed to the oppression of homosexuals and women. It seems that Kristeva is condemning some kind of separatism that simply denies the existence of the other. Yet it is unclear what kind of "denial" of oppressive biblical teachings about the "war of the sexes" would not be perverse. Certainly to deny that these teachings exist or even that they are an important part of Western culture may be perverse. But to resist them and attempt to create new discourses of sexual difference does not seem perverse. From reading many of Kristeva's texts, I get the impression that she might agree. But in this strange passage from *About Chinese Women* she goes on to say that the solution is to go on waging the "war of the sexes" until "some other economy of the sexes installs itself." (1974c, 145) Can we have nothing to do with that installation? Must we simply accept oppressive religious discourses until that time, whenever it may come? Are we merely to wait? A more appropriate question might be, "What is Kristeva's attachment to biblical metaphors?"

One of Kristeva's latest books, *Black Sun*, is full of Christian imagery. Her main thesis is that the melancholic is a radical atheist mourning the loss of God, or the maternal "Thing." In *Black Sun* she frequently uses metaphors of rebirth, resurrection, and forgiveness in order to describe psychic dynamics and the analytic process. For example, she compares the psychic rebirth that results from Christian forgiveness to the psychic rebirth that results from forgiveness in analysis:

> Indeed, any modern imprecation against Christianity—up to and including Nietzsche's—is an imprecation against forgiveness. . . . [T]he *solemnity* of forgiveness—as it functions in theological tradition and as it is rehabilitated in aesthetic experience, which identifies with abjection in order to traverse it, name it, expend it—is inherent in the economy of psychic rebirth. At any rate, that is how it appears under the benevolent impact of analytic practice. (1987, 190)

Kristeva believes that forgiveness leads to a complete identification with the "constantly *threefold* (real, imaginary, and symbolic)." (1987, 207; italics mine) This "miraculous device of identification" with this "threefold" secular Trinity, which comes through forgiveness, gives the wounded subject a "second life," a rebirth. (1987, 207) Forgiveness constitutes a loving bond with a nonjudgmental other who "allows me to be reborn." (1987, 205) When successful, the analytic transference leads to this "miraculous" identification with a loving other who cures through forgiveness. The analyst forgives her patient and allows her to be born again. Through these strange Christian metaphors, Kristeva suggests that in analysis humanity prepares to pay its debt to the "Allmighty" (because analysis is so expensive?) and that the analysand finds forgiveness. It seems difficult, then, not to interpret analysis as a "lay religion."

In addition to importing metaphors from Christianity, Kristeva also praises Christianity because the "imaginative capability of Western man is fulfilled within Christianity." She claims that imaginative capability is "the ability to transfer meaning to the very place where it was lost in death and/or nonmeaning." This imaginary capability is at the same time a "miracle" and a "shattering." It is a "self-illusion." (1987, 103) In Christianity it is the illusion of the borders of meaning and nonmeaning that Kristeva identifies as "Satan and God, Fall and Resurrection." (1987, 101) She suggests that Christianity fulfills our imaginative capability because it names nonmeaning and death through the illusions of Satan and the Fall. She maintains that the Western tradition has inherited "a specific economy of imaginary discourses" that supports a heterogeneous subjectivity posed between meaning and nonmeaning, the symbolic and semiotic, God and Satan, the Resurrection and the Fall.

For Kristeva, these imaginary discourses, Christianity in particular, provide a "tense link between Thing and Meaning, the unnameable and a proliferation of signs, the silent affect and the ideality that designates and goes beyond it, the *imaginary* is neither the objective description that will reach its highest point in science nor theological idealism that will be satisfied with reaching the Symbolic uniqueness of a beyond." (1987, 100) Is analysis, then, a new religion that serves the same function as the "solemn" Christian imaginary and that provides the tense and tenuous link between the Thing and meaning, but in a different setting, on the couch? In these extreme moments in Kristeva's texts, moments marinated in Christian/Catholic imagery, moments in which humankind is fulfilled by Christianity, a dangerous ethnocentrism is on the prowl.

Analyzing the Analyst

Perhaps Kristeva's strangest, and most Eurocentric, invocation of a biblical metaphor is in the conclusion of an autobiographical article entitled "My Memory's Hyperbole." (1984c, 276) There she concludes her intellectual history with a dream of Judeo-Christian Europe in an alliance with the United States against the Third World:

> While the Latin American or Arab Marxist revolution is brewing on the doorstep of the United States, I feel closer to truth and liberty when I work within the space of this challenged giant, which may, in fact, be on the point of becoming a David before the growing Goliath of the Third World. I dream that our children will prefer to join this David, with his errors and impasses, armed with our erring and circling about the Idea, the Logos, the Form: in short, the old Judeo-Christian Europe. (1984, 276)

By comparing the Third World to the monster Goliath and the United States to the small David, Kristeva figures the Third World as threatening Other. The so-called "Third World" is set up as the Other against which Western culture can establish its identity. Kristeva's Eurocentrism flies in the face of her analysis of love and her call to embrace the stranger/foreigner in *Strangers to Ourselves*.[9]

What is Kristeva's attachment to biblical fantasies and the Christian/Catholic imaginary in particular? Does she employ biblical metaphors merely for the effect of this powerful currency? This explanation would not make sense in a market where, as Kristeva claims, Christian symbols have lost their value. Perhaps within the circle of her intellectual contacts, biblical metaphors have a certain currency. In "My Memory's Hyperbole" she explains *Tel Quel's* "unappreciated" involvement with studies of the sacred:

> . . . our own thoughts on writing and the various mythemes of the sacred (from the sacrificial rite that institutes the Symbolic to the Virgin, and the topos of the incarnation) have had a swift and artful dissemination whose toughness and corrosiveness have not always been appreciated. In short, these thoughts, as various articles and works of fiction published in *Tel Quel* demonstrate, have nothing to do with a religious psychology or ideology but rather with certain phantasmic and linguistic knots on which the power of the sacred is built. (1984c, 268)

Here Kristeva defends herself and her friends from *Tel Quel* by arguing that their interest in the sacred is purely in order to understand how its imaginary and symbolic dynamics work. This still does not explain why she imports these sacred images and symbols into her descriptions of psychoanalytic processes. Is she trying to harness the power of this waning sacred? She does suggest that psychoanalysis must operate through the imaginary in order to retain/replace some of the mystery and spirituality of the sacred. (1984b, 25) This, in fact, is one of the reasons that she claims that political discourse cannot replace religious discourse; it cannot account for mysteries and spirituality.

Could Kristeva be nostalgic for the power of the old sacred? Could she be the melancholic atheist mourning the death of God? She does begin *Black Sun* with a lament that only the melancholic can write about melancholy. Since *Black Sun* is about melancholia, Kristeva must herself be melancholy. In an interview, however, Kristeva insists that her discussion of Christianity in *Tales of Love* is not nostalgia. Rather, she claims that it is "more a questioning about the discourse that can take the place of this religious discourse which is cracking now." (1984b, 25) She believes that psychoanalysis, or possibly art, can take its place. For her this does not necessarily mean, however, that psychoanalysis becomes a new religion. Rather, in her best moments, Kristeva suggests that it means that psychoanalysis fills the cracks of religion. In her worst moments, a few of which I have discussed above, she is nostalgic, mourning the death of God.

What kind of narrative fiction might be able to explain Kristeva's nostalgia for strong, living religion? Perhaps Kristeva provides a place to begin in *In the Beginning Was Love* when she describes her relationship to religious faith as a child:

> I am not a believer, but I recall having been born into a family of believers who tried, without excessive enthusiasm perhaps, to transmit their faith to me. My unbelief was not, however, a matter of oedipal rebellion and signal of a rejection of family values. In adolescence, when Dostoevsky's characters first began to impress me with the violence of their tragic mysticism, I knelt

before the icon of the Virgin that sat enthroned above my bed and attempted
to gain access to a faith that my secular education did not so much combat
as treat ironically or simply ignore. . . . But the vitality, not to say excitabil-
ity, of my adolescent body came between mournful images of death and
everyday reality, and my macabre thoughts soon gave way to erotic day-
dreams. (1987, 23–24)

In this passage Kristeva defends her disbelief by assuring us that it is not
an oedipal rebellion against her family's values and that she tried to believe but could not. Still, this is a romantic memory of herself as a child,
kneeling before the Virgin, a time of innocence before her own sexual
desires were aroused. Is it important that while Kristeva was an adolescent
in Bulgaria, religion and certain literature were outlawed by the government? Her family values, insofar as they were religious, were not the
State's values. In addition, Kristeva remembers that her family valued
literature and "pushed" her into a "cultural milieu." (1986, 217) Could
Kristeva's attachment to biblical metaphors, then, be nostalgia for her
childhood attachment to her family, especially her mother, forever associated with the icon of the Virgin, which she presumably hung above the
bed? Could these metaphors be Kristeva's melancholy mournings for her
lost mother/land?

In her latest book (as of this writing), *Strangers to Ourselves*, Kristeva
suggests that an exile on foreign soil will resurrect the abandoned religion
of her ancestors in an "essential purity."[10] (1989, 39) And what could
be "purer" than Kristeva's psychohistorical analyses of Catholicism à la
Christianity in general? She is fascinated with Christianity in its "essential purity." The religion that meant nothing to the exile in her own country becomes the authority of law in a new country. The exile prefers this
maternal law, the tradition of her motherland to that of her new country.
(Cf. 1989, 150.) Although Kristeva's maternal religion, Catholicism, exists
in France, it is possible that foreign law (with its apparent arbitrariness),
combined with mourning for the lost motherland, led the exile back to
her abandoned religion. After all, Kristeva is this exile. Until the recent
changes in Eastern Europe, she had been exiled from Communist Bulgaria
since she moved to Paris in 1965, married a Frenchman, and became a
French citizen.

Is Kristeva herself the "stranger" that she describes in *Etrangers a nous-
memes*? Of course, in the end, for Kristeva, we are all *Etrangers's* strangers
and *Tales of Loves's* extraterrestrials. But as an alien in a foreign country,
Kristeva has a special relationship to this stranger whom she describes.
Like the experience of *Etrangers's* stranger, this relationship seems painful
and exhilarating. Keeping in mind that Kristeva is a foreigner in the juridical sense that she analyses in parts of her book, her position in *Etrangers*
is strange ("etranger a lui-memes?"). There the stranger is someone else

and not her. She talks about her own experience with strangers in France. She tells personal anecdotes. But they are stories of other strangers.

For example, she mentions a foreign woman who was a virgin when she arrived in Paris before the events of May '68. During the political upheaval this woman engaged in "group sex" and impressed her lover with her audacity. (1989, 48) Kristeva suggests that this kind of sexual freedom is characteristic of foreigners who leave the morals of their homes behind. In addition, she describes the laws governing "mixed marriages," which can give foreigners some of the rights of citizenship. But she does not refer directly to her own experience as a foreigner. What of Kristeva's own experience arriving in Paris, as she did, before the events of May '68? What of her own "mixed marriage"? In *Etrangers* she claims that nowhere is one stranger than in France because of the French pride in their "polished and dear" speech. (1989, 57–58) Does she know this from her own experience? Yet in *Etrangers* Kristeva distances herself from her own foreignness and speaks from the position of the French intellectual, realizing that she, like the immigrants, is a stranger to herself.

Kristeva does not always assume the position of the French intellectual. As she points out in *Etrangers*, great artists and scholars will be claimed by the countries in which they live in spite of their immigrant or alien status, even while their country people suffer from discrimination. (1989, 60) Certainly France has claimed Kristeva; and in the United States she is considered a French intellectual. At times, however, she has been quick to point out that she cannot be called a "French intellectual" because she is not French. (1986, 222) Usually in these moments Kristeva wants to set herself apart politically. For example, she claims that she is not a French intellectual in order to separate herself from (naive) French leftists. Or, she claims that her relationship to feminism is different from that of other (naive) French and British or American feminists because she grew up in Eastern Europe where women had more economic, political, and professional equality. (1979a, 39) In addition to these moments in which Kristeva uses her foreignness in order to prove her political savvy, there are moments in which she alludes to or invokes her foreignness in a romantic daydream, or in an analytic countertransference, or in political and personal frustration.

In *About Chinese Women* Kristeva refers to her childhood in Bulgaria and her "Asian ancestors" in order to distance herself from Western culture and possibly affirm her connection to China. In a romantic moment she claims that China is less disorienting for her "who recognized my own pioneer komsomol childhood in the little red guards, and who owe my cheekbones to some Asian ancestor." (1974c, 12) Could Kristeva be the "Asiatic princess" of *Etrangers* "writing her memoirs in a borrowed language"? (1989, 19) Or does her foreignness better allow her to imagine the out-of-placeness of this Asiatic princess, writing her life in a second language? Is this the analyst's countertransference?

Or is this what Gayatri Spivak calls Kristeva's "naturalization transformed into privilege"? (1981) Spivak persuasively argues that Kristeva's concern with China is self-centered. Her questions about Chinese women are always really questions about herself. The women of China are silent in Kristeva's *About Chinese Women*. And Spivak argues that Kristeva turns a few possibly marginal books and articles about China into facts. Spivak suggests that Kristeva's scholarly use of China is imperialist. She uses China and Chinese women as objects against which she can define herself. Her romanticization of China is nothing more than naturalization transformed into privilege. She sees herself in those little red guards and those high cheekbones of the silent women of China because it was only herself for whom she was looking. Spivak claims that "[a]s she investigates the pre-Confucian text of the modern Chinese woman, her own prehistory in Bulgaria is not even a shadow under the harsh light of the Parisian voice." (1981, 164; see also Lowe 1991)

I would add that when we do see the shadow of the Bulgarian it is only to more distinctly foreground the Parisian voice. In her account of Chinese women, when Kristeva recognizes herself in them, she also recognizes herself superior to them. While they cannot speak, she can. While they cannot see how quaint and romantic and privileged they are in their society, she can. She can see what they cannot because she speaks with a Parisian voice. With her Bulgarian voice, like the woman of Huxian Square, she says nothing.

In Kristeva's latest works, *Tales of Love*, *Black Sun*, and *Strangers to Ourselves*, she adopts a more personal tone than in some of her earlier works. In many of her early works, especially *Revolution*, she maintains her scholarly position, the position of the French intellectual. In the latest works, however, there are frequent passages where Kristeva will use the personal pronouns "I" and "you." In these passages, she is usually offering the analyst's countertransference fantasies. She is identifying with John and Juliet's lack of love, or Dostoevsky's need for forgiveness, or Camus's stranger. She speaks as if she is speaking for them. She performs the task of the analyst and provides words, symbols, fantasies, in order to name the unnameable. She uses these fantasies in order to link the symbolic and semiotic. Often protected within quotation marks, these imaginary confessions are still the analyst's fantasies. The words that Kristeva provides for the love sick, the extraterrestrials, the melancholics, and the strangers speak her Unconscious as well as theirs. In some passages her pain is left unprotected without quotation marks. She speaks *as*, not *for*, the love-sick, the extraterrestrial, the melancholic, and the stranger. "My pain," says Kristeva, very much in her own voice, "is the hidden side of my philosophy, its mute sister." (1987a, 4)

In an unusually personal early essay, "The Novel as Polylogue," about Philippe Sollers' novel *H*, Kristeva writes an almost delirious confession of her pain and passion. High on *H*, her words are "more throbbing than meaning." (1974b, 163) This essay throbs with pain and sexual passion. Kristeva describes the pain of exile:

> To put it bluntly, I speak in French and about literature because of Yalta. I mean that because of Yalta, I was obliged to marry in order to have a French passport and to work in France; moreover, because of Yalta I wanted to "marry" the violence that has tormented me ever since, has dissolved identity and cells, coveted recognition and haunted my nights and my tranquility, caused hatred to well within what is usually called love, in short, has raked me to death.
>
> Above all, you must not forget that this all takes place within language. Hence, not possible in Bulgarian, once again because of Yalta, and of course, past history. As a result, I had recourse to French: Robespierre, Sade, Mallarmé. . . .
>
> And I have since been wedded to a torrent. It is a desire to understand to be sure or, if you prefer, a laboratory of death. For what you take to be a shattering of language is really a shattering of the body, and the immediate surroundings get it smack on the chin.
>
> A body, a text that bounces back to me echoes of a territory that I have lost but that I am seeking within the blackness of dreams in Bulgarian, French, Russian, Chinese tones, invocations, lifting up the dismembered, sleeping body. Territory of the mother. (1974b, 161–63)

Fifteen years later Kristeva describes this same experience in *Etrangers*; here it is as the theoretician and not as the stranger. In *Etrangers* she says that the stranger has lost her mother. (1989, 14) The stranger suffers because she cannot speak her maternal language: "Not to speak one's maternal language. To inhabit the resonance, the cut logics of the nocturnal memory of the body, of the bitter-sweet sleep of the child." (1989, 26–27) The stranger lives in resonances of the maternal language, which are always also the resonances of the maternal body. Yet for Kristeva, these become mere memories buried beneath the new language that feels like a "new body," a "new skin," a "new sex." (1989, 27)

Has Kristeva taken on her new skin and shed the old? It seems odd that she begins her autobiographical essay, "My Memory's Hyperbole," with her arrival in France, as if this is the beginning of her life, or even her intellectual life. It may be the beginning of her new life as a French intellectual. But what has happened to the Bulgarian? Is Kristeva describing her own experience in *Etrangers* when she asks who are the murderers, the natives who never speak about their parents, or "myself who builds my new life as a fragile mausoleum"? Perhaps Kristeva builds her new life in France as this fragile mausoleum in which she tries to contain her Bulgarian past, maternal language, maternal body. Perhaps her theory of the semiotic in language is one way of resurrecting her own lost maternal language. Could the maternal rhythms and tones that Kristeva hears in all language be the invocations in her dreams of her lost Bulgarian mother/

land? Certainly Kristeva's interest in language acquisition and the nuances of sounds could be related to her own experience speaking French in France with natives. As she says, "this all takes place within language."

In addition, her supposition of the semiotic element in language could be related to her experience as a foreigner in France. Like the fetishist, she becomes fixated on part of her loss, the loss of her maternal language. Like the fetishist, with her theory of the semiotic Kristeva both admits and denies the loss of maternal language. The theory of the semiotic allows her to postulate the existence of the maternal language within her new language even while she admits that this maternal element is always out of reach of the new language.

In psychoanalytic terms, Kristeva retains an image of the phallic mother, denies her castration, by postulating the maternal within the paternal. That is, she postulates the maternal within the Symbolic or paternal, and thereby endows the maternal with the phallic power of the paternal. Maternal generation and procreation become associated with, and more powerful than, paternal power. Compare this to Kristeva's suggestion that fetishism appears as a solution to the depression over the loss of the mother through a denial of the father's function. She maintains that the depressive's father is deprived of phallic power, which is instead attributed to the mother. And this father does not allow any idealization of the Symbolic except as he becomes the "maternal father." (1987, 45) Yet, Kristeva's postulation of the heterogeneity of language, with its strong maternal element, seems to turn language into a type of maternal father.

Kristeva's theory of melancholia and depression goes even further than traditional psychoanalytic theory in analyzing the loss of the mother/land. The melancholic mourns the loss of the maternal "Thing" that, although always lurking, can never be fully recovered in language. Kristeva claims that the melancholic buries this "Thing" below language and then cannot recover it. It could be argued that this is precisely what Kristeva does by proposing the existence of the semiotic "Thing." She buries the semiotic below language and then maintains that it can never be fully recovered. In fact, she suggests (and rejects) this reading of her postulation of the "Thing":

> To posit the existence of a primal object, or even of a Thing, which is to be conveyed through and beyond a completed mourning—isn't that the fantasy of a melancholy theoretician? . . . Positing the existence of that other language and even of an other of language, indeed of an outside-of-language, is not necessarily setting up a preserve for metaphysics or theology. The postulate corresponds to a psychic requirement that Western metaphysics and theory have had, perhaps, the good luck and audacity to represent. (1987, 66)

Her argument here is that the "Thing" is postulated as the cause of conveyability only because conveyability is already possible and taking place. In other words, the postulation of a "Thing" that is prior to representation—its cause and its telos—is itself a representation. And taken as such, it does not have to become a replacement for God or Being. As Kristeva points out, however, this postulation is necessary for religion or metaphysics. Moreover this postulate is a "psychic requirement" for Western culture. For Kristeva, the "advantages" of Western culture's postulate are that it provides a way of allowing subjects to see a relationship between themselves and something outside of themselves; and it allows them to avoid pain by not facing it directly. Kristeva argues that Westerners believe in the conveyability of the "Thing" and therefore it can be represented in its absence. Thereby, the pain of loss is replaced by the joy of mastering signs. (1987, 67)

Still, I wonder how merely asserting that the postulation of the "Thing," or the semiotic element of language, is a necessary requirement for Western culture allows Kristeva to sidestep metaphysics. On the contrary, it seems that the claim that an extralinguistic, or nonsymbolizable element within the linguistic, in a psychic necessity is itself a metaphysical claim. The implication of this is that Kristeva is postulating a replacement for God or Being that she calls a "necessary psychic requirement." Then she is arguing that this is not what it seems because she knows that even this unnameable is a name, a representation. What Kristeva seems to be arguing is that the unnameable is not a religious or metaphysical supposition because it is already a name, the "Thing," the "semiotic." But what this demonstrates is the very obsession with conveyability that she attributes to Western culture. In a sense, Kristeva is saying "my unnameable is not metaphysical because I realize that I have already named it. I have made the unconveyable conveyable." That is to say that Kristeva, by decree, asserts that her attempt to name the unnameable is not metaphysical because she realizes that it is metaphysical and therefore doesn't really believe in it. She suggests that it is her skepticism of herself that takes her attempts beyond metaphysics. I am skeptical of her success in going beyond metaphysics through such a slight of hand.

In addition, Kristeva's attempts to go beyond metaphysics can be read as a manifestation of her own melancholia as a theorist. The attempt to convey the unconveyable is what Kristeva describes as an attempt to overcome mourning for the lost maternal "Thing." The melancholic lives in mourning. She is not able to replace the lost mother with words. Kristeva attempts to describe what she sees as a melancholic culture, Western culture. So if her theory itself is melancholic, we might expect that because she is part of Western culture. This image of a melancholy Western culture, however, may be merely the result of the imagination of a melancholy theorist. Moreover, Kristeva's embrace of Western culture is always in the shadow of her "fragile mausoleum," her Eastern European and

Asian ancestors. Perhaps the melancholia that she sees in Western culture is a projection of her melancholia in the face of her lost mother/land. She sees her lost mother/land hiding everywhere within her new culture.

Kristeva's own analysis provides further support for this interpretation. In *Etrangers* she suggests that by devouring her love for a lost mother, the stranger transfers the universal necessity of a stage onto an elsewhere that will be seen as the "simple axis of movement," "the key to the soul," or a musical tone. (1989, 46) Kristeva, like her stranger, transfers the preoedipal stage of development onto an elsewhere, the unrepresentable semiotic. In addition, her translation from Bulgarian into French is analogous to the translation that she describes between the semiotic and the Symbolic, the mother and the name. "If I did not agree to lose mother," says Kristeva, "I could neither imagine nor name her." (1987, 41) Kristeva gives up her own maternal language and then imagines the maternal element in language as a "simple axis of movement," "the key to the soul," a musical tone. Is this tone the tone of her dreams, the tone of her childhood that comes to her in Bulgarian, French, Russian, Chinese, the tone that she associates with her lost maternal tongue?

The melancholic, however, is melancholy because she cannot give up the maternal. She is forever trying to replace the lost maternal in order to separate from it. She cannot replace the lost mother in her own maternal tongue; it only becomes more difficult in a foreign tongue. She is forever mourning the loss of the maternal territory, her mother/land. (Cf. 1983, 234.) Kristeva confesses her "own precociously lost love" early in *Tales of Love* when she asks why it is that only homosexuals proclaim their love for her:

> I have chanced to note that when analysands of either sex made their love known to me, pretending to forget the expedient of the analytical contract, it involved men or women who called themselves homosexual. . . . Why homosexuals? Could they have guessed an uneasiness on my part in dealing with their uneasiness about a subjugating mother, precociously and encroachingly loving, abandoned or abiding, but always underhandedly fascinating? Do they set up, in my place, instead of an object of love, my own preciously lost love? Probably. (1983, 11–12)

In Kristeva's own underhandedly fascinating way, she confesses her love for her lost mother. She also describes an "uneasy" countertransference to homosexual love, a countertransference that brings her too close to her own love. Kristeva sees herself in the homosexual who imagines the lost maternal in the place of the analyst even while she admits her own homophobia.

For Kristeva, homosexuals replace the symbolic father with an imaginary mother. Like the homosexual whom Kristeva describes, she too replaces the symbolic father of psychoanalysis with an imaginary father who is the mother, a maternal father, the imaginary link between the maternal semiotic and the paternal symbolic. She longs for a real maternal body that lies beyond the Symbolic, even while she realizes that it is always already a representation. Kristeva's precociously lost love is the homosexual love for her mother, from whom she is doubly estranged, separated from both maternal body and maternal language.

Keeping with traditional psychoanalysis, in her early writings especially, Kristeva operates as if the homosexual is a deviant. Because of this some of her critics argue that Kristeva is homophobic. (Butler 1989; O'Conner 1989) In her later writings, however, she is more open to multiple sexualities. She says that "I have the deep conviction that every person has a very particular sexuality. This sexuality and this kind of love organization is what interests me and not the group of *the* homosexuals, *the* heterosexuals, and so on." (1984b, 24) Her ambiguity in relation to homosexuality is one of the places where the contradictions in her writing are more frustrating than productive. Perhaps because of the strong influence of traditional psychoanalysis Kristeva's own lesbian desires are always repressed within her texts. When she describes homosexuality as a desire for the mother, she is describing her own individual sexuality.

Several of Kristeva's critics have argued that she makes all lesbian relations into mother-child relations and overlooks or denies the love of one woman for another. Jane Gallop, Elizabeth Grosz, and Judith Butler, in particular, argue that Kristeva denies lesbian loves. Gallop asks why there is no lesbian in "Stabat Mater." She suggests that perhaps the lesbian is the phallic mother with whom Kristeva cannot identify. (1982, 130) Within Kristeva's analysis, however, feminine sexuality is fundamentally homosexual. Feminine sexuality is determined by a lesbian relationship between daughter and mother. Lesbian love is everywhere repressed beneath the surface in "Stabat Mater." Elizabeth Grosz asks why there is no lesbian love in *Tales of Love*. Once again I see lesbian love pushed into every corner of *Tales of Love*. Hints of an erotics of the purely feminine and female homosexuality appear in the text at those points where Kristeva seems frustrated with and weary of the same old love stories. Lesbian love appears in the condensations and displacements of Kristeva's texts. She recognizes a lesbian love. But once again it is the daughter's love for her mother and the mother's for her child, the foundation of feminine sexuality:

> ... lesbian loves comprise the delightful arena of a neutralized, filtered libido, devoid of the erotic cutting edge of masculine sexuality. Light touches, caresses, barely distinct images fading one into the other, growing dim or veiled without bright flashes into the mellowness of a dissolution, a liquefaction, a merger.... It evokes the loving dialogue of the pregnant mother with the fruit, barely distinct from her, that she shelters in her womb. Or the light rumble of soft skins that are iridescent not from desire

but from that opening-closing, blossoming-wilting, an in-between hardly established that suddenly collapses in the same warmth, that slumbers or wakens within the embrace of the baby and its nourishing mother. Skin; mouth; empty, excited, or filled opening of the lips—they coat such emanations, float, cradle, drug. Relation or consciousness, daydream, language that is neither dialectical nor rhetorical, but peace or eclipse: nirvana, intoxication, and silence. (1983, 81)

Perhaps Grosz is right that what is missing in *Tales of Love* is the love of one woman for another. Kristeva's lesbian love takes her back once again to her mother. Even while her own language is full of desire, barely able to stop itself, Kristeva denies desire in lesbian love. She wants it to remain outside of "phallic eroticism." Her lesbian love is an escape valve for the pain of phallic desire. Yet phallic desire is painful precisely because it leaves out this lesbian love. Behind all of Kristeva's writing is a longing for her one true lesbian lover, her mother. Kristeva is proclaiming, yet hiding, her sexual desire for her mother as one adult woman to another. So while it is true that her homoerotic fantasy is the fantasy of a mother-daughter relationship, it is also a relationship between two women, a relationship that could only be sublimated into a relation with a mother-substitute, another woman.

Judith Butler is right when she says that for Kristeva women are melancholy heterosexuals longing for lesbian love. (1989, 111) All women are lesbians perverted by compulsory heterosexuality. Kristeva seems to believe that the contortions that Freud describes as normal feminine sexuality—the change of love object and erogenous zone—leave women permanently scarred. I don't agree, however, with Butler that the only other alternative that Kristeva leaves for women is psychosis. She suggests that there are as many sexualities as there are individuals. Like Butler, she endorses the multiplication of sexualities. She refuses the dualism between homosexuality and heterosexuality. (1984b, 24) If this multitude of sexualities is not recognized it is because traditional psychoanalytic discouse, among others, naturalizes a binary structure, what Butler, following Wittig, calls the "heterosexual matrix."

I see Kristeva's work as an intervention into traditional heterosexist psychoanalytic discourse. She rarely discusses sexual difference as such because she is trying to break open a discourse that continues to insist on a binary structure. Moreover, Kristeva's work as an analyst and her analysis in *Black Sun* attempt to provide women with new fantasies with which they can live with what Kristeva sees as their primary loss, the loss of their mothers. Certainly this says as much, possibly more, about Kristeva herself than feminine sexualities. She is a melancholy theorist longing for her lost lesbian love.

Kristeva's books moan with the pain of this open wound, an incomplete mourning. Like the stranger, she is the theorist who occupies the place of this scar. (Cf. 1989, 142) For Kristeva the theoretician is posited on the place of the scar because she is trying to elaborate at a distance a phenomenon very close to her own pain. And the theoretician has to reveal this pain. (1984b, 24) Recall that Kristeva claims that "Stabat Mater," with its two columns, is supposed give an image of "a sort of wound, a scar."[11] (1984b, 24) "Stabat Mater" tells the story of a woman's, Kristeva's, experience of childbirth as a reunion with her own mother. The two columns give the image not only of a wound but also of the maternal sex that both separates and reunites mother and daughter. Possibly foreshadowing *Black Sun*'s maternal "Thing," in *Tales*, Kristeva refers to the mother's sex as the "maternal Thing." (1983, 369) The comparison between *Black Sun*'s "Thing" and *Tales*'s "Thing" suggests that the maternal Thing can be read as the maternal sex. This reading supports my argument that Kristeva takes us deeper into the maternal body. Between the two columns both the child and the mother's mother are born. Between these two columns lie the pain and joy of separation and reunion. Kristeva's own pain, posited on the place of this scar, rivets her to her subjugating, precociously and encroachingly loving, abandoned mother. She says that it is this pain of her exile from her mother/land that leads her to analysis. (1986) It is interesting that she claims that her exile leads her to analysis and that analysis can produce in exiles great scholars and artists. (1989, 49–50)

The uneasiness of Kristeva's relation to her lost mother/land can also be read in her relation to one of her philosophical Foremothers, Simone de Beauvoir. Kristeva argues that matricide is necessary in order to separate from the mother and go through mourning. But she claims that for women it is difficult if not impossible. (1987, 27–29) Some women, says Kristeva, carry the "living corpse" of their mother with them. (1980b, 137) Perhaps Simone de Beauvoir is one of Kristeva's living corpses. She very rarely mentions Beauvoir by name.[12] Yet at the time when she arrived in France, and still considered herself a feminist, Beauvoir was the leading voice of French feminism. There are several places where Kristeva criticizes the existential feminists without mentioning Beauvoir by name, in spite of the fact that Beauvoir is the most well-known existential feminist. (1979a, 36, 39; 1980, 10; 1983, 234, 374) Is her reluctance to mention Beauvoir's name matricide? Or, is it a symptom of her inability to lose this Foremother in order to be able to name her?

The peculiarity of Kristeva's relationship to Beauvoir is manifest in the introduction to her biographical essay "My Memory's Hyperbole." She begins this intellectual autobiography by referring to Beauvoir's *La Cérémonie des adieux*. This introductory paragraph, however, in which she both valorizes and denigrates Beauvoir, does not seem to have anything to do with her autobiography that follows. In this brief and biting account of Beauvoir's work, Kristeva refers to "the naive cruelty of this exceptional woman," who "as a chronicler . . . knew how to construct an entire cultural phenomenon," the phenomenon of "a sexuality more contained than unveiled." (1984c, 261) After setting up the image of Beauvoir as cold, cruel chronicler, Kristeva claims that the gap between unconscious and conscious prevents her (Kristeva) "from being a good witness" and that *making history* has become impossible. In other words, unlike Beauvoir, she cannot be a "good witness" to a cultural phenomenon and thereby create history. She is not Beauvoir. She begins her own autobiography by passionately separating herself from Beauvoir, her Foremother. The fact that Kristeva feels the need to separate herself from Beauvoir at the outset of her autobiographical essay suggests that she is an heir to Beauvoir's philosophy even while she rejects it. In addition, the Beauvoir text to which Kristeva refers is Beauvoir's own autobiography. It is strange that Kristeva begins her autobiography by disassociating it from Beauvoir's.

And just as Kristeva rejects existential feminism without ever mentioning Beauvoir, she does not credit Beauvoir when it might be appropriate to do so. Although on the surface it seems that Beauvoir's position on motherhood is almost the opposite of Kristeva's, the foundations of Kristeva's position are already manifest in Beauvoir's *The Second Sex*. For example, Beauvoir claims that in becoming a mother, a woman takes the place of her own mother. (1948, 493) She also analyzes pregnancy as a conflict between the species and the individual. (1948, 498) And perhaps most important for Kristeva's theory, Beauvoir suggests that pregnancy is an oscillation between subject and object within the maternal body.[13] (1948, 504) These three elements are crucial to Kristeva's account of pregnancy and the herethics that can provide the beginnings of her secular discourse on motherhood.[14] In addition, Kristeva's concern to develop a new ethical discourse in which the ethical subject is never merely an autonomous individual regulated by law could be informed by Beauvoir's *Ethics of Ambiguity*. In the *Ethics of Ambiguity* Beauvoir argues that human beings can be ethical agents only because their individuality presupposes the social relation. Like Kristeva after her, she claims that there can be no ethics if we presuppose a completely autonomous subject who is regulated by law.

Why does Kristeva either ignore Beauvoir or so bitterly criticize her? On my reading, Kristeva's relation to Beauvoir is a symptom of her own uneasiness with the maternal. Applying Kristeva's theories to her own writing, I see a melancholy theoretician mourning the loss of her mother/ land. As an exile, Kristeva is cut off from her motherland and maternal language. For Kristeva the maternal becomes a source of pain and ecstasy. Her fantasies are filled with joyous reunions with the maternal body and language, whether through poetry, art, or pregnancy. They are also filled with images of horrifying abject mothers. In order to separate from this "encroachingly loving" mother without brutal matricide Kristeva sets up, in her place, a theoretical womb: the nourishing semiotic *chora*, the un-representable maternal Thing. Then Kristeva writes and writes in order to fill the void left in the place of the lost mother/land. She tries to fill the *chora* with words even while she attempts to bring it to words. Hers is a struggle that takes place within language, estranged from her mother-tongue, living in/with a foreign tongue. Like the melancholic whom she describes in *Black Sun*, Kristeva keeps writing because she is looking for the total foreign word in order to capture the unnameable maternal Thing that she carries with her in her fragile mausoleum. (1987, 42)

VI

POLITICS IN THE AGE OF PROPAGANDA

Political Perversions

Like many intellectuals in Paris before May '68, including her *Tel Quel* colleagues, Kristeva was politically active with the Communist party; she says that the *Tel Quel* group had endorsed a certain Maoism. (1984c, 273) Like many intellectuals after May '68, however, including the *Tel Quel* group, Kristeva became disillusioned with practical politics. In "My Memory's Hyperbole," she says that they realized that they were practicing political perversion. (1984c, 273) Here she defines political perversion as "a coherent structure determined by an ideal . . . which nevertheless uses the abjections of reality, one that is neglected or even foreclosed, on behalf of libidinal or sublimated gratifications." She says that *Tel Quel's* ideal was theoretical while their gratification was the development of their own work. She points out that the Communist party insured that alternative sorts of theory and literature got published. *Tel Quel* took advantage of this in order to get fairly well known in France. (1984c, 272–73) Kristeva claims that once they recognized this perversion, they remained aloof from the Communist party and practical politics. But it was already too late; they became well known in France.

In Kristeva's analysis, most politics is a sort of perversion. She claims that if the ideal in politics is not theoretical, like hers, then it is moral. Modern politics becomes fixated on the ideal, for its own sake, which covers over the libidinal gratifications sought through this ideal. Kristeva maintains that this is true of some feminists who use political ideals in order to further their careers and publish books. (1979a, 50) The more that these libidinal gratifications are repressed, the more transcendent political ideals become. In what she identifies as a crisis in religion, political ideals replace religious ideals. Politics, says Kristeva, has become a modern religion. (1984b, 25; 1986, 223)

For Kristeva political interpretation, like religion, is a search for one transcendent Meaning. Like religion, it becomes a way of explaining and legitimating certain traditions and life-styles. It becomes a kind of cultural imaginary in which drives are controlled or indirectly discharged. Unlike religion, however, political interpretation cannot account for nonmeaning. Kristeva argues that while it is a fantasy, politics must maintain itself as rational and meaningful, whereas religion can defer to mysteries and miracles. (1981, 312–13) This is one of the disadvantages of political discourse. It cannot account for nonmeaning that is part of our experience. For this reason, Kristeva argues that political discourse cannot fill in the cracks in religious discourse. It cannot solve the crisis in religious discourse. (1984b, 25) Moreover, like religious discourse, which does not acknowledge its unconscious drives, political discourse can easily lead to totalitarianism, persecution, and war.

In "Women's Time" Kristeva defines religion as the speaking being's necessity to replace the process of its significations with a fixed representation, a meaning. (1979a, 50) The result is that this representation becomes reified, even deified. It becomes an end in itself rather than a moment in a process or the symptom of misfired repression. In this sense, ideals are religious; and all wars will be holy wars. (1980a, 210) As Kristeva points out, Stalinism and fascism are political interpretations, in some sense the logical consequence of the search for one Meaning. (1981, 303–304) Insofar as they fix an ideal, even political interpretations with emancipatory goals can become totalitarian. This is Kristeva's complaint with contemporary feminist movements. In order for political movements to be emancipatory, they must acknowledge that their fixed ideals are built on exclusions and persecutions. They must admit that their ideals are illusions created in the contexts of particular psychic struggles. For Kristeva, psychoanalysis cuts through the illusions of political interpretation. (1981, 303–304; 1984b, 25) She argues that she can do more with psychoanalysis in order to help people and enact change than she can with practical politics. (1986, 222)

Psychoanalysis makes the ultimate meaning and final causes provided by political ideals and interpretations analyzable. Psychoanalysis can disclose other meanings and nonmeanings within the one Meaning of political interpretation. Kristeva suggests that in this way, psychoanalytic discourses can mobilize resistance to totalitarian discourse. (1981, 303–304) In the closing remarks in "Psychoanalysis and the Polis" Kristeva sets out the "political function" of psychoanalysis:

> The task is not to make an interpretive summa in the name of a system of truths—for that attitude has always made interpretation a rather poor cousin of theology. The task is, instead, to record the *crisis* of modern interpretative systems without smoothing it over, to affirm that this crisis is inherent in the symbolic function itself and to perceive as symptoms all constructions, including totalizing interpretation, which try to deny this

crisis: to dissolve, to displace indefinitely, in Kafka's words, "temporarily and for a lifetime." (1981, 319)

Psychoanalysis has the odd task of representing all representations as symptoms of the crisis in representation—that it always includes the unrepresentable. This claim, which seems to employ the logic of classical representation even while it undermines it, raises some fundamental problems that accompany antifoundational theories. For example, the claim that all representations are symptoms of the crisis in representation is itself a representation. Therefore, if the claim is true, then the statement is false, in the sense that it is merely a symptom of something else. Or, if the statement is true, then the claim is false, because there is a representation that is universally true.[1]

Kristeva's claim asserts a representation that seems to operate as a stable representation and yet at the same time denies that very possibility. The psychoanalytic premise, like the antifoundational premise, has a double effect. On the one hand, since any counterclaims can be analyzed as mere symptoms, her claim becomes impossible to refute. Like Freud's famous suggestion that there is no "no" in the Unconscious and therefore "no" means "yes," all resistance to psychoanalysis proves that psychoanalysis is true. On the other hand, since it does not stop analyzing any representations, including its own, it provides a scientific model of tolerance and self-reflection that gives rise to continual modifications and possibly short-circuits totalitarianism. It gives rise to multiple interpretations, multiple representations, none of which can claim to be stable or unified. The analyst is always subject to unconscious processes and countertransference. The analyst is always also an analysand.

A Politics of Difference

If psychoanalysis can provide a way to acknowledge the processes through which we become invested in fixed representations, then we may be more tolerant of the excluded elements that are both essential to, and results of, these processes. Kristeva suggests that there might be fewer deaths if we acknowledged the death drive. What this amounts to is beginning to analyze our aggression, frustration, hate, and love that appear as unanalyzable in political and religious discourse. For example, in *Strangers to Ourselves* Kristeva claims that even the rights of "man" and "citizen" (*droits de l'homme et du citoyen*) are not fundamental. Even they are analyzable.

Kristeva argues that real political dissidence is not waging one fundamental ideal against another. It is neither taking up a position nor absorbing conflict. Rather, for her, it is analyzing conflict in an "attempt to bring about multiple sublations of the unnameable, the unrepresentable, the void." (1977b, 300) What she is suggesting is that we need to bring about multiple sublations of what appears in politics and religion as unrepresentable. Multiple sublations are fantasies that open up further analysis rather than closing it off. They are not stable identities or alternative positions. Kristeva emphasizes the need to steer between stable identities/positions, which become forms of religion on the one hand and lead to the dissolution of identities on the other.

The dissolution of identities is one position trying to absorb all others. This dissolution still operates within a logic of identity that relies on a stable and fixed identity. The dissolution of different identities into one— the melting pot—merely replaces a multitude of stable identities with one overarching stable identity. So while Kristeva maintains that politics must be informed by a psychoanalysis that recognizes unconscious structures, at the same time she emphasizes the importance of a politics of individuals. That is to say, she is not content to analyze signifying systems, including political institutions, merely in terms of their structures. In addition, she is not willing to reduce politics to party or class struggles. She rejects political interpretations that merely absorb individuals into groups:

> My reproach to some political discourses with which I am disillusioned is that they don't consider the individual as a value. . . . That's why I say that, of course, political struggles for people that are exploited will continue, but they will continue maybe better if the main concern remains the individuality and particularity of the person. (1984b, 27)

Kristeva endorses the political action of psychoanalysts and artists because they intervene on an individual level. (1984b, 27) She maintains that her own work has been primarily concerned with individuals rather than classes or groups. As a social scientist, she claims that she has tried to balance theoretical generalizations with an emphasis on the individual differences. (1984b, 27) She suggests that her psychoanalytic practice continually challenges her with individual differences.

While it is true that Kristeva analyzes individual artists and includes transcripts from her practice, most of her work seems clearly focused on generalizations about the very structure of the Western psyche, if not the human psyche. And while in interviews and essays she acknowledges that her theories are the result of her own individual history, much of her writing takes on a very detached scientific tone. In spite of her concern for the individual, the problem of theoretical generalizations that do not dissolve individuality is rarely explicitly addressed in Kristeva's writings. Even so, much of her writing grapples with the problems of identity and how to think of individual differences without absorbing them into a stable and unified identity. This is why in her own writing, Kristeva claims to have concentrated on texts that break down identity. (1974e, 138)

In *Strangers to Ourselves,* for example, she has turned her attention to political identity and difference. In her analysis of political identity and difference, Kristeva does recognize that struggles in the name of group identities will and must continue in order to overcome oppression. She acknowledges that feminist movements have made great advances by using the group identity "woman." (1974e, 138) Still, this tactic has its dangers. Kristeva warns that it must be practiced with care, or politics of liberation become mere politics of exclusion and counter-power. Political interpretations that claim group identities can lead to "dogmatism," "violence," and the annihilation of personal differences. (1984b, 27)

Strangers to Ourselves is about how we can live with difference. As early as "Women's Time," however, Kristeva had set out the premise of her theory. There, in the context of analyzing feminism, she argues that we must address difference within personal identity itself. She suggests that this is the central step toward a "demassification of the problematic of *difference*," which can acknowledge difference without attempting to totalize it, annihilate it, or reconcile it. In this way, the violence directed toward the other can be disintegrated "in its very nucleus." (1979a, 52) The subject can understand the other, sympathize with the other, and more, take the place of the other, because the subject *is* other. (1989, 25) As Kristeva is quick to point out, this does not mean that subject and other share their strangeness, their otherness. (1989, 38) They are not the *same* in this strangeness. Rather, the subject can relate to an other as other because she is an other to herself.

Just as Kristeva brought the speaking body back into language by putting language into the body, she brings the subject into the place of the other by putting the other into the subject. For Kristeva, just as the pattern and logic of language are already found within the body, the pattern and logic of alterity are already found within the subject. And this is why the subject is never a stable identity, but always a subject-in-process/on trial. Kristeva's strategy is to make the social relation interior to the psyche:

> This process could be summarized as an *interiorization of the founding separation of the sociosymbolic contract,* as an introduction of its cutting edge into the very interior of every identity whether subjective, sexual, ideological, or so forth. This in such a way that the habitual and increasingly explicit attempt to fabricate a scapegoat victim as foundress of a society or a countersociety may be replaced by the analysis of the potentialities of *victim/executioner* which characterize each identity, each subject, each sex. (1979a, 52)

This paragraph from "Women's Time" becomes the central argument of *Strangers to Ourselves.* Kristeva argues that what we exclude as a society or a nation—in order to be a society or a nation—is interior to our very identity. It is our own Unconscious that is projected onto those whom we exclude from our society/nation. (1989, 271) In this way we protect our own proper and stable identity both as individual subjects and as nation-states; when we flee or combat strangers or foreigners, we are struggling with our own Unconscious. (1989, 283) The stranger or foreigner is within us.

As Kristeva has argued throughout her writings, identity is formed on the basis of exclusion. For example, in *Revolution in Poetic Language*, she discusses the exclusions necessary for subjects to enter language. In *Powers of Horror*, she discusses the exclusions necessary for religious and moral codes to bond societies. In *Tales of Love*, she discusses the exclusions necessary for narcissistic identity. In *Black Sun*, she discusses the exclusions necessary for subjects' "at-homeness" in language. Finally, in *Strangers to Ourselves* and *Lettre Ouvertre à Harlem Désir* she discusses the exclusions necessary for nation-states to exist.

In *Strangers to Ourselves* Kristeva suggests that the exclusions that are necessary in order for the nation-state to exist can be analyzed as analogues to the exclusions that are necessary for narcissistic identity. Like psychic identity, group identity forms itself by excluding the other. (1989, 61) In the case of psychic identity, it is necessary for individuals to distinguish themselves from others through this type of exclusion in order to communicate. (1989, 61–62) Just as the individual must learn to deal with the return of the repressed or excluded other, so too the nation-state and its citizens must learn to deal with those elements that are excluded and foreign. Kristeva maintains that this problem is condensed in the person of the stranger or foreigner, the main character of her *Strangers to Ourselves*:

> . . . the problem of strangers operates according to a classical logic, that of the political group and its apex, the Nation-state. This logic which, susceptible to perfection (democracies) or of degeneration (totalitarianism), recognizes that it rests on certain exclusions and which, in consequence, encircles other formations—moral and religions, including absolutist aspirations—in order to affront precisely that which it has separated, under the circumstances of the problem of strangers and their most egalitarian regulation. (1989, 143)

The problem, then, is how we are to confront that which we have excluded in order to be, whether it is the return of the repressed or the return of strangers. For Kristeva, fundamentally, the problem is how we are to confront alterity. She suggests that in order to understand how and why we confront strangers in the ways we do, we must understand the stranger within "ourselves."[2] That is to say, in order to understand our social relations with others, we must understand our relation to the other within ourselves. Kristeva believes that this analysis can help us to find a way to "live with others, to live *otherness*, without ostracism but also without levelling" difference. (1989, 10) It is a question of cohabitation, says Kristeva, not of absorption. (1989, 11) Just as we must learn to live with the other within us, so too must we learn to live with the others around us.

In a world that is moving toward a global economy and global politics, this is necessary in order to live well, perhaps at all. As the identities of nation-states begin to break down, personal and group identity is thrown into crisis. This can be seen in Eastern Europe, where the drastic changes in national identities have given rise to various sorts of ethnic unrest. Without a stable national identity, among other factors, groups and individuals define themselves in terms of violent exclusion of others. Kristeva argues that the fact that there are strangers/foreigners is a symptom of our difficulty living as others with others. (1989, 150–51) In our world it seems completely normal that there are strangers/foreigners. Kristeva tries to make this normalcy appear strange.

She asks, if foreigners can get the rights of citizenship, then why can't they get the right to vote? What is it that makes nationality? Is it automatically acquired or chosen? Kristeva analyzes nationality, dividing it into citizens by soil and by blood. She analyzes the relationship between the rights of the citizen and the "rights of man [sic]." She points out that the stranger is a scar between citizen and "man." (1989, 142) Is the stranger a citizen or a "man"? Kristeva argues that states separate off the rights of noncitizens in order to define themselves as states. Yet, who are these noncitizens? Are they not "other men"? Kristeva argues that without the rights of citizens they never fully have the rights of "man." She points to a paradox in the very notion of the stranger/foreigner. She argues that the stranger/foreigner is defined through the legislation of a government. Yet it is through that very legislation that strangers/foreigners exist. In other words, legislation defines stranger/foreigners into existence. Legislation creates foreigners and the very concept of "foreign." (1989, 141) Therefore, states find foreigners only because they have created them. Kristeva tries to make all of these categories—citizen, man, foreigner—which seem natural in our contemporary political world seem strange.

By making the notion of stranger/foreigner strange to us Kristeva attempts to dislodge any notion of the identity of the stranger. Her analysis provokes a transference in the reader to the place of the stranger. Through the concept of the stranger Kristeva *makes us* strangers to ourselves. She demonstrates how what seems to be a normal, meaningful distinction between native/foreigner and citizen/noncitizen is not only a symptom of the inability to adjust to social relations but also a paradox. Through her analysis of Western political philosophy, Kristeva opens up the possibility of considering the unconscious dynamics at work in our own traditions.

She conjures the uncanny even while she analyzes it and can make a Western reader experience her own tradition as other, as the other within. Always the analyst, Kristeva creates fantasies to help bridge the space between pain, frustration, violence, and anger and conscious rational thought.

Kristeva suggests that psychoanalysis can provide a new way of identifying the other, the stranger, not in order to reify and exclude it/her, but in order to welcome it/her. This was Freud's project. (1989, 284) Freud tried to show that alterity is within us and created psychoanalysis as an invitation to live with it. Kristeva maintains that psychoanalysis sets up an ethics that respects the irreconcilable. (1989, 269) Psychoanalysis accepts, even invites, difference, nonmeaning, otherness. Kristeva argues that, in turn, this ethics of psychoanalysis implies a politics.

After over a decade of denouncing politics, in the conclusion of *Strangers to Ourselves*, Kristeva provides the foundation for a politics that she argues grows out of psychoanalysis:

> The ethic of psychoanalysis implies a politic: it would be a question of a cosmopolitanism of a new type which, transversal to governments, to economies and to markets, works for a humanity whose solidarity is founded on the consciousness of its unconscious—desiring, destructive, fearful, void, impossible. (1989, 284)

Psychoanalysis calls on us to work toward this humanity whose solidarity is founded on a consciousness of its unconscious. (1989, 284) Kristeva instructs us to recognize the difference in us as the condition of our being with others. (1989, 285) For the first time in history, says Kristeva, in the absence of any community bond other than economic, without either a community embracing our particularities or the power to transcend them, we must live with differences in moral codes. She imagines a "paradoxical community" that is "made of strangers who accept themselves insofar as they recognize themselves as strangers to themselves." She concludes that "[t]he multinational society will be thus the result of an extreme individualism, but conscious of its sicknesses and its limits, only aware of irreducibility given to help one another in their weakness, a weakness in which the other name is our radical strangeness." (1989, 290)

Feminism

Kristeva's notion of a politics of difference has given rise to her many criticisms of feminist movements. Although she continues to maintain a concern for the feminist movement and argues that it has been important in securing rights for women, she claims that her break with feminism, and politics in general, occurred after her trip to China in 1974. (1984c, 275) In spite of her "farewell" to feminism, Kristeva occasionally praises the feminist movement.[3] In a 1977 interview she says, "I am quite dedicated to the feminist movement but I think feminism, or any other movement, need not expect unconditional backing on the part of an intellectual woman."[4] (1977d, 106) In addition, she says that feminism has sufficient strength to endure self-criticism. And most of her remarks about feminism are cutting criticisms. Evidently feminisms/feminists are not strong enough to endure criticism by name, however, since Kristeva never specifically names the theorists or activists responsible for the feminisms that she criticizes. (1984b, 27)

In "My Memory's Hyperbole" Kristeva attributes her break from feminism to her disillusion with the Cultural Revolution in China. Like her colleagues in *Tel Quel*, Kristeva was hopeful that Maoism would provide a true socialist alternative to Soviet communism or capitalism. She says that during her visit to China she felt the "profound, unflagging, sly presence of the Soviet model." (1984c, 275) This trip turned her away from politics, which seemed hopeless, and toward psychoanalysis. In this autobiographical essay, however, the paragraph immediately following her statement that her trip to China marked her "farewell to politics, including feminism," suggests that her move away from feminism involved personal circumstances, about which we can only fantasize:

> The eruptions, encounters, loves, passions, as well as the more or less liberated or controlled eroticism that have shaped each person's biography constitute, I am convinced, the deepest influences on an individual path. In this essay, I simply present the visible surface effects. Only a diary, a novel, could perhaps one day restore the wild indecency of it. (1984c, 275)

Out of fear of, or respect for, this "wild indecency," I will not speculate on what encounters lurked behind Kristeva's break with feminism as she traveled through China with Philippe Sollers, Roland Barthes, Marcelin Playnet, and François Wahl. Perhaps Kristeva's recent novels, *Les Samourais* and *Le vieil homme et les loups* will "restore the wild indecency of it."

Kristeva argues that some feminisms, like politics in general, have become a type of religion. (1979a, 50; 1977b, 298) Specifically, she rejects feminisms that rally around the ideal of "woman" or the "feminine." (1980a, 58; 1980b, 134) She criticizes feminist movements that maintain some fixed notion of a feminine essence or "woman" because they cover over differences between individual women. (1977a, 36) She goes so far as to suggest that "scorn for femininity" might be the solution. (1976, 157) Kristeva argues that there is no such thing as "woman," except as we use her to fight for abortion rights and the pill. (1974c, 16) She concludes that feminism should not fight for "woman" but against "woman"; feminism must always be negative in that it denies any and every concept of "woman." (1974e, 137, 166)

Kristeva criticizes feminisms that tend to classify by groups ("woman," "heterosexual," "homosexual") because it is impossible to speak of all women, or all heterosexuals, or all homosexuals. (1984b, 23–24; 1980b, 135) Groups are made up of individuals with important differences and to identify people according to these types of classifications is to deny these differences. For Kristeva this is the danger of what she calls "herd" feminism, which hews too close to its ideal of identity. (1980b, 135) She maintains that feminism must renounce this religious belief in its own identity in order to analyze its own relationship to its power. (1977e, 141) Even "our" identity as women must be called into question. Every individual, says Kristeva, has his or her own unique sexuality. (1984b, 24) And the women's movements should demand attention to these individual differences. (1980b, 133) In spite of the fact that, as Kristeva admits, at first the "we women" of feminism got things done, now this "we" has become problematic insofar as it covers over individual differences in the same way that the universal concept "man" has done. (1980b, 135)

This is the same problematic that Kristeva addresses in *Strangers to Ourselves*. There she argues that the "we" is a mirage but at the same time a condition for all community. (1989, 37) She points out, however, that even while each individual participates in this "we," as its source, each individual is also its victim. This has become the fate of contemporary feminism. Individual women have become the victims of feminisms' totalizing "we." Therefore, Kristeva endorses only those aspects of the feminist movement that have served to break down identity and render it ambiguous. (1984b, 23) Jacqueline Rose coins a possible slogan for Kristeva's feminism: "No politics without identity, but no identity which takes itself at its word." (1986, 157)

In fact, Rose sees Kristeva's project as one that is central to feminism: "how to challenge the very form of available self-definition without losing the possibility of speech." (1986, 158) Like many Anglo-American feminists, Kristeva is struggling with this double-bind, which brings into focus problems of identity and difference that revolve around language and representation. How can we use language in order to change notions of identity and difference when it is language or representation through which stereotypical notions of identity and difference are perpetuated? Rose sees a crucial insight into this double-bind in Kristeva's writing. She suggests that Kristeva understands "that identity is necessary but only ever partial and therefore carries with it a dual risk—the wreck of all identity, a self-binding allegiance to psychic norms." (1986, 150)

Kristeva's work is always trying to steer between these two extremes, anarchy on the one hand and totalitarianism on the other. Rose points out that "Kristeva herself has said over and again that her own aim is to avoid both of these alternatives: no absolutism of the 'thetic' which then gets erected as a theological law, but no denial of the 'thetic' which brings with it the fantasy of 'an irrationalism in pieces.'" (1986, 149) Kristeva's attention to the borders, however, makes for a tension in her work, a tension manifest in contemporary feminism itself: How can we talk about identity and difference without either resorting to absolutes or giving up identity altogether?

Unapologetically Rose claims that "I do not think we should be surprised, therefore, nor too comfortably critical or dismissive, when Kristeva proceeds to fall, at various points throughout her work, into one or other side of the psychic dynamic which she herself describes." (1986, 151) Rose concludes:

> Kristeva's work splits on a paradox, or rather a dilemma: the hideous moment when a theory arms itself with a concept of femininity as different, as something other to the culture as it is known, only to find itself face to face with, or even entrenched within, the most grotesque and fully cultural stereotypes of femininity itself. Unlike some of her most virulent detractors, however, Kristeva at least knows that these images are not so easily dispatched. (1986, 157)

While I agree with Rose that there are places in her texts where Kristeva does fall into one extreme or the other, overall she carefully analyzes tensions and crises without glossing over their rough spots and turning them into domesticated catchphrases. She realizes that the double-bind of identity—what Rose calls the paradox or dilemma—is a bomb that must be very carefully, very slowly dismantled. While some feminist utopian visions and manifestos can and have been useful for feminism, there is also a need for theory that faces up to the problems and tensions in feminism head on. Some of Kristeva's critics attribute the problems that she analyzes in theories of difference to her theory itself. In a sense, they blame the messenger for the message. They attribute the problems that Kristeva identifies with "woman" and "feminine" to Kristeva herself.

Most of the feminist criticism of Kristeva's work has centered on the relationship between "woman" and "feminine" as they function in her writings. Depending on how they read these terms, and the relationships between them, feminist critics tend to come down on different sides of whether or not Kristeva's theories are valuable for feminist theory. For example, Elizabeth Grosz maintains that Kristeva's:

> ... critical attitude to feminist texts is, I suggest, a function of the slippage she effects from the concept of woman to that of the feminine, a displacement of the question of identity by *differentiation*. By means of this manoeuvre, she is able, on the one hand, to evacuate women of any privileged access to femininity, and on the other, to position men, the avant-garde, in the best position to represent, to name or speak the feminine. (1989, 95)

The result, claims Grosz, is that Kristeva denies sexual difference by denying women any specific sexual identity. Grosz complains that Kristeva refuses to see "the *sexed body* as the site of the inscriptions of masculine and feminine attributes." (1989, 96)

While there is legitimate textual ground for interpreting a slippage in Kristeva's texts, I think that this slippage can be productively read as Kristeva's struggle against representing sexed bodies as only two types of bodies and of attributing certain characteristics to particular body types. Unlike Freud or Lacan, Kristeva prefers to discuss difference in general rather than sexual difference in particular. I think that she avoids sexual difference because she does not want to perpetuate traditional accounts of binary sexes by focusing on the limiting way in which sexual difference operates in Western culture. She does not, however, avoid a discussion of sexual difference altogether. She locates the beginnings of sexual difference in the child's relation to its mother.

Here Kristeva's theory might seem vaguely reminiscent of the theories of American psychologists Carol Gilligan and Nancy Chodorow, who also attribute what they call "gender identity" to the child's relationship to the mother. There is an important difference, however, between the American notion of gender identity and the French notion of sexual difference. Sexual difference is the fundamental difference between the sexes. It determines how we "read" different bodies. The psychoanalytic account of sexual difference is concerned with what American feminists refer to as the sex behind the gender. Whereas traditionally American feminists have seen sex as a biological fact and gender as its cultural representation, Kristeva sees sexual difference as socially constructed in a very deep sense. This is because, for Kristeva, there is always only a representation of a body; there is no body in-itself. The body is always already implicated in signification. Through the dialectical oscillation between symbolic and semiotic elements, the body is always and at the same time operating within the Symbolic even while it troubles and exceeds it. Therefore there is no separation between the sexed body and the way in which it is perceived or represented. If Kristeva was asked to define her terms in the American context, I think that she would agree with Judith Butler that sex is always already gendered.

Kristeva's concern with difference in general underlines her concern to multiply representations of various sexed bodies that do not limit us to just masculine or feminine or male or female. In this endeavor to multiply representations of various sexed bodies, Kristeva has an ally in Judith Butler. Judith Butler's monumental *Gender Trouble* (1990) forces feminists' hands on the sex/gender distinction. Butler argues that sex is always already gendered. For Butler, like Kristeva, there is no natural sexed body. There are not two types of sexed bodies. Butler, like Kristeva, is concerned to multiply sexualities and sexed bodies. And Butler, like Kristeva, argues that feminism can and should operate without fixed identities of woman, feminine, or even female. Following Foucault, Butler suggests that this kind of specificity is part of a repressive structure that works to exclude and limit rather than include and multiply. Like Butler, Kristeva is concerned with feminism's use of identity politics.

In "Women's Time" Kristeva identifies two generations of feminism, both of which she accuses of using "woman" as a religious ideal. The first (pre-'68) feminism is the feminism of suffragettes and existentialists. It is a struggle over the identity of woman as rational citizen, deserving of the "rights of man." The ideal "woman" contains the same characteristics of the ideal "man" and the struggle is to insert her in man's linear history. The second (post-'68) feminism is the feminism of psychoanalysts and artists. It is a struggle against reducing the identity of woman to the identity of man by inserting her into his linear time. These feminists assert a unique essence of woman or the feminine that falls outside of phallic time and phallic discourse. Kristeva argues that this strategy not only makes feminism into a religion but also traps women in an inferior and marginal position with regard to society:

> Certain feminists, in France, particularly, say that whatever is in language is of the order of strict designation, of understanding, of logic, and is male. Ultimately, theory, science, is phallic, is male. On the other hand, that which in language, according to the same feminists, is feminine, is whatever has to do with the imprecise, with the whisper, with impulses, perhaps with primary processes. . . . I think that this is, so to speak, a Manichean position which consists in designating as feminine a phase or a modality in the functioning of language. And if one assigns to women that phase alone, this in fact amounts to maintaining women in a position of inferiority, and in any case of marginality, to reserving them the place of the childish, of the unsayable, or of the hysteric. (1980b, 134)

To some, Kristeva's description of these "certain feminists" may sound like a description of her own theory. As her writing evolves, however, Kristeva has been careful to separate the maternal element in language from either the feminine or women. She argues that language is heterogeneous. It is composed of both maternal semiotic elements and paternal symbolic elements. But this has nothing to do with men and women. Both men and women use language. The semiotic elements are not inherently the reserve of women while the symbolic elements are the reserve of men. On the contrary, Kristeva argues that men risk less by playing with the semiotic elements in language. This is because of their relationship to the maternal function in Western culture. If men and women have a different relation to language, for Kristeva, this is because of the *representations* of the maternal (and paternal) functions in the West.

Kristeva argues that women are first of all speaking beings. (1980b, 145)

And the Symbolic order is the domain of speaking beings. She thinks that
rather than try to do away with the Symbolic order, women should place
themselves within it. But she makes it clear that this is not to say "all
women should master the dominant discourse." Kristeva argues that "we
must no longer speak of 'all women.'" Each one of us, says Kristeva,
should find her own language. (1980b, 135) This language will be part of
the Symbolic order. Women cannot merely jump outside of the Symbolic
order; nor should they want to. This is why Kristeva criticizes feminists
who argue that the Symbolic is essentially patriarchal and must be abandoned. Kristeva insists that without the Symbolic dimension, there would
be no human life, there could be no love. And she wants nothing to do
with feminists who would do away with love:

> ... what I call love is openness to the other, and it is what gives me my
> human dimension, my symbolic dimension, my cultural and historical di-
> mension. So if one says that it's patriarchy which produces that, long live
> patriarchy. ... I would look with horror on a humanity which would de-
> capitate or wipe out this symbolic moment. If that's what some feminists
> propose, I don't want any of it. (1980b, 144)

Rushing after Phallic Power

In addition to calling feminism a religion, Kristeva calls feminism a
power-seeking ideology. (1980a, 208) She rejects feminisms that merely
want to take over "phallic power." (1983, 61, 227, 232) She claims that
these feminists are "Electras, militants in the cause of the father."[5] (1974c,
152) For Kristeva, the question for feminists is how to avoid the centraliza-
tion of power and not how to take over that power. She argues that feminist
separatists, for example, want to set up a countersociety that is based on
the same logic of exclusion of the society that they oppose:

> As with any society, the countersociety is based on the expulsion of an
> excluded element, a scapegoat charged with the evil of which the commu-
> nity duly constituted can then purge itself; a purge which will finally exon-
> erate that community of any future criticism. Modern protest movements
> have often reiterated this logic, locating the guilty one—in order to fend off
> criticism—in the foreign, in capital alone, in the other religion, in the other
> sex. Does not feminism become a kind of inverted sexism when this logic
> is followed to its conclusion? (1977a, 45)

Kristeva argues that it is not the case that these utopian societies start
out with a more "libertarian" logic and then, over time, become corrupted
by patriarchal society. Rather, she insists that "the very logic of coun-
terpower and of countersociety necessarily generates, by its very structure,
its essence as a simulacrum of the combated society or power." (1977a,

46) She concludes that this type of feminism mistakes its own "sulking isolation" for political protest. (1977b, 298)

Another of Kristeva's complaints about certain feminisms is their view of motherhood. In fact, in the passage from the 1977 interview that I quoted earlier in which Kristeva argued, somewhat defensively, that an "intellectual" woman could not accept feminism unconditionally, she went on to explain that she could not accept the way that existential feminism made women feel guilty for wanting to have children. (1977e, 106) By this time, Kristeva herself had given birth. She claims that one reason why feminist movements fail is that they do not take up the question of maternity and its impact on women. (1984d, 20) She argues that "real female innovation (in whatever field) will only come about when maternity, female creation and the link between them are better understood." (1977b, 298)

In "Stabat Mater" Kristeva chastises feminists for circumventing the *real experience* of motherhood by accepting the Western myth that motherhood is identical with femininity. Therefore, in order to discard the myth of the feminine, they believe that they also have to discard motherhood. Rather than discard motherhood, Kristeva suggests that what we need is a secular discourse of motherhood in order to replace a religious myth in crisis, the myth of the Virgin Mary.[6] She begins to develop such a discourse at the end of "Stabat Mater" with her description of "herethics." As I have analyzed earlier, she believes that an analysis of motherhood and the mother/child relationship can provide the foundation for a new ethics and a new conception of difference and alterity. Kristeva maintains that this should be the central focus of feminism. Feminism, like all contemporary politics, should be concerned with difference. The question that feminists should be asking is: How can we live with others without either leveling their difference or ostracism? In Kristeva's view, however, the feminist movement has been guilty of both leveling difference and ostracism.

But since Kristeva does not attribute the theories that she rejects to specific theorists, it is difficult to assess her claims. She often refers to "many feminists in France." She does specifically criticize existentialist feminism; here she must be thinking of Simone de Beauvoir's *The Second Sex*, which is the primary text of existentialist feminism. She does not, however, challenge Beauvoir directly.[7] Her complaint against feminists in France who essentialize the feminine as impulses and her disparaging reference to feminine writing might be obliquely aimed at Luce Irigary or Hélène Cixous. But, once again, Kristeva does not name names.

While Kristeva is aware of the tension between generalizing as a theorist and treating individuals in their individuality in other contexts, this tension remains unconscious when she is talking about feminism.[8] For example, she maintains that she uses the split columns in "Stabat Mater" in order to call into question the theorist's objectivity and ability to universalize from her observations. She claims that she wants to point to the theorist's involvement with her subject. (1984b, 24) By extension this concern should apply to Kristeva's treatment of feminism, but it does not seem to. It seems strange that with her emphasis on not leveling individual particularities and focusing on individual women, she attacks feminism and feminists as a group, never treating them in their individuality. Not only does this seem to fly in the face of her theory, but also it seems a gross injustice to feminisms, whose particularities and varieties are multiplying along with the particularities and varieties of women and men who work on them. Since there is a plurality of feminisms and feminist theories, especially in France, perhaps Kristeva's criticisms can be seen as a warning to feminists, but cannot ground a rejection of feminism.[9] Moreover, some feminists in France, and elsewhere, are taking up the question of difference and alterity as one of their central research concerns.[10] But Kristeva never mentions or credits other "feminists" working on the problems of difference and alterity. If her writings are informed by some of this other work, she doesn't acknowledge it.

Perhaps she has gotten caught up in phallic competition. Or, alternatively, in terms of her own theory, her inability to name feminists and her difficulty naming women could be read as her inability to work through her mourning for the maternal "Thing." In *Black Sun* she argues that a person must lose her mother, the maternal "Thing" (and sublimate the loss), in order to be able to name her. Melancholics haven't sublimated the loss. Therefore they are still mourning the loss of the mother and cannot name her. Perhaps Kristeva's inability to name feminists is another symptom of the melancholy theoretician.[11]

Oppression as Misplaced Abjection

The most interesting and original aspect of Kristeva's thoughts on feminism is her account of women's oppression. In only a very few passages, Kristeva analyzes one of the causes of women's oppression. She argues that without a secular discourse or myth of motherhood that absorbs abjection, abjection is misplaced onto women. She claims that the mother is not a woman. That is to say, she is "alone of her sex." Everyone has a mother—dead or alive, unknown or known—to reckon with qua mother. Mothers are women apart from being mothers; and not all women are mothers. Therefore, mothers and women are not identical. But without a way of conceiving the mother that allows us to abject her and come to terms with that abjection, we abject all women:

> The image of the Virgin—the woman whose entire body is an emptiness through which the paternal word is conveyed—had remarkably subsumed the maternal "abject," which is so necessarily intrapsychic. Lacking that

safety lock, feminine abjection imposed itself upon social representation, *causing an actual denigration of women;* this in turn gave rise to increased antifeminism but even more so to a strong reaction on the part of women who were unwilling to bear, in narcissistic fashion, the representation of their own rejection of the maternal, which no available secular code could now guarantee. (1983, 374; my emphasis)

Kristeva argues that the crisis in the religious representation of maternity, the Virgin, leads to misplaced abjection and the denigration of women and increased antifeminism. In addition, she claims that it leads women to reject maternity for themselves because they identify so strongly with their own rejection of maternity. That is to say that without a myth/discourse of the maternal that can absorb abjection, they abject maternity. And pregnancy would turn them into this abject that they reject.

Although Kristeva's analysis is interesting, it is problematic for feminists. Regardless of its causes, women must reckon with all sorts of legislation and institutional structures that attempt to mandate maternity. As a result, some feminists have made a political decision to reject what appears as forced maternity in spite of the psychological causes of that institutional mandate. As usual, Kristeva demands that we fight the cause and not just the symptoms. Many women, however, may prefer to fight the symptoms than to give up the fight.

Another problem with Kristeva's suggestion is that she attributes the denigration of women to the crisis in the myth of the Virgin. Even at the apex of the myth's popularity, however, women were oppressed and expected to have children. In fact, the Catholic church has never been a champion of women. How can Kristeva's analysis explain women's oppression before the nineteenth century? In spite of this problem, I think that Kristeva's theory is useful for feminist consideration. It is not necessary to link a misdirected abjection to the crisis in the myth of the Virgin. After all, Kristeva does not endorse the myth of the Virgin. She merely points out that it is the only discourse of motherhood that is available to us; and that this discourse is inadequate.

What Kristeva is suggesting is that everyone must separate from their mother by abjecting her. If we don't have some imaginary construct that enables us to both separate from her and separate the maternal function from her, then we misplace abjection. Rather than perceive the "maternal container" as a horrible threat to our autonomy, we perceive women as a threat.[12] It is necessary that we feel continued dependence on the "maternal container" as a threat to our autonomy. Without the imaginary wherewithal in order to turn the threat into a representation of mother as Other, we turn women into the Other. Here it is important to reconsider the difference between mother and woman.

Kristeva's analysis in "Stabat Mater" in particular suggests that maternity provides an example of radical alterity within identity. What a representation of maternity provides, which a representation of woman does not, is alterity within identity. The mother provides a case of the other *as* the self and the other *in* the self. As such, only she can provide the necessary sense of separation within union that founds ethics. In other words, the child must separate from the mother, but the mother proves that the other is within. And just as the mother contains the child, the child contains the mother. (Certainly, biologically, the mother is in the child.) A representation of the mother as a subject-in-process, as an open subjectivity that contains alterity, sets up a model of autonomy that still allows for connection, identity, ethics, and love.[13] The woman as radical other, completely exterior to the self, does not. She is not reachable, lovable, or even identifiable, let alone "identical."

Separated from the mother, the child never forgets that it was once part of the mother's body. Without a discourse or myth that allows this primary and unique identity within a firmly established autonomy, the child feels its connection to the maternal body as a threat. Recall from my earlier analysis that this is especially true for men. Not only is a man's personal identity challenged by his past identity with his mother, but also his sexual identity is challenged. How can he be a man if he was once part of a woman? On the other hand, Kristeva argues that it is easier for men to abject their mothers because their sexual identity is not threatened by this denigration and separation. Women, however, abject themselves when they abject their mothers. (1980b, 138)

I find useful Kristeva's suggestion that women's oppression is caused, in part, by the representation of woman as mother. Her argument is different from other feminist positions that have considered women's oppression linked to reproduction or compulsory maternity for women. Kristeva maintains that it is not maternity or reproduction that are responsible for women's oppression but the representations of them. She suggests that we need to be able to consider the *maternal function* apart from women and individual mothers. If we can abject the maternal body as part of the maternal function and work through that abjection without abjecting the mother as a woman, then not only does the representation of woman change but also the representation of motherhood. Kristeva believes that the representations of woman and motherhood can be changed through the power of texts. Her analysis of philosophical, religious, and literary texts suggests that these texts have been historically situated social forces engaged in the production of representations, representations through which we live.

VII

IMPORTING "THE FRENCH FEMINISTS" AND THEIR DESIRES

> *. . . search for the woman-non-mother,*
> *the only radical other, the sister*[1]

Importing "The French Feminists"

More of the writings of Julia Kristeva have been translated into English than any of the other so-called "French Feminists." Hers has become an important voice in literary theory and criticism, cultural criticism, and psychoanalytic theory. Along with the work of the two other "French Feminists," who make up what Toril Moi calls the "new holy Trinity of French feminist theory," Hélène Cixous and Luce Irigaray, Kristeva's writings have influenced many American feminists—in the United States when we think of French feminists we think of Cixous, Irigaray, and Kristeva. Since I started this project on Kristeva, feminists have continually asked me to articulate the differences between Cixous, Irigaray, and Kristeva. And theorists continually group the three of them together in discussions of any one of them. And while I do not want to perpetuate this conglomerate of the "holy Trinity of French feminism," still there needs to be some analysis of the relationships between the work of these theorists who have too frequently been lumped together, usually in order to be dismissed.

Some American feminists avoid the French feminists, or read only secondary reports of their writing, because they claim that their writing is elitist and/or politically bankrupt. Much of the aversion to French feminism on the American scene, however, is due to a certain importation of Kristeva, Irigaray, and Cixous. And labeling Kristeva, Irigaray, and Cixous "The French Feminists" is an essential element of the problem with their importation.

What seems especially odd about calling Kristeva, Irigaray, and Cixous "The French Feminists" is that none of them were born in France and

none of them claim any kind of unqualified relation to feminism. Irigaray
was born in Belgium and her name is Basque. Kristeva was born and
raised in Bulgaria. Her mother-tongue is Bulgarian. She came to France
to study and stayed as an exile from Bulgarian-Soviet communism. "To
put it bluntly," says Kristeva, "I speak in French and about literature because of Yalta." (1974b, 161) Like Kristeva and Irigaray, Cixous has a problematic relationship to the French language. Cixous was born and raised
in French-occupied Algeria. Her mother-tongue is German.[2] As an Alge-
rian Jew she was an exile in her own country:

> . . . had this strange "luck": a couple rolls of the dice, a meeting of two
> trajectories of the diaspora, and, at the end of these routes of expulsion
> and dispersion that mark the functioning of Western history through the
> displacements of Jews, I fall. . . . Today I know from experience that one
> cannot imagine what an Algerian French girl was; you have to have been
> it, to have gone through it. To have seen "Frenchmen" at the "height" of
> imperialist blindness, behaving in a country that was inhabited by humans
> as if it were peopled by nonbeings, born-slaves. I learned everything from
> this first spectacle: I saw how the white (French), superior, plutocratic,
> civilized world founded its power on the repression of populations who
> had suddenly become "invisible," like proletarians, immigrant workers,
> minorities who are not the right "color." (1985, 70)

Even more problematic than the "French" in "The French Feminists"
is the "feminist." When American theorists and practitioners talk about
feminism they refer to a multifaceted conglomerate of different views and
strategies that cannot be easily reduced to a single element. When French
theorists and practitioners talk about feminism, however, they are referring to a specific political movement in France. So when "The French
Feminists" refuse to be identified as feminists this does not mean that
they would not identify with some of the goals and strategies of feminism
in the American context. What they are rejecting is a specific movement
in France that many of them think engages in, and merely replicates,
oppressive bourgeois logics and strategies for gaining power. "Feminism"
does not refer to the same thing on both sides of the Atlantic.[3] And recognizing this is crucial for learning anything from "The French Feminists."
Luce Irigaray says "I don't particularly care for the term *feminism*. It is
the word by which the social system designates the struggle of women. I
am completely willing to abandon this word, namely because it is formed
on the same model as the other great words of the culture that oppress
us." (1980a, 150; 1985a, 166) While she does maintain that in some situa-
tions, it may be necessary to reclaim "feminism" from the dominant culture, Irigaray prefers to discuss the struggles of women or even women's
liberation movements. She does not use "feminism" in her texts. Cixous
has been less diplomatic in her relation to feminism. She says "I am not

a feminist." (1977, 482) She claims that feminism is threatened by the direction that it has headed in France (and elsewhere): "I would not want anything to do with a feminism which lost sight of the dialectic articulation with other struggles, and that seems to me to be happening even with students, even with the women who write, who paint." (1967d, 33) And Kristeva wants nothing to do with feminism or "woman." She argues that, among other things, feminism has become a religion and a power-seeking ideology. (1977e, 141; 1980a, 208) She says that feminists—"Electras, militants in the cause of the father"—merely want to take over "phallic power." (1974c, 154; 1983, 61, 227, 232) And she maintains that we no longer need "woman." (1984b, 23; 1977a, 36)

So, how did this Belgian, this Bulgarian, and this Algerian-born woman, all of whom keep their distance from feminism, become "The French Feminists"? In 1972 Cixous's doctoral thesis, *L'Exile de James Joyce ou l'art du remplacement*, was published in English translation. In the same year articles by Kristeva began to appear in translation in journals such as *Semiotext(e)* and *Screen*. Throughout the '70s articles by Kristeva appeared in translation in *Diacritics*, *Semiotext(e)*, *Sub-Stance*, *Wide Angle*, and *Signs*. American scholars working in French and comparative literature departments knew her from her involvement with the influential French journal *Tel Quel*. Mary Ann Caws's 1973 article "Tel Quel: Text and Revolution" included a review of Kristeva's *Semiotiké Recherches Pour une Sémanalyse* (1969) and was the beginning of an ongoing series of articles in *Diacritics* on Kristeva's work.[4] *Diacritics* also published a translated excerpt from Cixous and Clément's *La Jeune Née* in 1977 along with a review by Verena Conley. In the same year Irigaray's "Women's Exile" appeared in *Ideology and Consciousness*. Also, in the last half of the '70s review articles on Irigaray's writing started to appear in *Diacritics*.

The work of Kristeva and Cixous reached an even wider audience with *Signs*'s publication of Kristeva's "On the Women of China" (1975) and Cixous's influential "The Laugh of the Medusa." (1976) In 1978 Kristeva, Cixous, and Irigaray were imported/reported together, along with other "French Feminists," in two important articles in *Signs*: Carolyn Burke's "Report from Paris" and Elaine Marks's "Women and Literature in France." The bulk of Burke's article is spent discussing the work of "three prominent French women, Julia Kristeva, Luce Irigaray, and Hélène Cixous." While Marks discusses an impressive list of women writing in France, she ends her article with comparisons of Irigaray, Cixous, and Kristeva.

The rising interest in French feminism in the United States was marked and fueled by Elaine Marks and Isabelle de Courtivron's 1980 anthology *New French Feminisms*. While Kristeva, Cixous, and Irigaray were important voices in this collection, they remained individual voices among

many others, including Simone de Beauvoir, Annie Leclerc, Claudine Her-
mann, Marguerite Duras, Antoinette Fouque, Catherine Clément, Xavière
Gauthier, Chantal Chawaf, Christiane Rochefort, and Monique Wittig. At
the turn of the decade, however, the "holy Trinity" began to emerge in the
United States. *The Future of Difference*, edited by Hester Eisenstein and
Alice Jardine, was also published in 1980. It included an entire section
entitled "Contemporary Feminist Thought in France: Translating Difference," in which portions of articles were devoted to one or more of the
future "holy Trinity of French feminist theory." In spite of the subtitle,
"Translating *Difference*," Domna Stanton's contribution, "Language and
Revolution: The Franco-American Dis-Connection" (appropriately titled),
more often than not condenses the different positions of Kristeva, Cixous,
and Irigaray into one. Overlooking their very different styles and projects,
Stanton equates them all with *"écriture féminine,"* a notion that Kristeva
explicitly rejects. (Kristeva 1974c, 1974e, 1979a, 1980b) And Cixous rejects the notion of a woman's writing, which is the way in which *écriture
féminine* was translated in the American context.[5] (Cixous 1984, 129)
Cixous's *"écriture féminine"* is translated by Keith and Paula Cohen as
"women's writing" in "The Laugh of the Medusa." The connotations, however, of women's writing and feminine writing are very different. The
feminine does not necessarily have to do with women's bodies; it is not
biologically determined. This translation problem could go some distance
to explain why American feminists were so quick to reject the notion of
écriture féminine as essentialist.

In 1981 the trio reappeared in several special journal issues devoted to
French feminism, *Yale French Studies*, *Signs*, and partial issues of *Feminist Studies*. The *Signs* special issue was extremely influential because of
its wider readership among American feminists and because it featured
translations of Kristeva's "Women's Time," Cixous's "Castration or Decapitation," and Irigaray's "And One Doesn't Stir Without the Other." The
only other French feminist featured in this volume was Christine Fauré
writing on women in history.

A pivotal text in the importation of "The French Feminists" to the
United States is Jane Gallop's *The Daughter's Seduction: Feminism and
Psychoanalysis*. (1982) Following her analysis of Juliet Mitchell's Freud
and her playful reading of Lacan, Gallop includes a chapter on Irigaray's
Freud, one on Irigaray's Lacan, another on French analyst Eugénie
Lemoine-Luccioni's Irigaray, one on Kristeva, and a final chapter on Cixous's Dora. As Gallop introduces them to her American audience, however, the daughters of psychoanalysis are Irigaray, Kristeva, and Cixous. In
1989 I heard Jane Gallop give a presentation at Miami University, where
she had been teaching when *The Daughter's Seduction* was published. In
response to a question from a member of the audience, Gallop became
defensive and responded that "*I* can name the French feminists—*Irigaray,*

Kristeva, and Cixous." And it is true that, in a sense, she *had named* the French feminists—Irigaray, Kristeva, and Cixous.

During the 1980s several articles appeared that linked Irigaray, Kristeva, and Cixous and/or referred to them as "The French Feminists." Most of the time this tactic was used in order to dismiss the theories of all three of them as "essentialist."[6] Ironically, the finishing touches of what Moi calls "the holy Trinity of French feminist theory" were probably added by Moi herself in *Sexual/Textual Politics: Feminist Literary Theory.* (1985) There, Moi devotes one section of her book to "The French Feminists." Moi defends her selection of Cixous, Irigaray, and Kristeva:

> In the following presentation of French feminist theory I have chosen to focus on the figures Hélène Cixous, Luce Irigaray and Julia Kristeva. They have been chosen partly because their work is the most representative of the main trends in French feminist theory, and partly because they are more closely concerned with the specific problems raised by women's relation to writing and language than many other feminist theorists in France. Thus I have decided not to discuss the work of women like Anne Leclerc, Michèle Montrelay, Eugénie Lemoine-Luccioni, Sarah Kofman and Marcelle Marini. (1985, 97)

And since Moi claims that "Irigaray's vision of femininity and of feminine language remains almost indistinguishable from Cixous's," why doesn't she limit herself to two French feminists in order to represent "the main trends in French feminist theory"? (1985, 143) Moi dismisses the Cixous/Irigaray trend in feminist theory as essentialist and ultimately apolitical. So for Moi, in spite of their good points, Cixous and Irigaray represent the bad feminism in France; and, in spite of her bad points, Kristeva represents the good feminism in France. Two years later, however, Moi is concerned to bring those theorists whom she had left out of the debate earlier back into it. In 1987 she edited a volume, *French Feminist Thought,* which only "sparingly" represents the work of Cixous, Irigaray, and Kristeva because "the French debate on sexual difference has many other participants." (1987, 5) Here, Moi capitalizes on her own earlier reinforcement of "The French Feminists" in order to argue that there is a need to open the debate with the Anglo-American context to more French participants.

Certainly the work of Kristeva, Irigaray, and Cixous is important to Anglo-American feminists. Their own ambiguous relationships to feminism, however, combined with the importance of other feminists writing in France whose work has been translated into English—most notably Simone de Beauvoir, Monique Witting, Marguerite Duras, Sarah Kofman, Catherine Clement, and others—makes it clear that "The French Feminists" is a product of a certain importation.

The Politics of Importation

At this point I will provide a hypothesis about the *politics* of the importation of "The French Feminists" *en masse*. French criticism was imported at about the same time that American feminist criticism was taking the most heat for ignoring differences among women. Specifically, American feminist theory and practice was called upon to account for its racism. At the same time that French feminist theory was being imported to the United States, black feminists, and other women of color, were criticizing the women's movement for excluding them. Along with other articles in the 1970s criticizing the women's movement for its racism, Rosalyn Terborg-Penn's "Discrimination against Afro-American Women in the Women's Movement" was published in 1978. And three important challenges to white feminist theory were published in 1981: bell hooks's *Ain't I a Woman* and Angela Davis's *Women, Race & Class* and *This Bridge Called My Back: Writings by Radical Women of Color*. All of these books include powerful criticisms of American feminists. The challenge from women of color continued in the early 1980s with the publication of *But Some of Us Are Brave* (1982) and *Home Girls: A Black Feminist Anthology* (1983).

bell hooks argues that white feminists use a logic of identity that can set itself up only on the back of another. hooks points out that

> . . . when the women's movement was at its peak and while women were rejecting the role of breeder, burden bearer, and sex object, black women were celebrated for their unique devotion to the task of mothering; for their "innate" ability to bear tremendous burdens; and for their ever-increasing availability as sex object. We appeared to have been unanimously elected to take up where white women were leaving off. (1981, 6)

hooks identifies the psychic defense of projecting onto an other those qualities that you reject in yourself. My hypothesis is that some American feminists projected the charges of essentialism that were coming from black feminists onto the French feminists. Overlooking their differences, and their theories of difference, some American feminists criticized the French feminists for their essentialism and elitism, the very charges that were being brought against American feminists themselves. In an essentializing move, some American feminists reduced the French feminists to one concept, feminine writing, and then projected all of the charges of excluding women onto their theories. Against the French feminists, American feminists could define themselves as nonessentializing, more inclusive, and more accessible to women. As Tina Chanter points out, the differences in philosophical traditions and training also contribute to American feminists' misreading of French feminists. (1991)

Breaking Up Is Hard to Do

Irigaray's Fling

Now I will take up where I find myself, negotiating the striking differences and similarities between the texts of Kristeva, Irigaray, and Cixous. The first striking difference between Irigaray, Cixous, and Kristeva is the difference between their writing styles and methods. In *This Sex Which Is Not One*—in answer to the question "What method have you adopted for this research?"—Irigaray claims that "the option left to me was to *have a fling with the philosophers*, which is easier said than done . . . for what path can one take to get back inside their ever so coherent systems?" (1985a, 150)

Irigaray maintains that woman appears in philosophy merely as its repressed Other. Within the history of Western philosophy, science, and literature, woman has served as man's Unconscious. So woman does not have an Unconscious because she *is* the Unconscious. (1985, 133–46) For Irigaray the task is to work from this position both inside and outside the system in order to deconstruct its hierarchy. (1980a, 159) She uses a "double-mimesis," both productive and reproductive, in order to engage the philosophers.[7] (1985a, 131, 150; 1985d, 82) And she uses her double-mimetic strategy in different ways in different texts in order to engage in inter(textual)course with different philosophers. In her attempts to displace the privilege given to masculine metaphors and structures in the writing of philosophers, Irigaray often literally reproduces a text, fragmenting it by adding her mimetic reflections of the text. She takes up the place of the Other that philosophy has assigned to woman/feminine and uses it in order to reflect a distorted and disruptive image of the Subject of philosophy.

For example, in *Speculum of the Other Woman*, Irigaray uses this strategy with both Plato and Freud. In two essays in *This Sex Which Is Not One*—"Cosi Fan Tutti" and "The Mechanics of Fluids"—she uses this strategy with Lacan. In *Amante Marine*, she has a fling with Nietzsche, writing her intro(sed)uction like a love letter. "The Fecundity of the Caress" is an intimate description of Irigaray's textual relationship with Levinas. And *L'Oubli de l'air* is her attempt to use her double-mimesis in order to deconstruct Heidegger's philosophy. It is interesting that in these texts, the proper names of these philosophers appear only buried in the text, if at all. Irigaray tries to reveal the ways in which philosophy has covered over the feminine/woman and at the same time open up a space for a different feminine sex.

In "Cossi Fan Tutti" Irigaray plays with Lacan's Seminar XX on femi-

nine sexuality by repeatedly quoting Lacan without invoking his name—
the Name of the Father. She takes Lacan's words and turns them against
his theory. She alternates between quoting Lacan's text and "reading"
Lacan's text. She reappropriates Lacan's text by repeating phrases from
them in her own reading of those texts. The effect of this procedure is
that Lacan's texts appear cut up into ridiculous pathetic little bits. For
example, here is a substantial selection of passages from "Cosi Fan Tutti"
(pieces of Lacan's Seminar XX are in italics):

> *The one who I presume has knowledge is the one I love. Women don't know*
> *what they are saying, that's the whole difference between them and me. . . .*
> The question whether, in his logic, they can articulate anything at all,
> whether they can be heard, is not even raised. . . . And to make sure this
> does not come up, the right to experience pleasure is awarded to a statue.
> *Just go look at Bernini's statue in Rome, you'll see right away that St.*
> *Theresa is coming, there's no doubt about it.*
> In Rome? So far away? To look? At a statue? Of a saint? Sculpted by a
> man? What pleasure are we talking about? Whose pleasure? . . . his? . . .
> *In other words, what we're saying is that love is impossible, and that the*
> *sexual relation is engulfed in non-sense. . . .* It is appropriate then to pro-
> ceed prudently—to bed. *We're simply reduced to a little embrace, like this,*
> *we'll settle for a forearm or anything else at all—ow.*
> Even for so little? . . . No doubt that part was not yet *corporealized in a*
> *signifying manner?* Not sufficiently transmuted into an *enjoying sub-*
> *stance. . . .*
> *Ow . . .* from the other side. What are we going to have to go through in
> order to bring about this transformation? How, how many times, are we
> going to have to be cut into *parts, hammered, recast* . . . in order to become
> sufficiently signifying? Substantial enough? All that without knowing any-
> thing about it. Hardly a twinge. . . . (1985a, 86–92)

Irigaray's "*Ow . . .* from the other side" cuts Lacan's texts into parts. By
productively reflecting his text back onto itself, Irigaray uses "the master's
tools" in order to hammer and recast his theory. She shows how the logic
of psychoanalysis is a logic that makes all difference into sameness, all
desire into man's desire. She argues that the Other created by psychoanalysis is an Other of the Same. (1958a, 98) That is to say, the logic of
psychoanalysis is a "hom(m)o-sexual" (homme-man, homo-same) logic.
(1985a, 171–72) There is only one sex, a sex that is one, unitary, solid,
man's sex. And *this sex which is not one* (does not exist and is more than
one) is feminine sexuality.

A couple of cleverly juxtaposed quotations from Lacan says it all: "The
one who I presume has knowledge is the one I love." "Women don't know
what they are saying, that's the whole difference between them and me."
Lacan presumes to know what women are saying. Who then, does he love?
The one who he presumes "has knowledge," that is, himself. For Irigaray

the logic of Western philosophy, including psychoanalysis, is all male self-love, "*hom(me)o*-sexual." Irigaray tries "to go back through the masculine imaginary, to interpret the way in which it has reduced us to silence, to muteness or mimicry." She is "attempting, from that starting-point and at the same time, to (re)discover a possible space for the feminine imaginary." (1985a, 164) And once we make space for a new imaginary, we will also have made a new Symbolic order. For the "symbolic order is an imaginary order which becomes law." (1980a, 159) Therefore it is necessary to open the space for a new imaginary in order to fundamentally change the Symbolic order.

For Irigaray what is at stake is a new economy of desire. She criticizes Lacan's notion of desire, which she says leaves women with no desire and no possibility of desiring. (1985a, 94–98) Within the current phallocentric economy of desire, women's desire—since it isn't allowed any articulation—shows up only as symptoms in the body of the hysteric. "Speaking (as) woman," then, is finding continuity between bodily gestures and language. (1985a, 137) "Speaking (as) woman" is finding a way to bring desire from the body into language. Only then can two sexes meet each other.

Irigaray argues that Lacan's phallocratic notion of desire does not allow for any positive relation between two sexes. (1985a, 94–98) The Phallus stands in for sexual difference in what becomes the endless deferral of desire. Within the Lacanian framework, desire can never be satisfied. Rather, it operates by substituting one object for an Other in an eternally frustrating attempt to have or be the Phallus.[8] Woman, as the/man's Other, is always merely the mimetic reflection of man's desire.

Irigaray suggests that this phallocratic economy of desire is operated by a mechanics of solids. Desire, through a closed circuit of metaphorical substitutions, always takes us back to the solid Phallus. Irigaray seems to dispute Lacan's thesis that his desire operates according to a logic of metonymy; it is, after all, the paternal metaphor that sets the metonymy of desire into motion. Irigaray maintains that Lacan's theory gives priority to metaphor over metonymy.[9] (1985a, 110) And the logic of metaphor requires a mechanics of solids—one object is substituted for another. With fluids, on the other hand, a smooth substitution cannot take place. Irigaray suggests that fluids operate according to a logic of metonymy. They can be associated, touch each other, but never completely substituted for an-Other.[10]

Irigaray attempts to recover the repressed mechanics of fluids that lies behind the mechanics of solids in the traditional psychoanalytic account of desire. She enlists the penis in order to show that it is operated by a mechanics of fluids, sperm (and blood). Behind the mechanics of solids that erects the ideal of the Phallus are bodies operating according to another mechanics, the mechanics of fluids. The phallocracy, however, covers over the exchange of fluids in both male and female bodies. It prefers form to matter. Only in a formal system can one object be substituted for another, can relations be seen in terms of substitution.

Within the economy of substitution, there is no reciprocal exchange *between* one and another. There is only exchange of one *for* another. For Irigaray, wherever matter is concerned individuals are not substitutable. Which is not to say that they have no relation. Rather, there can be relations only between two different sexes that are not reducible to one another, operating within an economy of desire that does not substitute/sacrifice one for the other.

For Irigaray, desire *is* difference. This difference is not Lacan's lack, which always leads to opposition and hierarchy, and in which one sex becomes a mere reflection of the other. Irigaray figures desire as "the interval," "the residue," "the between," "a dynamic force," "wonder," as "angels." (1987b) So, if for Lacan desire is the gap or lack between need and demand, for Irigaray it is the wonder-full excess between two sexes. Desire is between form and matter. It changes the relation between form and matter, between time and space, between man and woman. To reconceive (out) of desire is to reconceive all relations:

> The transition to a new age coincides with a change in the economy of desire, necessitating a different relationship between man and god(s), man and man, man and the world, man and woman. . . . Our age will only realize the dynamic potential in desire if the latter is referred back to the economy of the *interval*, that is if it is located in the attractions, tensions, and acts between *form* and *matter*, or characterized as the *residue* of any creation or work, which lies *between* what is already identified and what has still to be identified, etc. (1987b, 120)

Recuperating elements from patriarchal culture—Aristotelian philosophy and contemporary physics—Irigaray tries to open a space for a new desire, a place (interval in space/time) "that could be inhabited by each sex, body or flesh." (1987b, 128) It is a desire that acts "upon the porous nature of the body" and includes "the communion that takes place through the most intimate mucous membranes." (1987b, 128–29) It is "a love so scrupulous that it is divine." Irigaray says that "[a] sexual or carnal ethics would demand that both angel and body be found together." (1987b, 127) It is the sexed desiring bodies of angels. (1987b) The ethics of sexual difference is the divine-in-between, the embodied angel. Irigaray is concerned with the interval between body and divinity, matter and form. She calls for an ethics of passion through which each sex rejoices in the wonder of the other.

This is why she insists on discussing the *morphology* (from morphé, form) of the sexed body.[11] The morphology of the sexed body designates the interval between form and matter. And as such the "body" can "speak." Morphology operates according to the logic of metonymy, association, matter touching form. In phallocratic theory, however, the morphology of the male body is substituted for all bodies. Phallocratic theory denies that it is sexed. It purports to be neutral/neuter. Part of Irigaray's strategy, then, is to expose the ways in which the discourses of philosophy and science are sexed. She brings out the sex in their discourse by having a "fling" with the philosophers.

Cixous's Other Woman

If Irigaray has a *fling* with the philosophers, Cixous teases them with her playful irreverence. She refuses to play "the game of penis-check played by the imperialist superpowers of the triumvirate with the mean solemnity that makes history." (1985, 128) And while, as she says, "the penis gets around in my text," she won't allow herself "to be threatened by the big dick." (1976, 262) At the same time that she manipulates the penis in her texts, Cixous shouts "I want vulva. . . . 'Vulva!'"[12] (1975d, 110) Cixous sets out to shock the philosophers who have been so squeamish about the female body by exposing/creating it in her texts:

> Let them tremble, those priests; we are going to *show* them our *sexts*! Too bad for them if they collapse on discovering that women aren't men, or that the mother doesn't have one. But doesn't this fear suit them fine? Wouldn't the worst thing be—isn't the worst thing that, really, woman is not castrated. . . . (1985, 69)

Cixous creates feminine myths by reclaiming the feminine from its debasement in the Western culture. She rereads traditional myths and literature in order to throw off the masculine metaphors that have been forced onto the feminine. For example, she tells the story of Dora from Dora's perspective in her play *Portrait of Dora*. She retells the stories of Electra and Cleopatra in *Sorties*. She identifies with Medusa, Electra, Antigone, Cleopatra. She says that she has been them all. In this way, she reclaims these female characters and their myths. She brings them to life again. In her fiction, she tries to actualize her image of feminine writing. She creates new myths of femininity using a variety of shifting styles.[13] In "Castration or Decapitation" she compares psychoanalysis to fairy tales. There, she argues that in both psychoanalytic theory and the tales of "Little Red Riding Hood" and "Sleeping Beauty," woman is "laid" between two beds, "ever caught in her chain of metaphors, metaphors that organize culture." (1981, 44)

In order to be free of these masculine metaphors in which women have been caught, Cixous maintains that women must write their bodies. She seems to suggest that women need to create their own metaphors, metaphors that do not operate within a metaphorical economy of substitution. In this regard, she comes close to Irigaray's inversion of metonymy/metaphor. For Cixous it is women's bodies, particularly their sexuality, that has been left out of Western culture's "masculine" economy of the Same. And she tries to imagine a "feminine" writing that expresses/creates a feminine libidinal economy.

For Cixous the Unconscious is always a cultural phenomenon. The Unconscious that circulates in psychoanalytic discourse is a product of a masculine imaginary. Therefore, we need a new unconscious, a feminine unconscious. And if the Unconscious is a cultural product, then we can create this new unconscious through writing. "Things are starting to be written," says Cixous, "things that will constitute a feminine Imaginary, the site, that is, of identifications of an ego no longer given over to an image defined by the masculine. . . ." (1981, 52)

At the end of "Castration or Decapitation" Cixous describes how she would imagine feminine writing. It is important that for Cixous feminine writing cannot be theorized and therefore her text should not be read as a theoretical description. She considers herself a poet and not a philosopher. In "Castration or Decapitation," she is trying to create a feminine writing. She imagines a text that has neither origin nor end, a text with several beginnings, a text that goes on and on. This text "asks the question of giving—'What does this writing give?' 'How does it give?'" (1981, 53) It isn't predictable or knowable. It is a tactile text, "close to the voice, very close to the flesh." (1981, 54) For Cixous the relation between feminine writing, the feminine libido, and the body is crucial. Her texts are manifestos calling upon women to write their bodies because feminine writing derives from the body. This "body" of hers, however, is not merely the physical body. She is not proposing some kind of biologism. Rather, for Cixous the body is a complex of social and biological processes:

> I believe that anything having to do with the body should be explored from the functional to the libidinal, to the imaginary; and then how all of this is articulated at the symbolic level. It is beyond a doubt that femininity derives from the body, from the anatomical, the biological difference, from a whole system of drives which are radically different for women than for men. *But none of this exists in a pure state: it is always, immediately "already spoken," caught in representation, produced culturally.* This does not prevent the libidinal economy of woman from functioning in a specific manner which modifies her rapport with reality. (1976d, 28; my emphasis)

Because femininity is a matter of representation, it is crucial for women to write their bodies, their imaginations, their libidos. What is at issue is creating a new economy of representation that is not built on the repression of the feminine. Cixous argues that the phallocracy of Western culture has insured that a phallic representational economy has suppressed any other. Like Irigaray, Cixous maintains that men too have lost their bodies and their sexuality to the phallic economy that always returns to the Phallus. The phallic economy is premised on a logic of metaphorical substitution that always returns to the Phallus. And this phallic economy has been erected "in the face of this person [woman] who lacks lack [castration]."[14] It is her lack of lack upon which "manhood" is constructed, "flaunting its metaphors like banners through history." (1981, 47)

Like Irigaray, Cixous believes that the masculine economy of metaphors is an economy of the Same *("monosexuality")* in which feminine elements are always appropriated for its purposes. (1976, 254) The master has invented his own Other and this is why this Other can be domesticated. (1985, 71) Both Cixous and Irigaray are trying to imagine a *bisexuality* that does not deny difference. For Irigaray bisexuality is two different sexes engaging with their difference in discourse. For Cixous bisexuality means the location within oneself of difference, of two sexes. She maintains that we are all bisexual; our primary bisexuality is perverted by phallocentric culture. (1985, 83; 1976d, 22) Cixous imagines a bisexuality that is a process of exchange and not a struggle to the death. In "The Laugh of the Medusa" she claims that writing is not masculine or feminine but in between. It is bisexual. (1976, 254) The between seems to exist within each of us, the presence of difference within.

This is reminiscent of Irigaray's figure of the between, the interval. For Irigaray, however, the between is the residue of a meeting of the sexes; it is the excess/difference, wonder, of fundamentally different sexes coming together. Irigaray's bisexuality displaces the *(hom(m)osexuality* of phallocracy. While most of Irigaray's efforts are toward opening a space for the place of this meeting, Cixous tries to imagine the "newly born woman" who will occupy this place. While Irigaray tries to open a space for a new economy of desire, Cixous imagines a new feminine desire—something that Irigaray may admit is not possible until a place is opened.[15]

Like Irigaray, Cixous maintains that men have theorized their desire as reality. (1976, 255) Men imagine women as representative of castration, says Cixous, because "it's the jitters that give them a hard-on!" (1976, 255) She imagines a desire that is not the result of lack or castration, a desire that does not remain within psychoanalysis, a "desire-that-gives." (1976, 262–63) This is woman's desire. "I have always loved desire," says Cixous, "but not the one which believes itself to be determined by lack." (1974, 7) And when women speak and write their desire, culture will change:

> From the very moment that anything connected to desire begins to speak up, and begins to speak against the established forms, against what closes, what codifies, from the moment an anticode arises, it necessarily indicates that there is an open channel. It's a narrow channel, to be sure; it is perhaps, for the time being, only a crack, perhaps hardly a fissure. Nonetheless, it has always existed, otherwise the woman's movement would not exist, nothing would have ever come about to say whether *something else* existed. The

very question of a *something else* indicates that there is always otherness. (1979a, 72)

Kristeva's Difference

Kristeva is the "odd man out," so to speak, in the "holy Trinity" of French feminist theory. Her early work is written in traditional philosophical style. Her later work has become somewhat more poetic and often includes transcripts from analytic sessions. And most recently she has written novels. Even so, Kristeva claims that in her theoretical writing she is seeking the truth. (1986a) And she is not seeking a truth that is necessarily an alternative to the truths of patriarchy. Unlike either Cixous or Irigaray, Kristeva praises patriarchy:

> I think that culture—in particular Occidental culture, which is founded on patriarchy and expressed in the great religious which were—which still are—Judaism and Christianity—has produced profoundly true visions of the human being as the symbolic being, as the being who lives in language and who is not reduced just to the womb and to reproduction. Now love is a moment in the life of a speaking being who, all the while caught in the body, opens oneself to the symbolic dimension. . . . So if one says it's patriarchy which produces that, long live patriarchy. (1980a, 143–44)

Unlike Irigaray's texts in which the "Fathers" names appear only in the margins, or Cixous's texts where the "Fathers'" names are invoked with complete irreverence—"Old Lacan"—some of Kristeva's texts could serve as catalogues of the great male theorists of Western culture. Much of her writing, especially her early writing in the '60s and '70s, is loaded with invocations of the "Fathers'" names: Althusser, Artaud, Barthes, Bataille, Baudelaire, Beneviste, Céline, Chomsky, Comte, Derrida, Diderot, Feuerbach, Frege, Freud, Goethe, Hegel, Heidegger, Heraclitus, Hjelmslev, Husserl, Jakobson, Joyce, Kant, Kierkegaard, Lacan, Lautréamont, Lenin, Lévi-Strauss, Lukács, Mallarmé, Mao, Marx, Nerval, Nietzsche, Plato, Saussure, among others! Kristeva very much identifies with the her theoretical "Fathers," especially Freud. In *Black Sun* Kristeva claims that Names gathered in a text may have mere sign-value for the lost mother. (1987, 157) In fact, part of my project in this book is to suggest that in Kristeva's texts the Father can be read as a screen for the mother.[16] And Kristeva's most famous "discovery," the semiotic, can be read as the melancholy theorist's mourning the loss of her motherland and mother-tongue.

Unlike Irigaray or Cixous, Kristeva does not believe that writing is sexed. She maintains that "writing ignores sex or gender and displaces its difference in the discreet workings of language and signification." (Moi 1987, 111) Kristeva criticizes "certain feminists in France" who argue that language and theory are phallic and that the feminine is imprecise, impulse, whispered, in language. (1980b, 134) This view assigns women to an inferior position, reserving for them the position of "the unsayable," "the hysteric." (1980b, 134) If these "certain feminists" are Cixous and Irigaray, Kristeva overlooks their various claims that it is phallocentric culture that assigns women the position of unsayable or hysteric. And they are trying, using different strategies, to recuperate this repressed feminine.

In addition, unlike Irigaray or Cixous, Kristeva, in her early work, argues that any difference between a masculine and feminine unconscious has to do with relations to the penis/Phallus. (1975, 241; 1979a, 41) Following Lacan, Kristeva suggests that the child can imagine its reunion with the lost mother only by identifying with the penis—representative of the Phallus—which the child imagines fulfills her desire. In fact, Kristeva is more likely to refer to the "penis" than Lacan's "Phallus." As Elizabeth Grosz points out, Kristeva accepts the oedipal structure while Irigaray— and I would add Cixous—does not.[17] This is more true of Kristeva's early writings than it is of her later writings. In all of her writing, Kristeva is concerned with the preoedipal dynamics, which she claims Lacan has ignored. In her early writings from the '60s and '70s, however, Kristeva still maintains that it is within the family structure, the oedipal structure, that the child moves from the preoedipal to the oedipal, from what she calls material "rejection" to desire.[18]

In her later writings from the '80s, Kristeva argues that the oedipal structure is not as Lacan imagined it to be. She argues that there are several paternal functions and not just the function of Law or prohibition. (1983, 1987) In *Tales of Love* Kristeva claims that Freud's libido is male and that its mirage of power remains constituted "by the appeal of the tumescent-detumescent penis." (1983, 75) There, Kristeva also imagines the possibility of an "erotics of the purely feminine." She imagines the possibility of a feminine outside of phallic economy. She imagines "lesbian loves" that "comprise the delightful arena of neutralized, filtered libido, devoid of the erotic cutting edge of masculine sexuality." (1983, 81) Still, for Kristeva this image remains a mere passing fantasy. It cannot last. Either it gives way to "erotic mania" or death. Kristeva retreats from her lesbian fantasy and insists that the loving soul required some confrontation with, relation to, the Phallus. (1983, 81, 224) Unlike Cixous, who mocks the lack lack, Kristeva is comfortable talking about feminine castration. (1987, 80, 81)

In *Black Sun* Kristeva diagnoses feminine sexuality as it operates within patriarchal culture. Without suggesting any alternatives—except maybe psychoanalysis—Kristeva says that feminine sexuality within Western culture may be inherently tied to melancholy and depression. While Cixous identifies sexual difference on the level of *jouissance*, Kristeva, staying within the framework of a revised oedipal structure, suggests that sexual difference is the result of different relations to the mother. (Cixous 1985, 82; Kristeva 1980b, 137; 1987) She argues that matricide is a "vital necessity" in order for the subject to go through mourning for the lost maternal "Thing." (1987, 27–28) Compare this to Irigaray's argument that matricide is only "necessary" in *phallocratic* psychoanalytic theory. (1985d, 85) Because matricide is difficult, if not impossible, for women, Kristeva argues that there is a greater frequency of female depression. Women cannot rid themselves of the dead mother. Rather, they carry her around with them locked into the crypt of their psyches. Kristeva claims that this addiction to the maternal Thing is a symptom of feminine sexuality. (1987, 71) And whereas for men the loss of the maternal object isn't as devastating because in the heterosexual relation they get a mother-substitute, for women in the heterosexual relation it is more difficult because they cannot look forward to this "reunion." This is why Kristeva suggests that women may actually have to repress pleasure itself in order to enter into a heterosexual relation. While Kristeva seems concerned to provide therapeutic fantasies to her patients that might help them to cope with their depression, she accepts the depressing effects/affects of the larger fantasies of Western culture.

In most of her latest work Kristeva addresses the crisis in the Western psyche or imaginary, but she does not specifically address any crisis in relation to women. This is because, unlike Cixous and Irigaray, Kristeva believes that sexual difference is not fundamental. Rather, it is difference or alterity itself that is fundamental to the psyche. She argues that women's protests revolve around difference, individual difference, sexual difference. The question of difference is always the question of how difference itself is marked or represented in culture. The question, then, is not a question of sexual difference in particular, but a question of difference in general. In *Strangers to Ourselves* Kristeva argues that the human psyche, regardless of sexual difference, contains the other. Alterity is within. And on both an individual level and a social level we need to learn to deal with the return of that repressed alterity.

In this regard, Kristeva's theory is more like Cixous's notion of bisexuality than Irigaray's. Cixous has argued that all people are originally bisexual. They contain difference, the other sex. Kristeva has also said that all speaking subjects are bisexual. (1974e, 165) She also maintains that desire between sexes depends on both difference and sameness. (1980b, 142) For Irigaray, on the other hand, the notion that the other is within reduces the other to the same. Irigaray insists on a radical alterity between totally different elements that cannot be incorporated into each other. For Irigaray, desire is difference, residue, interval. Elizabeth Grosz puts the difference between Irigaray and Kristeva's *difference* very succinctly when she says:

> Where Kristeva uses [the concept of difference] to designate the difference
> *internal* to each subject, Irigaray uses it to refer to the differences *between*
> one sex and another. For Kristeva, Irigaray's project is logocentric and
> steeped in a metaphysical tradition; for Irigaray, Kristeva's position is anti-
> feminist and phallocratic. (1989, 104)

Another striking difference between Kristeva and Irigaray is their analysis of metaphor and metonymy. While Irigaray privileges metonymy in
order to displace what she sees as the priority given to metaphor in psychoanalysis, Kristeva privileges metaphor in order to displace what she
sees as the priority given to metonymy in psychoanalysis. (1983, 29; 1987,
102) Kristeva criticizes Lacanian theory because it more or less starts with
the mirror stage, which quickly turns into the *mise en abîme* of desire,
what Lacan calls the "metonymy of desire." Lancanian analysis begins
after the Name of the Father has been imposed and the subject has more
or less completely entered language. Kristeva argues that there is a complicated dynamic, what she calls the "metaphor of love," which precedes
the mirror stage and desire. These preoedipal processes are associated
with the maternal function. Kristeva brings out the importance and com-
plications of the maternal function, which she argues both Freud and
Lacan have ignored. In this way, Kristeva offers her own significant revi-
sions of the oedipal structure and psychoanalysis. At the same time that
Kristeva breaks down the traditional emphasis put on the Father of the
Law, she opens up the possibility for treating psychosis, a possibility foreclosed by Lacanian analysis.

There are some similarities between Kristeva, Cixous, and Irigaray.
Ironically, in spite of the charge that they are essentialists, all three of
"The French Feminists" reject the concept "woman" and the notion of
"woman's nature." All of them, in different ways, argue that "woman"
and "man" are the products of ideology. For example, Cixous claims that
"woman" and "man" operate in the "ideological theater." All of them
emphasize the necessity of changing the representational system in order
to radically alter the socioeconomic scene. In addition, all of them believe
that representation has to do with the imaginary and that by changing
our imaginary we can change the Symbolic order. Finally, all of them
prefer ears to eyes. Cixous imagines a writing that touches through the
ear. (1981, 54) Irigaray claims that the man's eye is a substitute for the
penis. (1985, 144–45, 95, 184) And Kristeva talks about listening and the
ear of the virgin. All three of them listen with attentive ears to language
that sings and to songs within language. In *Sorties* Cixous describes a
voice that sings. (1985, 93) Irigaray longs for the sounds in women's language, songs heard only by an attentive ear. (1985a, 112; 1985, 193) She
talks of angels who "set trances or convulsions to music, and lend them

harmony." (1987b, 127) And Kristeva's work as a whole always comes back to the maternal music in language.

For me the strangest thing about the work of these three writers taken together is that they always resist any categorization. When I first began working on this project I set out to criticize Kristeva's writing from a feminist standpoint. Like other critics I tried to use my criticisms of Kristeva against all of "The French Feminists." But the more that I tried to find the similarities between these writers, the more I saw differences. Now, writing this concluding chapter after my project is nearly complete, I set out to describe those differences. But as I tried to think through these differences, they began to disappear. Reading "The French Feminists" forces the reader to confront the Other repressed through the process of reading itself. With regard to these writers I could not sustain either the position that there *are* fundamental differences between their theories or that there *are not* fundamental differences between their theories. Whichever I went looking for, I would always confront the Other.[19]

CONCLUSION
OUTLAW ETHICS

In an interview with *psyche & po*, Kristeva says that her research is the work of a woman because she concentrates on discourses that break down identity. (1974e, 138) She claims that her "work obeys ethical exigencies" because she is a woman and concentrates on discourses that break identity. She suggests that women are more aware of ethics because of their marginal relation to the Symbolic; and her texts in particular carry an ethical imperative to break fixed identity through practice. (1974e, 138)

Just as Kristeva brought the speaking body back into language by putting the logic of language into the body, and brought the subject into the place of the other by putting the other into the subject, she brings *jouissance* back into the foundation of ethics by founding ethics in *jouissance*. Once again she employs two strategies in order to undermine the law of ethics and the ethics of law. She argues that the law is material and bodily. And she argues that ethics requires bodily drive force. For Kristeva, just as the pattern and logic of language is already found within the body and the pattern and logic of alterity is already found within the subject, the logic and law of ethics is already operating within the desiring body.

Her concern is to link the ethical with negativity so that it won't degenerate into either conformity or perversion. Without negativity, ethics is mere conformity. And without ethics, negativity is mere perversion. (1974, 233) At the limit, without negativity ethics is tyranny; and without ethics negativity is delirium. By linking ethics and negativity, Kristeva tries to steer between tyranny and delirium. Here again Kristeva attempts to unravel the double-bind of identity. She proposes an ethics that oscillates between Law and transgression. Her revolutionary ethics is another consequence of her struggle with identity and her politics of difference.

Three of the discourses with which Kristeva attempts to break down identity and link negativity with ethics are poetic language, maternity, and psychoanalysis. She suggests that "the ethics of a linguistic discourse may be gauged in proportion to the poetry that it presupposes." (1974a, 25) In addition, the ethics of a social discourse may be gauged by how much poetry it allows. All of the great tyrannies and repressive systems have legislated and censored poetry. From Plato's imaginary Republic to Stalin's brutal dictatorship, censorship has been the sign of repression, tyranny, and death. Poetry signals tolerance in a society. The openness to poetry is the openness to difference.

In the case of poetic language symbolic identity is full of difference and yet maintains its integrity as language. Here the heterogeneity in language is at its most apparent. Poetic language is language that is also not language, language that is other to itself. Meaningful but nonsignifying aspects of language—rhythm, tone, music—are just as important in poetry as the signifying elements of language. In poetry it is obvious that words are both meaningful for what they signify and meaningful for how they sound and how they affect the listener. Poetry points to the heterogeneity of language. Kristeva argues that it shows how signification comes to be out of nonsignifying semiotic bodily drives. By pointing to signification in process, poetry also points to a subject-in-process. For, as Kristeva says, any theory of language is also a theory of the subject.

Poetry's subject-in-process/on trial requires a new ethics that Kristeva says operates as "the negativizing of narcissism within practice." (1974, 233) Within ethical practice, negativity works to "make visible the process underlying" signification. (1974, 233) By making the process visible, negativity calls into question any stable identity. By calling into question stable identity, negativity is the catalyst for a narcissistic crisis in identity. Kristeva (re)turns this crisis to the very structure of narcissism. Drives are part of the narcissistic structure; they are part of identity. So identity is always heterogeneous.

This means that Kristeva's new ethics is also heterogeneous. It can never be fully articulated or represented with symbols because it is driven by an element that is heterogeneous to the symbolic. She says that "[t]he ethical cannot be stated, instead it is practiced to the point of loss, and the text is one of the most accomplished examples of such a practice." (1974, 234) For Kristeva, texts can be ethical. She sees her own writing as an ethical project.

But as Ewa Ziarek argues, the alterity within poetic language is less shocking than the alterity within maternity because while poetry may seem esoteric, maternity is a fact of everyday life. (Ziarek, 1990) As Ziarek points out, maternity is the most powerful model of alterity within because it exists at the heart of the social and the species:

> Kristeva's semiotic analysis of the maternal body inscribes, after all, the abyss and alterity into the very site of domesticated normalcy (or what is perceived as such) and the generation of the species. If the avant-garde poet can be thought of as a modern Dionysus, pregnant madonnas invading that

Nietzschean position could evoke only the specter of . . . monstrosity. (1990, 23)

Maternity is the very embodiment of alterity within. It cannot be neatly divided into subject and object. "It is an identity," says Kristeva, "that splits, turns in on itself and changes without becoming other." (1977b, 297) Pregnancy is "the splitting of the subject," the subject-in-process/on trial. (1979, 49) Like poetic language, pregnancy is a case where identity contains alterity as a heterogeneous other without completely losing its integrity.

I agree with Ewa Ziarek that Kristeva's rendering of the maternal body as the site of an "infolding" of sameness and otherness problematizes the very notions of identity and difference. (1990) With the maternal body the borders between identity and difference break down. The maternal function is an infolding of negation and identification that precedes the paternal function. Kristeva finds the difference and negation within identity.

In *Tales of Love* Kristeva uses maternity as a model for an outlaw ethics, what she calls "herethics." Herethics is founded on the ambiguity in pregnancy and birth between subject and object positions. It is an ethics that challenges rather than presupposes an autonomous ethical agent. Herethics sets up one's obligations to the other as obligations to the self and obligations to the species. This ethics binds the subject to the other through love and not Law. As I explained in chapter 2, the model of ethical love is the mother's love for the child, which is a love for herself and a love for her own mother. The mother's love is also the willingness to give herself up, to embrace the strangeness within herself. (1983, 262–63)

Like herethics, psychoanalysis posits a subject-in-process/on trial that is based on a relation of alterity within. The ethics of psychoanalysis is founded on the relation between the conscious and Unconscious. The notion of the Unconscious makes any stable or unified subject, truth, meaning, impossible. Even the individual is full of difference, other to itself. Kristeva says that psychoanalysis analyzes a series of splittings— birth, weaning, separation—as indispensable to an individual's identity. (1987, 132) Psychoanalysis is a science of subjects-in-process/on trial. It records the evolutions and devolutions of these strangers. By examining the common underlying dynamics of limit cases it shows us that we are all *étrangers à nous-mêmes*. Kristeva argues that like subjects undergoing psychoanalysis, pregnant Madonnas, and avant-garde poets, we are all subjects-in-process, strangers to ourselves. It is on the basis of this psychoanalytic insight that Kristeva begins to develop a politics of difference.

Operating at the borders of meaning, psychoanalysis is constantly threatened by totalitarianism on the one side and delirium on the other. Kristeva says that "[s]ituating our discourse near such boundaries might enable us to endow it with a current ethical impact." (1974a, 25) But the ethics of psychoanalysis is a precarious ethics. Between the two extremes, however, lies what Kristeva calls "the modern version of liberty," which she says is played out in the analytic session. (1981, 319) Recall that the analytic session provides a space for liberty because the analyst's ethics is not normative but "directed." It is directed to a space where the analysand can embrace the Other in her—that alien Other that is both her Unconscious and her cultural heritage—in order to live with her crisis in value. (1987, 55) According to Kristeva, it is this crisis in value that is the empty signature of our culture. And the direction of analysis is not to deny the crisis, but to elaborate it.

For Kristeva, only the elaboration of *jouissance* in all of its forms can control its expansion. This elaboration is always interactive and social. For her, the analytic session is the exemplary relationship that can sublimate drive force, eros and the death drive, in order to begin to ground an ethics. Recall that for Kristeva psychoanalysis provides the basis of a morality:

> . . . [Psychoanalysis's] vital efficacy is inseparable from its ethical dimension, which is commensurate with love: the speaking being opens up to and reposes in the other.
> . . . No restrictive, prohibitive, or punitive legislation can possibly restrain my desire for objects, values, life, or death. Only the meaning that my desire may have for an other and hence for me can control its expansion, hence serve as the unique, if tenuous, basis of a morality. (1987, 60–61, 63)

The psychoanalytic session is an interaction between two subjects-in-process, in which the analysand's desires are reflected back from the other and elaborated so that they can be expressed in productive ways. Because the subjects are always in process/on trial, meaning and morality are always in process/on trial. Morality, like the subject, is an ongoing process that requires the elaboration of desire in order to avoid a violent, possibly, deadly, discharge of drive force.

For Kristeva, to recognize the subject-in-process is to recognize the death drive and eros. It is to recognize drive force that transgresses the Law. She says that the subject-in-process speaks to the ethical concern "because it assumes that we recognize, on the one hand, the unity of the subject who submits to a law—the law of communication, among others; yet who, on the other hand, does not entirely submit, cannot entirely submit, does not want to submit entirely." (1986a, 8) To recognize the subject-in-process expands our conception of the social. The social becomes both Law and transgression, both Meaning and nonmeaning. It becomes a social-in-process/on trial. And human life becomes an open system. (1986a, 8)

In *Revolution in Poetic Language* and *Polylogue* Kristeva argues that "the subject of a new political practice can only be the subject of a new discursive practice." (1977, 20) She claims that "an other sociality is required by a subject in process/on trial which averts with the very same gesture the madness and the subordination cleaving him to the law." (1977, 21) The subject-in-process not only requires a new ethics, but also a new sociality. Ethics and sociality are one in the same. For Kristeva, both are founded on an embrace and articulation of *jouissance*.

Kristeva proposes an ethics that is not a question of morals or submission to the Law. (1986a, 8) Rather, it is a question of the boundaries of the Law—what is on the other side of the Law. Her reformulation of ethics results in an ethics that is not based on restriction and repression. When sociality is reconceived as grounded in pleasure and violence, *jouissance* rather than the repression of *jouissance*, then the ethical imperative is reconceived as the necessity to articulate that *jouissance*:

> Ethics used to be a coercive, customary manner of ensuring the cohesiveness of a particular group through the repetition of a code—a more or less accepted apologue. Now, however, the issue of ethics crops up wherever a code (mores, social contract) must be shattered in order to give way to the free play of negativity, need, desire, pleasure, and *jouissance*, before being put together again, although temporarily and with full knowledge of what is involved. (1974a, 23)

Kristeva identifies the beginning of the reformulation of ethics with Marx, Nietzsche, and Freud. And post-structuralism and deconstruction, with their code shattering, have given new life to the discussion of ethics. In this context, ethics has a new urgency. Kristeva points out that the urgency of this new ethics, "between law and transgression," comes from its borders: fascism and Stalinism. (1974a, 23) The urgency comes from the fact that Hitler can (can't) read Nietzsche and Stalin can (can't) read Marx. What is an ethics between Law and transgression? How can we talk about ethics in this context? How can we afford not to?

Ethics operates somewhere between Stalinism, the tyranny of the Law, and fascism, the brutal transgression of Law. Ethics, as an open system, moves between Law and transgression, always in process, on trial, under revision. Transgression becomes law that itself gives way to transgression; even the Law is put in process/on trial, interactive, never absolute. And in order for people to live together ethically, we must acknowledge this transgression. Kristeva likens the oscillation between Law and its transgression to the Freudian oscillation between eros and the death drive. (1986a, 8) She suggests that we must encode transgression so that it can be understood by the social. By acknowledging the death drive, we broaden our conception of the social. We face our *jouissance* so that we might articulate it rather than kill some one.

Kristeva's models for ethics—poetry, maternity, and psychoanalysis—

are all alternatives to juridical models of ethics that presuppose autonomous subjects who relate to each other through the force of law. The models that Kristeva proposes operate outside/before the Law in the sense that the law or obligation is already internal to the "subject." The Law is turned inside out; it is within the body. In other words; there is no need for an external law that insures the social relation. The social relation is inherent in the subject.

This theory does away with the solipsism that threatened Descartes and Husserl. It does not have to explain how an autonomous subject would know anything about, let alone care about or feel obligated to, any other. In addition, it does not require a sympathy for others that is founded on their similarity, even identity, to the subject. The subject does not have to imagine that the other is the same as himself. He does not have to impose a Kantian imperative or golden rule in order to insure that he will be treated justly or kindly by others. Rather than love the other as himself, the ethical subject-in-process will love the other *in* herself. She will love what is different. She will love alterity because it is within but not because it is homogeneous. She can imagine an ethics of love because the ethical relation is interior to her psyche.

Some critics, however, among them Andrea Nye, Nancy Fraser, and Eléanor Kuykendall, have argued that Kristeva's ethics does not allow for any effective ethical agent. Nye maintains that Kristeva's theory does not allow for any relation between adults and lacks any account of interpersonal relationships. (1987, 681–82) Fraser argues that "neither half of Kristeva's split subject can be a feminist political agent. Nor, I submit, can the two halves joined together." (1990, 98) And Kuykendall argues that Kristeva's ethics does not allow for a "female agency." (1989, 181) Her claim is that for Kristeva the feminine falls outside of ethics. (1989, 189)

To say that the feminine falls outside of ethics is not to say that women are not the subjects of ethics. The feminine is not synonymous with women. And if Kristeva suggests that the feminine falls outside of ethics, she does so in order to bring it back to ethics. What has been repressed in Western culture, including the feminine, must return in order to talk about a nontotalizing, nonrestrictive, ethics. Kristeva bases her notion of ethics on a loving embrace of the return of the repressed. She maintains that in order to have an ethics of life, women *must be* involved. (1967a, 262) But, she does say that in order for women to be the subjects of ethics, we must go beyond feminism. She is referring to a feminism that merely replaces one restrictive law with another; she refers to a feminism that is as intolerant of others as patriarchy is of it.

Kristeva suggests that women can "conceive and construct a new comprehensive legitimacy for their *jouissance(s)*, an ethics guaranteed not by constraint but by a logic, that is always a poly-logic, of love." (1977f, 115–16) This ethics that is a poly-logic of love is an ethics of difference. It is an ethics-in-process through which changing varieties of difference are possible to embrace. In order for women, and everyone on the margins of the social, to be the subjects of ethics, we must reconceive of ethics.

Kristeva's newly conceived ethics, which combines ethics and negativity, can be seen as another kind of feminist ethics, a feminist ethics that goes beyond restrictive laws whether they are matriarchal or patriarchal. Kristeva is concerned to formulate an ethics that allows all individuals to avoid sheer conformity to the Law, on the one hand, and complete ostracism from the social, on the other; she wants an ethics in which women are neither mere conformists nor absolute outlaws. She wants an ethics that unravels the double-bind of identity. Jacqueline Rose sees this as a feminist concern.

> Ethics plus (as) negativity describes a subjective position which avoids conformity (the first without the second), and esoterism or marginality (the second without the first), capturing alternatives which have historically presented themselves to feminism: between an equality which risks absorption into the law, and an absolute difference which can only defy it. (1986, 159)

The problem of how to arbitrate between women's identity or equality and women's difference has been a central problem for feminists for centuries. In order not to get trapped in the double-bind of identity, Kristeva suggests that women must articulate their *jouissance* within the Symbolic without relinquishing any of their difference. This project requires both symbolic law and negativity. It requires that women take up their identity as an identity-in-process in order not to be linked to that identity in an oppressive way. Women need to take up identity always tentatively and never completely in order to avoid the annihilation of difference.

Struggles for emancipation are struggles that question the status of the subject. As Foucault says, on the one hand, "people struggling for emancipation assert the right to be different and they underline everything which makes individuals truly individual. On the other hand, they attack everything which separates the individual, breaks his links with others, splits up community life, forces the individual back on himself and ties him to his own identity in a constraining way." (1983, 211–12)

As Judith Butler so persuasively argues in *Gender Trouble*, feminism needs to give up the notion that it requires a unified subject in order to operate effectively. (1990) As soon as feminism defines its unified subject it has the effect of exclusion and domination. Paradoxically, as soon as feminism defines its subject so that it can start representing that subject, it ceases to represent its subject. In other words, as soon as feminism defines "woman" it excludes all sorts of women. As soon as feminism defines its constituents, it loses constituents. Kristeva's ethics of a subject-in-process suggests possible ways of negotiating this double-bind of identity. Insofar as Kristeva's concern with ethics is a concern for unraveling this double-bind, her theories can inform a feminist ethics.

Elizabeth Grosz, however, argues that Kristeva's herethics in "Stabat Mater" is not a feminine or feminist ethics in any sense. She maintains that "[e]thics becomes necessary, for Kristeva, insofar as the maternal debt *needs to be spoken.*" (1990, 91) While it is the case that Kristeva's "Stabat Mater" calls for a new discourse of maternity, it does so not (only) to articulate the maternal debt. Rather, the new discourse of maternity is needed in order to articulate a new ethical relationship between subject and other. Kristeva's concern with maternity is a concern with alterity. What needs to be spoken is a new discourse of alterity, an alterity within, so that human beings can love each other and so that ethics is possible. So it is not (only) the maternal debt that must be spoken; rather, it is the logic of the maternal body that must be spoken. What needs to be spoken is what has been repressed within patriarchal culture and patriarchal theory.

What her critics do not acknowledge when they argue that Kristeva's ethics is not feminist or that it excludes women is that she is challenging traditional notions of ethics that presuppose a unified subject who affirms only the self-same. If Kristeva's theory excludes women from traditional ethics, that is because she wants us to go beyond traditional ethics. The logic of traditional ethics can lead to exclusion and repression, which can in turn lead to oppression and murder. For within traditional ethics, which presuppose an autonomous unified subject, ethical imperatives are externally imposed. An obligation to an other cannot come from this isolated unified subject because the very existence of the other is always presented as an afterthought and/or a fight to the death. Within Kristeva's model, on the other hand, the other is always within and originary to the subject, who is always in process. There is already a relationship between the subject and the other. Sociality itself is founded on this *ongoing* relationship. The subject-in-process is not bound to its other through external restrictions.

The relation between the subject-in-process and its other, part of that process, is not a Hegelian struggle for recognition. Rather it is an embrace of what has been lost through the traditional logic of identity. The Hegelian notion of desire founds the social relation on lack and struggle, whereas the Freudian notion of eros or identification founds the social relation on love. Kristeva maintains that desire "emphasizes *lack*, whereas *affect*, while acknowledging the latter, gives greater importance to the movement toward the other and to mutual *attraction*." (1983, 155) She concludes that eros, attraction, and love are the only hope for the social relation. (1980a, 142)

Kristeva not only presents an ethics modeled on psychoanalysis but also an alternative view of psychoanalysis. It is not a tyrannical superego or paternal Law that restricts the relation between the subject and the return of the repressed. For her, a breakdown in sociality is not a breakdown in the superego or the paternal Law. (1983, 378) Rather it is a breakdown of love, maternal love. It is love that binds the subject to its other. Kristeva presents a revolutionary psychoanalytic theory that challenges Freudian and Lacanian theory with their emphasis on the paternal function. She recovers and begins to articulate the maternal function in order to reconceive of ethics and sociality.

Kristeva's is an outlaw ethics. Ethics is not a matter of enforcing the Law. Rather, it is a matter of embracing the return of the repressed other, the foreigner, the outcast, the woman, the Unconscious, *jouissance* in all of its manifestations. Kristeva suggests that if we can bring about multiple sublations of this other that has been excluded, then we won't need to kill it. If, through this outlaw ethics-in-process, we acknowledge the death drive, then there might be fewer deaths.

NOTES

1. The Prodigal Child

1. Freud quotes this passage. (1938, 207)
2. I will come back to the preoedipal transference in chapter 3.
3. Cf. Lacan 1954, 174.
4. For Lacan, the desire to be the object of the mother's desire is added to, or possibly substituted for, the Freudian oedipal desire to have the mother. If the child wants to "have" the mother it is only because that is what it thinks that she wants.
5. At this point I use the masculine pronoun because, in her early work especially, Kristeva follows both Freud and Lacan in presuming that the subject of psychoanalysis is male. This presumption is what has made sexual difference extremely difficult for psychoanalytic theory. In spite of the masculine presumption in much of her work, I argue that Kristeva is working toward undermining the traditional psychoanalytic account of binary sexual difference. I elaborate on Kristeva's theory of sexual difference in the next chapter.
6. I discuss Lacan's account of sexual difference later in this chapter.
7. Much of my analysis in the rest of this chapter and in chapter 3 is devoted to Kristeva's challenge to Lacan's mirror stage and castration.
8. Sarah Kofman argues that there is a contradiction in Freud's description of the transformation of the girl's active masculine sexuality to her passive feminine sexuality. Kofman argues that in Freud's scenario, the little girl actively assumes her passivity in a masculine way and therefore never really achieves the passivity that Freud describes: ". . . *being* like the mother, as such, implies the desire to *have* a penis-child with the father, for the girl's identification during the preoedipal phase can end only by making her play a masculine role, the role of a phallic mother, and will prevent her, properly speaking, from becoming a mother and a woman." (1980, 217) Here Kofman is playing on the distinction between "being" and "having," which gains an added importance with Lacan.
9. Following Janine Chasseguet-Smirgel, Jessica Benjamin argues that it is maternal power and not maternal lack that motivates the child's (male and female) revolt against the mother. (1988, 94–99) The girl, Benjamin explains, wants to separate from maternal control and this is why she identifies with the idealized father, who represents autonomy. (1988, 100) It is not, then, his penis *per se* that the little girl wants. Benjamin says that "it is not anatomy, but the totality of a girl's relationship with the father, in a context of gender polarity and unequal responsibility for childrearing, that explains woman's perceived 'lack.'" (1988, 86)
10. Freud is at his worst when talking about female sexuality. By the time he wrote his most developed work on female sexuality, his theories were already under attack. In most of his other writings, Freud is careful to avoid anything that sounds like biological determinism. In his work on female sexuality, however (perhaps feeling the threat of castration himself—the authority of the father of psychoanalysis had been challenged), Freud too often sounds as if gender identification is the result of biological determinism. These sorts of remarks have prompted serious feminist criticisms of Freud's account of penis envy, castration, and the oedipal complex. For example, Kate Millet argues that feminists should

reject psychoanalysis because of Freud's masculine bias. (1969) Juliet Mitchell suggests that we can divide the good Freud from the bad Freud, so to speak. She maintains that some aspects of Freud's theory can be useful for feminists if we correct those places where Freud makes misogynist mistakes on female sexuality. (1974) Luce Irigaray turns Freud's techniques against his own writings in order to expose masculine bias. (1974) Sarah Kofman argues that Freud's theory traps women in a prison. She claims that some of Freud's theories on female sexuality are the result of his fear of feminine power. (1980) Like Kofman, Jane Flax points out that Freud likens psychoanalysis to a weapon when it comes to female sexuality. In addition Flax argues that Freud's anxieties about gender relations (the "battle between the sexes") lead him to presuppose gender-biased antinomies: nature/culture, feminine/masculine, body/mind, patient/analyst, other/self, preoedipal/oedipal, female/male. (1990) And Jessica Benjamin maintains that Freud was simply mistaken about women's desire. (1988)

11. Sarah Kofman's analysis of the mother-son relationship as the most complete relationship for Freud supports my reading here. (1980, 214–16)

12. Oddly enough, since there is no Other of the Other (because it is so radically Other and to give it an Other would be to make it like us, the subjects, and not so radically different after all), woman is her own "Other because she has no Other." (1982, 93)

13. "Man" is used here in both its generic and specific senses.

14. Teri Stratton suggested this in comments on an earlier version of this chapter. I appreciate her comment.

15. Lacan and his followers argue that if psychoanalysis is phallocentric, it is because our culture is phallocentric. For example, Jacqueline Rose argues that psychoanalysis does not produce the definitions of masculine and feminine and invest or divest them of power. Rather, psychoanalysis merely accounts for *how* these definitions are produced. (1982) Does psychoanalysis, then, merely repeat the same old phallocentric stories or can it give new stories in order to initiate social change? Must we merely resurrect the sins that we have inherited from our fathers, or can we hang them out to dry?

16. Stratton concludes that for Lacan the Phallus is more feminine than masculine insofar as it signifies the repressed Unconscious because the feminine is closer to the Unconscious. Phallocentrism, she argues, is "properly feminine." (1990, 34)

17. I elaborate on Kristeva's notion of the semiotic later in this chapter.

18. For a brief introduction to Lacan's theory of drives, see Jacqueline Rose's introduction to *Feminine Sexuality.* (Lacan, 1982)

19. See the section on negativity below.

20. I elaborate on Kristeva's challenge to the paternal function in chapter 3.

21. This translation is mine with help from Nadja Hofmann. I am responsible for any errors.

22. For a useful discussion of the influence of Barthes, Benveniste, Bataille, and Saussure on the work of Kristeva, see John Lechte's *Julia Kristeva.* (1990)

23. It seems that Kristeva's fascination with scientific evidence, even positivist methods, undermines her attempts to revive a living, speaking body with "semanalysis."

24. In her essay devoted to Lacan's theories of the relation between the unconscious and language, "Within the Microcosm of 'The Talking Cure,'" Kristeva begins by saying that "it would be strange for a psychoanalyst, asked to present her own reading of Jacques Lacan's texts and practice, to consider herself either a propagator or a critic of his work. For the propagation of psychoanalysis . . . has shown us, ever since Freud, that interpretation necessarily represents appropria-

tion, and thus, an act of desire and murder." (1983a, 33) Kristeva's qualification before her critical interpretation of Lacan's work, which she emphasizes is her *own* interpretation, is in itself strange. If Kristeva means what she seems to say—when asked as a psychoanalyst to interpret, it is strange to consider herself a propagator of psychoanalysis—then I have two questions: What is it about the *calling* that weighs on her self-presentation? and, As a self-identified psychoanalyst engaging in interpretation, isn't she necessarily propagating psychoanalysis? Perhaps Kristeva's essay can be read as an "(obsessional) defense" (1983a, 48) about the association of her work with Lacan's.

25. For example, Kristeva criticizes Lacan for presupposing an always already there of language in *Revolution in Poetic Language* (1974, 130–31) and *Tales of Love* (1983, 44).

26. Kristeva's *Powers of Horror* is devoted to analyzing at least two ways in which sacrifice and violence are controlled and sublimated within the social code: religious ritual and literature. I discuss Kristeva's analysis of abject literature and its role in sublimating sacrifice and violence in the next chapter.

27. To use some of Kristeva's favorite imagery, in Christian lore the maternal body is penetrated by the Word so that the Word may become flesh. So that the Word may become eternal, so that it may become the Word of God, that flesh must be sacrificed on the cross. This echoes Nietzsche's argument in *On the Genealogy of Morals* that once socialized, human's pre-social instincts can no longer be discharged in their direct and natural manner. Consequently, since they must be discharged, they are turned inward and discharged against the body itself. For a comparison of Nietzsche and Kristeva on language, see my article "Revolutionary Horror: Nietzsche and Kristeva on the Politics of Poetry." (1989) See also Jean Graybeal's *Language and "The Feminine" in Nietzsche and Heidegger.* (1990)

28. Kristeva, however, argues that art is actually a better example of the relationship between the semiotic and the symbolic. Unlike sacrifice, which regulates *jouissance* so that it cannot disrupt the social, art allows the flow of *jouissance* into the symbolic, which can disrupt that symbolic. (1974, 79–80) I come back to this in chapter 4.

29. I explain how the semiotic uses the law against itself in chapter 4.

30. Compare this to a passage in Lacan's 1953–54 seminar, where he claims that the symbol opens up the world of negativity. (1954, 173–74)

31. Lacan also identifies a "negativation" that is prior to the "no." (1954, 173–74) Kristeva, however, suggests that his negativity is already a symbolic operation. I am not persuaded by Kristeva's interpretation of Lacan, but it is beyond the scope of my project to evaluate her interpretation here.

32. This translation is mine with help from Nadja Hofmann. All errors are mine alone.

2. The Abject Mother

1. From Kristeva's "Stabat Mater." (1976, 263)

2. When Kristeva criticizes existential feminism, she must be thinking of Beauvoir. I analyze Kristeva's relationship to Beauvoir in chapter 5.

3. Primary narcissism is an important issue in Kristeva's *Tales of Love*. There she associates it with what she calls the "Imaginary Father." The imaginary father will be the topic of the next chapter. In this particular essay, "Stabat Mater," Kristeva describes primary narcissism as a primary identification with the mother. (1976a, 234)

4. Kristeva gives four reasons why an identification with the Virgin maintains primary narcissism even while it contains it. First, the Virgin denies the other

sex, the sex of man. Hers is an immaculate conception and she has no need of another sex. Thus, she does not have to acknowledge an other. Second, the Virgin has the power of Mother of the Church and Queen in Heaven. However, since she is still subject to God and the child-god, she avoids megalomania. Third, the Virgin wards off any desire to murder or devour the mother "by means of a strong oral cathexis (the breast), valorization of pain (the sob), and incitement to replace the sexed body with the ear of understanding." (1976a, 257) Fourth, the Virgin is excluded from time and death. She is taken to heaven through Assumption without dying. This too protects the mother against death. It also protects the paranoiac against separation from the mother. Also, the Virgin is one of a kind, unlike other women, "alone in her sex." (1976a, 258, 256) This insures that she is the only one who exists. It guarantees that the primary identification is safe from the threat of any other possible identifications or objects.

5. The Virgin cannot account for the mother-daughter relationship, the relationship between (different) women. Kristeva suggests that relationships between women are always, in some sense, mother-daughter relationships; and, we need a discourse of motherhood that can account for this. Finally, the Virgin can no longer stand for a repudiation of the other sex (masculine) through the person of the child. The child as god (love) no longer fulfills the need for a relationship with an other. It can no longer be the "alter ego" that breaks feminine paranoia (1977a, 279) (See also "The Splitting Mother" below.) Love for and of a child is no longer enough for some women. Thus, today, argues Kristeva, women turn to politics, art, and science for fulfillment.

6. This analysis of feminine castration will become clearer after I elaborate Kristeva's notion of the maternal "Thing" below and after I develop my reading of her imaginary father in the next chapter.

7. This reading is fortified by Kristeva's identification of the "Thing" with the mother's sex in *Tales of Love.* (1983, 369)

8. "Between birth and birth" is the place that Lyotard describes as the object of our longing. It is the space between our birth and our realization that we were born, a place forever lost to us.

9. For a discussion of the psychoanalytic account of the mother's desire, see chapter 1.

10. Kristeva argues that becoming abject is the body's defense against cannibalism. If it is disgusting, it won't be eaten. (1980a, 78–79)

11. See 1983, 368. This splitting of the mother is complicated by another possibility that is central to Kristeva's discussion of Céline in *Powers of Horror.* There she argues that the abject can *become* sublime. (1980a, 59) The phobic can sexualize the abject and take sexual pleasure in it. Kristeva maintains that this eroticized abject is the "object" of perverts and artists.

12. A version of this section appeared in my "Kristeva's Imaginary Father and the Crisis in the Paternal Function." (1991)

13. There are critics of Kristeva's notion of herethics; for example, Eléanor Kuykendall and Andrea Nye. I will address their criticisms in my conclusion when I can develop the relationship between Kristeva's herethics and what she identifies as the ethics of psychoanalysis, which founds a politics of difference. I think that it is useful to assess Kristeva's herethics in the context of her recent analyses of the ethics of psychoanalysis.

14. Even this is problematic—witness Kristeva's account of the cult of the Virgin Mother and, I might add, the rhetoric of antiabortion crusaders in the United States, who argue that the fetus is a unified subject in its own right.

15. Lacan suggests that within the child's imaginary the relationship with the

other is a Hegelian struggle for recognition. (1954, 146–47, 170–73, 222–23; 1955, 166) For a more detailed account, see my analysis in the next chapter.

16. "Silence," says Kristeva, "weighs heavily nonetheless on the corporeal and psychological suffering of childbirth and especially the self-sacrifice involved in becoming anonymous in order to pass on the social norm, which one might repudiate for one's own sake but within which *one must* include the child in order to educate it along the chain of generations." (1976a, 260) This poses problems for feminist mothers who hope to change the status quo. Do they raise their children with traditional patriarchal values and sacrifice the feminist struggle? Or do they raise them with countercultural values and risk their being misfits?

3. The Imaginary Father

1. Parts of this chapter appeared in my "Kristeva's Imaginary Father and the Crisis in the Paternal Function." (1991)

2. See, for example: Eléanor Kuykendall's "Question for Julia Kristeva's Ethics of Linguistics" (1989, 184); Domna Stanton's "Difference on Trial: A Critique of the Maternal Metaphor in Cixous, Irigaray, and Kristeva" (1989, 160); Dorothy Leland's "Lacanian Psychoanalysis and French Feminism: Toward an Adequate Political Psychology" (1989, 98); Nancy Fraser, "The Uses and Abuses of French Discourse Theories for Feminist Politics." (1990)

3. I have slightly modified Roudiez's translation in this quotation. I think that Kristeva's reading of Lacan is problematic here. Lacan, it seems to me, suggests a dialectic between the symbolic and imaginary rather than the substitution of one for the other. But at this time I cannot attempt to develop this intuition.

4. I will come back to this imaginary love later in this chapter.

5. Within the framework of traditional psychoanalytic theory, it is possible to read Kristeva's thesis that the logic of the symbolic is already at work in the maternal body as a form of fetishism. Kristeva herself describes fetishism as the attribution of phallic power to the mother that results in the "maternal father." (1987, 45) Indeed, my own emphasis on the maternal function in Kristeva's writings could be read in the same way. For the beginnings of an analysis of Kristeva's fetishism, see chapter 5.

6. Even so she says that for Freud the father of pre-individual history "is something different from the overwhelming presence of the mother which is loving, but which is also too much desiring, too much in close proximity to the child, and in this way she perhaps cannot give enough space for symbolic elaboration." (1984b, 22) At the same time that Kristeva is calling for the "ambiguisation of identity" and the breakdown of the paternal function, she is reluctant to say that the mother can play the role of the Third. She is fundamentally concerned that the Third is "an intrapsychic and social instance that is not the physical envelope of the mother." (1984d, 21) Still, Kristeva does not say that the mother cannot play the role of the Third. She says that *for Freud* the mother cannot play the role of the Third.

7. Elizabeth Grosz criticizes the way in which Kristeva separates the maternal from women's bodies. (1990, 161) She argues that Kristeva denies the specificity of women's bodies.

8. Kristeva distinguishes between "Thing" *(Chose)* and "Object" *(Objet)* in *Soleil Noir.* (1987, 22–25) The Thing is prior to the Object. It represents the quasi-presymbolic connection to an archaic mother. The depressive, maintains Kristeva, mourns the loss of the Thing and not the Object. Refer back to the last chapter for a more detailed analysis of the maternal "Thing."

9. Cf. *Tales of Love,* where Kristeva discusses the relationship between the mother, her love, perversion, and death.

4. Revolutionary Language Rendered Speechless

1. See the most theoretical sections of her first two books, *Semeiotiké: Recherches Pour Une Sémanalyse* (1969) and *Le Texte du Roman* (1970) and various early articles (1966–1976) collected in *Polylogue* (1977).

2. "Psychoanalysis," of course, comes from Freud, who introduced the term. "Semiology" comes from Saussure, who introduced the term in his *Course in General Linguistics.* (1916) Kristeva is especially influenced by modifications in the meaning of "semiology," some drastic, by C. S. Pierce and, her teacher, Roland Barthes.

3. In some of her early writing, Kristeva refers to semanalysis as "semiotics."

4. For a discussion of Nietzsche's "monumental time" see Kristeva's "Women's Time." (1979a) For a useful analysis of "Women's Time" see Tina Chanter's "Female Temporality and the Future of Feminism," in Fletcher and Benjamin, eds., *Abjection, Melancholia and Love.* (1990, 63–79)

5. Nancy Fraser suggests that Kristeva's logic of transformation threatens to foreclose the possibility of analyzing real political transformations. (1990)

6. The translations of previously untranslated material quoted here are mine.

7. Lacan identifies with the father of psychoanalysis and invokes his authority. Lacan's relationship to Freud can be read as an ambivalent relationship to paternal authority. Lacan very consistently emphasizes his identification with Freud. He humbly claims to be the only dutiful son. This overemphasized identification, in light of Lacan's often creative readings of Freud, is at the same time a protection against castration and a type of autocastration. Lacan both identifies with a strong paternal authority in order to make it his own and undermines his own authority by constantly deferring to Freud's.

8. Chapters 1 and 2 above also contain analyses of the semiotic.

9. See especially Andrea Nye (1987) and Judith Butler. (1989)

10. For an explanation of the dialectic that gives rise to language see chapter 1.

11. The absolute signified cannot be the end point of signification precisely because it would put an end to signification. There would be no need to say any more; we keep talking because of the overdetermination of the signifier.

12. Parts of this section were published in my "Revolutionary Horror: Nietzsche and Kristeva on the Politics of Poetry." (1990) In that article I much too simply and quickly equated Kristeva's semiotic with a "prelinguistic" sphere. The semiotic is clearly not prelinguistic in any straightforward sense.

13. "Revolutionary Horror: Nietzsche and Kristeva on the Politics of Poetry." (1990)

14. See Jacqueline Rose "Julia Kristeva Take Two" (1986, 154). Ewa Ziarek. (1990)

15. I have already indicated in my introduction that Kristeva's work itself can be read as an oscillation between semiotic and symbolic.

16. Kristeva's views on women's marginality have remained basically the same throughout her writings. At a lecture that she gave at Ohio State University in October 1988, Kristeva still held the position that women have difficulty entering the symbolic.

17. In chapter 5 I argue that Kristeva is carrying the corpse of the dead mother. In that chapter I will come back to some of the suggestions that I have made here.

18. Cf. Foucault 1983, 211–12.

5. Revolutionary Analysis

1. Kristeva quotes this passage in *Black Sun*. (1987, 220)

2. Jane Gallop discusses Kristeva's authoritative posturing in *The Daughter's Seduction*, chapter 8. (1982)

3. Nancy Tiezen argues that Kristeva gives priority to whatever activities she happens to be engaged in at the time of her writing. She thereby legitimates, even privileges, her own work. (1990, 111–12)

4. I have altered the parentheses in the Roudiez translation in order to keep with the original. See *Histoires d'amour*, 27.

5. Now, I wonder, did Kristeva's patient accept her fantasy as the *truth* about his symptoms, or did he accept it as a fantasy? If it works, it seems that he must have accepted it as the truth. In this case, is it merely another truth/illusion posed as an absolute that replaces his old truths? Or does he accept this "truth" as an illusion. In order for Kristeva to be consistent, it seems that her patients must accept her fantasies as fantasies. They must accept her meanings as illusions. And they cannot accept them as truth in any traditional sense. This raises another question: Does Kristeva *present* her fantasies as fantasies or as truths? It seems that Kristeva presents her fantasies as truths. In her accounts of her own practice she does not explicitly claim to present her interpretations and meanings as illusions. Moreover, it seems that if she did present her interpretations as her own fantasies, they would not have the same, or desired, effect on the analysand. That is to say that, if the analysand accepted Kristeva's fantasies *as* fantasies, then the analysand would not really believe them and her behavior/symptoms may not change.

6. In this context, by fantasy I mean simply any image, interpretation, or goal conjured at least partially through the imagination.

7. I will come back to this discussion in the next chapter.

8. For Kristeva all primary transference is to the maternal body, even if it is a transference to an object. Recall my analysis of Kristeva's attribution of place names and demonstratives to the child's first symbolic substitutions for the maternal body. See chapter 1.

9. Kristeva's remarks are especially haunting after the Persian Gulf war, in which the force of the United States army virtually crushed Iraq's "Third World" army. The United States administration represented the Iraq army as a growing Goliath, a huge, fierce, threatening monster. Sadam was compared to Hitler, pure evil. And against this pure evil Bush and America could become good, pure good. Only by defining ourselves against an evil Other can we become good.

10. All quotations from *Etrangers à nous-mêmes* are my own translations.

11. See my analysis in chapter 2.

12. For example, she mentions Beauvoir in passing in "Stabat Mater," where she criticizes Beauvoir for seeing the defeat of woman in Piero della Franscesca's nativity. (1976, 246) She uses Beauvoir as an example of leftists with naive images of America in "Why the United States?" (1977c, 285) She refers to Beauvoir in connection with Stendhal's relation to woman in *Tales of Love*. (1983, 363)

13. These similarities first occurred to me when I heard Gayatri Spivak describe an ethics implicit in Beauvoir's account of pregnancy, which seemed to me very close to Kristeva's herethics. (1989)

14. I describe Kristeva's account of herethics and both traditional and alternative discourses of motherhood in chapter 2.

6. Politics in the Age of Propaganda

1. For example, this problem can be more easily seen in Nietzsche's claim that there is no truth. Obviously, this claim operates as a kind of statement of truth: the truth is that there is no truth. Either the statement is false and allows for the

possibility that the claim is true, or the statement is true and the claim is false. In one sense, the problem may boil down to the logician's truth: anything follows from a contradiction. Nietzsche's thesis, then, may have a double effect. It will multiply interpretations—anything follows. And it will insure that Nietzsche's theories cannot be refuted—anything follows. However, the power in Nietzsche's paradoxical claim is that while it undermines all other truths, it also undermines itself. While Nietzsche's claim may appear as a traditional truth claim, its "truth-effect" is different from a traditional truth claim. This claim, which at the same time asserts and denies, has a different *effect* than traditional truth claims. The same is true of Kristeva's claim that all representations are symptoms of the crisis in representation.

2. Insofar as it problematizes the notion of identity and difference, Kristeva's analysis problematizes the very notions of "we," "us," "ourselves."

3. For example, see 1984b, 23, 27; 1974e, 138; 1974c, 16.

4. This remark is quoted and translated in *Desire in Language*. (1980, 10)

5. Gayatri Spivak questions Kristeva's unexamined use of the Electra myth. (1981, 162–63)

6. See my analysis in chapter 2.

7. See my analysis of the relationship between Kristeva and Beauvoir in the previous chapter.

8. In her chapter on Kristeva in *Sexuality in the Field of Vision* Jacqueline Rose criticizes Kristeva for identifying feminism as a monolithic entity. She cites several places in which Kristeva dismisses feminism as a monolithic entity: "Subjet dans le langage et pratique politique," 26; "La femme, ce n'est jamais ça," *Tel Quel* 59 (Autumn 1974): 24; *Powers of Horror*, 208. (1986, 158)

9. For good introductions to the plurality of feminisms in France, see Marks and de Courtivron, eds., *New French Feminisms*, or Toril Moi, ed., *French Feminist Thought*.

10. For example, Luce Irigaray, Hélène Cixous, Sarah Kofman, and Michele Le Doeuff, among others, in France, Alice Jardine, Gayatri Spivak, and Judith Butler, among others, in the United States. I suspect that there are feminists thinking, in one way or another, about the problem of difference, and its impact on women, all over the world.

11. For my reading of Kristeva as a melancholy theoretician see the previous chapter.

12. Luce Irigaray makes the more radical argument that we need a new discourse of maternity that does not construct identification with the maternal body as a threat to be overcome. For a comparison of Irigaray and Kristeva on this point, see my "Traversing Love and Desire: Irigaray and Kristeva on Metaphor and Metonymy," in D. Bauer and K. Oliver, eds., *Feminism and Language* (Bloomington: Indiana University Press, forthcoming).

13. See chapters 2 and 3 for more in-depth analysis of identity and alterity in maternity.

7. Importing "The French Feminists" and Their Desires

1. Quoted from Kristeva's *Sémiotikè*, 314, in Alice Jardine's "Introduction to Julia Kristeva's 'Women's Time.'" (1981, 12)

2. See Brian Duren's "Cixous' Exorbitant Texts." (1981)

3. For discussions of the difference between "feminism" in the United States and France and the translation between these two contexts, see Elaine Marks and Isabelle de Courtivron's introduction of *New French Feminisms* (1981); Gayatri Spivak, "French Feminism in an International Frame," *Yale French Studies* 62 (1981); Alice Jardine, *Gynesis: Configurations of Woman and Modernity* (1981);

Notes to pages 165–177

and especially Dorothy Kaufmann-McCall, "Politics of Difference: The Women's Movement in France from May 1968 to Mitterand," *Signs* 9:2. (1983)

4. For example, in the last half of the 1970s *Diacritics* included articles on Kristeva's writings by Philip Lewis (1984), Verena Conely (1975), James Creech (1975), and Josette Féral. (1978)

5. Thanks to Elissa Marder who pointed this translation problem out to me.

6. Ann Rosalind Jones's article "Writing the Body: Toward an Understanding of *L'Écriture Féminine*," published in *Feminist Studies* (1981), was one of the first and most important articles to attack "The French Feminists." Like Stanton before her, Jones also condenses some of their differences in order to dismiss Kristeva, Irigaray, and Cixous as proponents of an essentialist notion of *"écriture féminine."* See also Monique Plaza "'Phallomorphic Power,' and the Psychology of 'Woman'" (1978); Dorothy Leland, "Lacanian Psychoanalysis and French Feminism: Toward an Adequate Political Psychology" (1989); Domna Stanton, "Difference on Trial: A Critique of the Maternal Metaphor in Cixous, Irigaray, and Kristeva" in Allen and Young, eds., *The Thinking Muse: Feminism and Modern French Philosophy* (1989); Susan Suleiman, "Writing and Motherhood," in Garner et al., ed., *The (M)other Tongue: Essays in Feminist Psychoanalytic Interpretation* (1985); For a related criticism of the universalist or imperialistic tendencies of Kristeva, Irigaray, and Cixous, see Gayatri Spivak's "French Feminism in an International Frame." (1981)

7. For an insightful discussion of Irigaray's mimesis, see Naomi Schor's "The Essentialism Which is Not One." (1989)

8. For more on Lacan's notion of desire see chapter 1.

9. In her *Essentially Speaking*, Diana Fuss discusses the way in which Irigaray displaces the priority given to metaphor. There, Fuss argues that for Irigaray, woman's body is both a metaphor and metonymy for a feminine imaginary. (1989)

10. On my reading, Lacan's description of desire seems in keeping with what Irigaray describes as the mechanics of fluids. In addition, if Irigaray is suggesting the Lacan's metonymy of desire poses as a metaphor, I think that Lacan would agree. Lacan maintains that desire is an endless series of substitutions that pretend to operate according to a logic of metaphor, equal exchange, but really operate according to a logic of metonymy, never equal. However, while Lacan emphasizes that this never equal is experienced as a lack, Irigaray interprets it as excess. My reading of Kristeva brings her closer to Irigaray in this regard. See chapter 3.

11. For a discussion of Irigaray's use of morphology and its relation to anatomy, see Elizabeth Grosz, *Sexual Subversions* (1989), especially 111–12.

12. This passage is quoted and translated in Verena Andermatt's "Hélène Cixous and the Uncovery of a Feminine Language," *Women and Literature* 7:1 (Winter 1979): 42.

13. Moi indicates that Christiane Makward argues that there are twelve different styles in Cixous's novel *LA.* (Moi 1985, 115) (See Makward, "Structure du silence/du délire: Marguerite Duras, Hélène Cixous," *Poétique* 35 [Septembre 1978]: 314–24.)

14. Here, Cixous is alluding to Freud's theory that women are inferior to men—their superegos are underdeveloped—because they don't undergo the castration complex.

15. In this regard, Irigaray is more Heideggerian than Cixous.

16. For my argument that Kristeva's father is a screen for the mother, see chapter 3.

17. For a very insightful comparison of the theories and strategies of Kristeva and Irigaray, see Elizabeth Grosz' *Sexual Subversions* (1989) especially 103–104.

18. I discuss Kristeva's theory of material rejection and the move to desire in chapter 1.

19. Kit Belgum pointed out that I don't acknowledge the "otherness" of Anglo-American feminism when I group these theorists together in order to criticize them, especially since theorists such as Toril Moi have a complex relation to the Anglo-American scene.

REFERENCES

Cixous, Hélène

1969. *L'Exile de James Joyce ou l'art du remplacement.* Paris: Grasset. Translated as *The Exile of James Joyce or the Art of Replacement,* by S. Purcell. New York: David Lewis, 1972.

1969a. *Dedans.* Paris: Grasset.

1970. *Les Commencements.* Paris: Grasset.

1972. *Neutre.* Paris: Grasset.

1972a. *Portrait du soleil.* Paris: Editions Denoël.

1974. *Prénoms de personne.* Paris: Seuil.

1974a. *Révolutions pour d'un Faust.* Paris: Seuil.

1974b. "The Character of 'Character,'" trans. K. Cohen. *New Literary History,* vol. 5, 383–402.

1975. *La Jeune Née* (with Catherine Clement). Paris: UGE, 10/18. Translated as *The Newly Born Woman,* by B. Wing. Minneapolis: University of Minnesota Press, 1985.

1975a. "Le Rire de la Médusa." *L'Arc* 61, 39–54.

1975b. *Portrait de Dora.* Paris: des femmes.

1975c. *Souffles.* Paris: des femmes.

1975d. *LA.* Paris: Gallimard.

1975e. "At Circe's, or the Self-Opener," trans. C. Bové. *Boundary 2,* vol. 3, 387–97.

1976. "The Laugh of the Medusa." *Signs* 1, 875–99. Reprinted in *New French Feminisms,* ed. Marks and Courtivron. New York: Schocken, 1980, 245–64.

1976a. *LA.* Paris: Gallimard.

1976b. "La Missexualité ou jouis-je?" *Poétique* 26, 240–49.

1976c. "Le sexe ou la tête?" *Les Cahiers du GRIF* 13, 5–15.

1976d. "Interview with Hélène Cixous," by Christiane Makward. *Sub-Stance* 13.

1976e. "Fiction and Its Phantoms: A Reading of Freud's das Unheimliche," trans. R. Dennomé. *New Literary History,* vol. 7, 525–48.

1977. "Entretien avec Françoise van Rossum-Guyon." *Revue des sciences humaines* 168, (Oct.–Dec.) 479–93.

1977a. *La Venue à l'écriture* (with Leclerc and Gagnon). Paris: UGE, 10/18.

1977b. *Angst,* trans. J. Levy. Paris: des femmes. London: John Calder, 1985.

1978. *Préparatifs de noces au-delà de l'abîme.* Paris: des femmes.

1979. "L'Approche de Clarice Lispector." *Poétique* 40, 408–19.

1979a. "Rethinking Differences," in *Homosexualities and French Literature,* ed. Stambolian and Marks. New York: Cornell University Press.

1979b. *Vivre l'orange.* Paris: des femmes.

1979c. *Ananké.* Paris: des femmes.

1980. "Sorties," trans. A. Liddle, in *New French Feminisms,* ed. Marks and Courtivron. Brighton: Harvester, 90–98.

1980a. "Poetry Is/and (the) Political." *Bread and Roses,* no. 1, 16–18.

1980b. *Illa.* Paris: des femmes.

1981. "Castration or Decapitation?" *Signs* 7, no. 1, 41–55.

1981a. "Ou l'art de l'innocence. Paris: des femmes.

1982. "Introduction to Lewis Carroll's *Through the Looking Glass* and *The Hunting of the Snark*." *New Literary History* 13.

1982a. *Limonade tout était si infini*. Paris: des femmes.

1983. "Portrait of Dora." *Diacritics* 13, no. 1 (Spring), 2–32.

1983a. *Livre de Promethea*. Paris: Gallimard.

1984. Interview in Verena Andermatt Conley's *Hélène Cixous: Writing the Feminine*. Lincoln: University of Nebraska Press.

1984a. "Joyce: The (R)use of Writing," trans. J. Still. In *Post-Structuralist Joyce: Essays from the French*, ed. D. Attridge and D. Ferrer. Cambridge, Eng.: Cambridge University Press, 15–30.

1984b. "Reading Clarice Lispector's 'Sunday Before Going to Sleep,'" trans. B. Wing. *Boundary* 2, vol. 12, no. 2, 41–48.

1984c. "Aller à la mer," trans. B. Kerslake. *Modern Drama* 27, 546–48.

1986. *Inside*, trans. C. Barko. New York: Schocken.

1986a. "The Conquest of the School at Madhubai," trans. D. Carpenter. *Women and Performance*, vol. 3, 59–96.

1986b. "The Last Word," trans. S. Sellers and A. Liddle. *Women's Review*, no. 6, 22–24.

1986c. Interview with Susan Sellers. *Women's Review*, no. 7, 22–23.

1986d. "Entretien avec Hélène Cixous." *Théâtre/Public*, no. 68, 22–29.

1987. "Reaching the Point of Wheat, or A Portrait of the Artist as a Maturing Woman." *New Literary History*, vol. 19, 1–21.

1988. "Extreme Fidelity," and "Tancredi Continues," trans. A. Liddle and S. Sellers. In *Writing Differences: Readings from the Seminar of Hélène Cixous*, ed. S. Sellers. Milton Keynes: Open University Press, 9–36.

1989. "The 'Double World' of Writing," "Listening to the Truth," "A Realm of Characters," "Writing as a Second Heart." In *Delighting the Heart: A Notebook by Women Writers*, ed. S. Sellers. London: The Women's Press, 18, 69, 126–28, 198.

189a. "From the Scene of the Unconscious to the Scene of History," trans. D. Carpenter. *Future Literary History*, 1–8.

1990. *Reading with Clarice Lispector*, trans. Verena Andermatt Conley. London: Harvester Wheatsheaf.

1990a. "Difficult Joys." In *The Body and the Text: Hélène Cixous, Reading and Teaching*, ed. Wilcox, McWatters, Thompson, and Williams. London: Harvester Wheatsheaf, 5–30.

1991. *Coming to Writing*, trans. A. Liddle and D. Carpenter-Jensen. Boston: Harvard University Press.

Freud, Sigmund

All texts are cited from *The Standard Edition of the Complete Psychological Works of Sigmund Freud*, translated by James Strachey. London: The Hogarth Press, 1953–1974.

1891. *Aspasia*.

1897. Letter to Fliess.

1900. *Interpretation of Dreams*.

1905. *Three Essays on the Theory of Sexuality*.

1910. *A Special Type of Object Choice Made by Men*. Vol. 11.

1911. *Contributions on the Psychology of Love*. Vol. 11.

1912. *A Note on the Unconscious in Psycho-analysis*. Vol. 12.

1914. *On Narcissism*. Vol. 14.

1915. *The Unconscious*.

1916–17. *Introductory Lectures to Psychoanalysis.*
1921. *Group Psychology and the Analysis of the Ego.* Vol. 18.
1923. *The Ego and the Id.* Vol. 19.
1924. *The Dissolution of the Oedipal Complex.*
1925. *Some Psychical Consequences of the Anatomical Distinction between the Sexes.*
1932. "Femininity." Lecture XXXIII, *New Introductory Lectures.*
1938. *An Outline of Psychoanalysis.*
1938a. *Splitting of the Ego in the Process of Defence.*
1938b. Findings, Ideas, etc., vol. 23.

Irigaray, Luce

1973. *Les Langages des déments.* Paris: Mouton.
1974. *Speculum: de l'autre femme.* Paris: Les Editions de Minuit.
1975. "La Femme, son sexe et le langage." *La Nouvelle Critique* 82 (March).
1977. "Women's Exile." *Ideology and Consciousness* 1.
1979. "Etablier un généalogie de femmes." *Maintenant* 12.
1980. *Amante Marine: de Friedrich Nietzsche.* Paris: Les Editions de Minuit.
1980a. Interview in *Women Analyze Women,* ed. Elaine Baruch and Lucienne Serrano. New York: New York University Press, 1988.
1981. *Le Corps-acorps avec la mère.* Montreal: Les Editions de la pleine lune.
1981a. "And One Doesn't Stir without the Other." *Signs* 7, no. 1.
1982. *Passions élémentaires.* Paris: Les Editions de Minuit.
1983. *La Croyance même.* Paris: Editions Galilée.
1983a. *L'Oubli de l'air: Chez Martin Heidegger.* Paris: Les Editions de Minuit.
1983b. "Veiled Lips." *Mississippi Review* 11, no. 3.
1983c. "For Centuries We've Been Living in the Mother-Son Relation . . ." *Hecate* 9, no. 1–2.
1983d. "An Interview with Luce Irigaray," with Kiki Amsberg and Aafke Steenhuis, trans. R. van Krieken. *Hecate* 9, no. 1–2, 192–202.
1983e. "Luce Irigaray," interview with Lucienne Serrano and Elaine Hoffman Baruch, in *Women Analyze Women,* ed. Serrano and Baruch. London: Harvester Whestsheaf, 147–64.
1984. *L'Ethique de la différence sexuelle.* Paris: Les Editions de Minuit.
1985. *Speculum of the Other Woman,* trans. Gillian Gill. Ithaca: Cornell University Press.
1985a. *This Sex Which Is Not One,* trans. Porter and Burke. Ithaca: Cornell University Press.
1985b. *Parler n'est jamais neutre.* Paris: Les Editions de Minuit.
1985c. "Is the Subject of Science Sexed?" *Cultural Critique* 1. Reprinted in *Hypatia* 2, no. 3 (Fall 1987).
1985d. "Language, Persephone and Sacrifice." An interview with J. J. Maroney. *Borderlines* 4 (Winter), 30–32.
1986. "Women, the Sacred and Money." *Paragraph* 8.
1986a. "The Fecundity of the Caress," in *Face-to-Face with Levinas,* ed. R. A. Cohen. New York: SUNY Press.
1987. *Sexes et parentes.* Paris: Les Editions de Minuit.
1987a. "L'ordre sexuel du discours." *Langages* 85.
1987b. "Sexual Difference," trans. Seán Hand, in *French Feminist Thought,* ed. Toril Moi. London: Blackwell.
1987c. "Le sujet de la science est-il sexué? Is the Subject of Science Sexed?" trans. Carol Mastrangelo. *Hypatia* 2, no. 3, 65–88.

1989. "Equal to Whom?" *differences* 1, no. 2 (Summer), 59–74, trans. R. L. Mazzola.

1989a. "Sorcerer Love: A Reading of Plato's Symposium, Diotima's Speech," trans. E. Kuykendall. *Hypatia* 3, no. 3 (Winter).

1989b. *Le Temps de la Différence.* Paris: Libraire Générale Française.

1991. *Marine Lover of Friedrich Nietzsche,* trans. Gillian Gill. Ithaca: Cornell University Press.

1991a. *Irigaray Reader,* ed. Margaret Whitford. New York: Blackwell.

1991b. Interview with Raoul Mortley, in *French Philosophers in Conversation: Derrida, Irigaray, Levinas, Le Doeuff, Schneider, Serres.* London: Routledge, 63–78.

Kristeva, Julia

1966. "Word, Dialogue, Novel," in *The Kristeva Reader,* ed. Toril Moi. New York: Columbia University Press, 1986.

1968. "Semiotics," in *The Kristeva Reader.*

1968a. "Gesture: Practice or Communication," in *Semiotike: Recherches pour une sémanalyse,* 90–112. In *Social Aspects of the Human Body: A Reader of Key Texts,* ed. Ted Polhemus. New York: Penguin Books, 1978, 264–84.

1969. *Semeiotiké: Recherches pour une semanalyse.* Paris: Seuil.

1970. *Le Texte du roman.* The Hague: Mouton.

1971. "How Does One Speak to Literature," trans. Thomas Gora, Alice Jardine, and Leon Roudiez, in *Desire in Language,* ed. Leon Roudiez. New York: Columbia University Press, 1980.

1972. "The Semiotic Activity." *Screen* 14, no. 1, 25–39.

1972a. "Four Types of Signifying Practice." *Semiotext(e)* 1.

1973. "The System and the Speaking Subject," in *The Kristeva Reader.*

1973a. "Le Sujet en Proces," in *Polylogue.* Paris: Seuil, 1977.

1974. *La Révolution du langage poétique.* Paris: Seuil. Translated as *Revolution in Poetic Language,* by Margaret Waller. New York: Columbia University Press, 1984.

1974a. "The Ethics of Linguistics," in *Desire.*

1974b. "The Novel as Polylogue," in *Desire.*

1974c. "About Chinese Women," in *The Kristeva Reader.*

1974d. "Phonetics, Phonology and Impulsional Bases," trans. Greenberg. *Diacritics* 4, no. 3, 33–37.

1974e. "Oscillation between Power and Denial," and "Woman Can Never Be Defined," in *New French Feminisms,* ed. Elaine Marks and Isabelle Courtivron. New York: Schocken Books, 1981.

1974f. "Luttes des femmes." *Tel Quel* 58 (Summer).

1975. "From One Identity to Another," in *Desire.*

1975a. "Motherhood according to Giovanni Bellini," in *Desire.*

1975b. "The Subject in Signifying Practice." *Semiotext(e)* 1, no. 3, 19–34.

1975c. "On the Women of China." *Signs* 1, no. 1 (Autumn).

1076. "The Father, Love, and Banishment," in *Desire.*

1976a. "Stabat Mater," in *Tales of Love,* trans. Leon Roudiez. New York: Columbia University Press, 1987.

1976b. "China, Women and the Symbolic." An interview by Josette Féral. *SubStance* 13.

1976c. "Signifying Practice and Mode of Production." *Edinburgh Review* 1.

1977. *Polylogue.* Paris: Seuil.

1977a. "Place Names," in *Desire.*

1977b. "A New Type of Intellectual: The Dissident," in *The Kristeva Reader*.

1977c. "Why the United States," in *The Kristeva Reader*.

1977d. Jean-Paul Enthoven, interviewer, "Julia Kristeva: *à quoi servent les intel-lectuels?*" *Le Nouvel Observateur*, June 20.

1977e. "Modern Theater Does Not Take (a) Place." *Sub-Stance* 18/19.

1977f. "A partir de Polylogue." *Revue des sciences humaines* 168, 495–501. Translated by Séan Hand as "Talking about *Polylogue*," in *French Feminist Thought: A Reader*, ed. Toril Moi. New York: Blackwell, 1987, 110–17.

1977g. "Chinese Women: The Mother at the Center." *Liberation* 20, no. 3 (March–April), 10–17.

1979. "The True-Real," in *The Kristeva Reader*.

1979a. "Le Temps des femmes," originally published in *34/44: Cahiers de recher-che de sciences des textes et documents*, no. 5. Trans. by A. Jardine and H. Blake as "Women's Time," in *Feminist Theory: A Critique of Ideology*, ed. N. Keohane, M. Z. Rosaldo, and B. C. Gelpi. Brighton: Harvester, 1982.

1979b. "Ellipsis on Terror and the Specular Seduction." *Wide Angle* 3, no. 2, 42–47.

1979c. "Il n'y a pas de maître à langage." *Nouvelle Revue de Psychanalyse, Re-gards sur la psychanalyse en France* 20 (Fall), 119–40.

1980, *Desire in Language*, trans. Thomas Gora, Alice Jardine, and Leon Roudiez, ed. Leon Roudiez. New York: Columbia University Press.

1980a. *Pouvoirs de l'horreur*. Paris: Seuil. Translated as *Powers of Horror*, by Leon Roudiez. New York: Columbia University Press, 1982.

1980b. "Interview with Julia Kristeva," in *Women Analyze Women*, ed. Elaine Baruch and Lucienne Serrano. New York: New York University Press, 1988.

1980c. "Postmodernism?" in *Romanticism, Modernism, Postmodernism*, ed. Harry Garvin.

1981. "Psychoanalysis and the Polis," in *The Kristeva Reader*.

1981a. "The Maternal Body." *m/f* 5–6.

1983. *Histoires d'amour*. Paris: Denoël. Translated as *Tales of Love*, by Leon Rou-diez. New York: Columbia University Press, 1987.

1983a. "Within the Microcosm of the 'Talking Cure,'" trans. T. Gora and M. Waller, in *Psychiatry and the Humanities*, ed. Smith, vol. 6. New Haven: Yale Uni-versity Press.

1983b. "Mémoires." *Infini* 1, 44.

1984. *Revolution in Poetic Language*, trans. Margaret Waller. New York: Columbia University Press, 1984.

1984a. Interview with Perry Meisel. *Partisan Review* 51, no. 1, 128–32.

1984b. "Julia Kristeva in Conversation with Rosalind Coward." *Desire, ICA Docu-ments*, 22–27.

1984c. "My Memory's Hyperbole." *New York Literary Forum*, vol. 12–14, 261–76.

1984d. "Histoires d'amour—Love Stories." *Desire, ICA Documents*, 18–21.

1984e. "The Last Word of This Adventure: Interview with Julia Kristeva," in Lou-ise Burchill, *On the Beach*, 26.

1985. "The Speaking Subject," in *On Signs*, M. Blonsky, ed. Baltimore: Johns Hopkins University Press.

1986. "An Interview with Julia Kristeva," by Edith Kurweil. *Partisan Review* 53, no. 2, 216–29.

1986a. "An Interview with Julia Kristeva," by I. Lipkowitz and A. Loselle. *Critical Texts* 3, no. 3.

1987. *Au commencement était l'amour*. Translated as *In the Beginning Was Love: Psychoanalysis and Faith*, by Author Goldhammer. New York: Columbia University Press, 1988.

1987a. *Soleil noir: Depression et mélancolie.* Paris: Gallimard. Translated as *Black Sun,* by Leon Roudiez. New York: Columbia University Press, 1989.
1987b. "La Femme tristesse." *L'Infini* 17, 5–9.
1987c. "La Vierge de Freud." *L'Infini,* 18, 23–30.
1987d. Interview with Alice Jardine. *Copyright* 1 (Fall), 22–29.
1987e. "The Pain of Sorrow in the Modern World: The Works of Marguerite Duras." *PMLA* 102, no. 2 (March), 138–52.
1988. "Imagination in Psychoanalysis." Lecture given at Ohio State University, October. A version of this lecture will appear in *Culturall Semiosis: Tracing the Signifier, Continental Philosophy,* vol. 6. New York: Routledge, forthcoming.
1988a. "Joyce 'The Gracehoper' or the Return of Orpheus," in *James Joyce: The Augmented Ninth,* ed. Bernard Benstock. Syracuse: Syracuse University Press.
1988b. "On the Melancholic Imaginary," in *Discourse in Psychoanalysis and Literature,* ed. Shlomith Rimmon-Kenan. New York: Methuen.
1989. *Etrangers à mous-mêmes.* Paris: Fayard, 1989. Translated as *Strangers to Ourselves,* by Leon Roudiez. New York: Columbia University Press, 1991.
1989a. "Jackson Pollock's Milky Way: 1912–1956." *Journal of Philosophy and the Visual Arts.*
1990. *Lettre ouverte à Harlem Désir.* Paris: Editions Rivages.
1990a. *Les Samouraïs.* Paris: Fayard.
1991. *Le vieil homme et les loups.* Paris: Fayard.

Lacan, Jacques

1953. "Some Reflections on the Ego." *International Journal of Psychoanalysis* 34.
1954. *The Seminar of Jacques Lacan, Freud's Papers on Technique, 1953–54,* Book I, trans. John Forrester. Cambridge, Eng.: Cambridge University Press, 1988.
1955. *The Seminar of Jacques Lacan, the Ego in Freud's Theory and in the Technique of Psychoanalysis, 1954–1955,* Book II, trans. Sylvana Tomaselli. Cambridge, Eng.: Cambridge University Press, 1988.
1966. *Ecrits 1 and 2.* Paris: Seuil.
1970. "Of Structure as an Inmixing of Otherness Prerequisite to Any Subject Whatever," in *The Languages of Criticism and Sciences of Man. The Structuralist Controversy,* ed. R. Mackesay and E. Donato. New York: Doubleday.
1972. "Seminar on 'The Purloined Letter.'" *Yale French Studies* 48.
1973. *The Four Fundamental Concepts of Psycho-Analysis.* London: Hogarth Press.
1077. *Ecrits: A Selection,* trans. Alan Sheridan. London: Tavistock.
1977a. "Desire and the Interpretation of Desire in *Hamlet." Yale French Studies* 55 and 56.
1980. "A Lacanian Psychosis: Interview by Lacan," in *Returning to Freud,* ed. S. Schneiderman. New Haven: Yale University Press.
1981. "The Oedipus Complex." *Semiotext(e)* 10.
1981a. "Ste Anne . . ." *Semiotext(e)* 10.
1982. *Feminine Sexuality,* trans. J. Mitchell and J. Rose. London: Macmillan.

Secondary Sources
On Cixous

Andermatt, V. 1977. "Hélène Cixous and the Uncovery of Feminine Language." *Women and Literature* 7, no. 1.
Coneley, Verena Andermatt. 1984. *Hélène Cixous: Writing the Feminine.* Lincoln: University of Nebraska Press.

————. 1984a. "Approaches." Boundary 2, vol. 12, no. 2, 1–7.
————. 1990. "Introduction" to Reading with Clarice Lispector. London: Harvester
    Wheatsheaf, vii–xviii.
Deleuze, Gilles. 1972. "Hélène Cixous ou l'écriture stoboscopique." Le Monde,
    August 11, p. 10.
Duren, B. 1981. "Cixous' Exorbitant Texts." Sub-Stance 32.
Kuhn, Annette. 1981. "Introduction to Cixous' 'Castration or Decapitation.'" Signs
    7, no. 1.
Lamont, Rosette C. 1989. "The Reverse Side of a Portrait: The Dora of Freud and
    Cixous," in Feminine Focus: The New Women Playwrights, ed. E. Baxter.
    Oxford: Oxford University Press, 79–93.
Makward, Christine. 1978. "Structures du silence/du délire: Marguerite Duras,
    Hélène Cixous." Poétique 35, 314–24.
Moi, Toril. 1981. "Representation of Patriarchy: Sexuality and Epistemology in
    Freud's 'Dora.'" Feminist Review 9, 60–74.
Picard, Anne-Marie. 1989. "'L'Indiade': Ariane's and Hélène's Conjugate Dreams."
    Modern Drama, vol. 32, 24–38.
Sankovitch, Tilde. 1988. "Hélène Cixous: The Pervasive Myth," in French Women
    Writers and the Book: Myths of Access and Desire. Syracuse: Syracuse
    University Press, 127–52.
Sellers, S., ed. 1988. Writing Differences: Reading from the Seminar of Hélène
    Cixous. Milton Keynes: Open University Press.
Singer, Linda. 1989. "True Confessions: Cixous and Foucault on Sexuality and
    Power," in The Thinking Muse: Feminism and Modern French Philosophy,
    ed. Allen and Young. Bloomington: Indiana University Press.
Stevens, Crista. 1990. "Hélène Cixous: Portraying the Feminine," in Beyond Limits,
    ed. L. Brouwer et al. Groningen: University of Groningen, 83–96.
Wilcox, H., et al., eds. 1990. The Body and the Text: Héle]gne Cixous, Reading
    and Teaching. London: Harvester Wheatsheaf.
Willis, Sharon. 1985. "Hélène Cixous's 'Portrait de Dora': The Unseen and the
    Un-Scene." Theatre Journal, vol. 37, 287–301.

                                    On Freud
Benjamin, Jessica. 1988. The Bonds of Love. New York: Pantheon Books.
Flax, Jane. 1990. Thinking Fragments. Berkeley: University of California Press.
Gallop, Jane. 1982. The Daughter's Seduction. Ithaca: Cornell University Press.
————. 1985. Reading Lacan. Ithaca: Cornell University Press.
Grosz, Elizabeth. 1991. "Lesbian Fetishism?" differences 3, no. 2, 39–54.
Kofman, Sarah. 1980. L'Enigme de la femme. Translated as The Enigma of Woman,
    by Catherine Porter. Ithaca: Cornell University Press, 1985.
Millet, Kate. 1969. Sexual Politics. New York: Doubleday.
Mitchell, Juliet. 1975. Psychoanalysis and Feminism. New York: Random House.

                                    On Irigaray
Adlam, D., and Venn, C. 1977. "Introduction to Irigaray." Ideology and Conscious-
    ness 1.
Bartkowski, Frances. 1980. "The Question of Ethics in French Feminism." Berk-
    shire Review 21, 22–29.
Berg, E. 1982. "The Third Woman." Diacritics 12.
Berg, Maggie. 1988. "Escaping the Cave: Irigaray and Her Feminist Critics," in
    Literature and Ethics, ed. Gary Wihl and David Williams. Toronto: Univer-
    sity of Toronto Press.
Bowlby, Rachel. 1983. "The Feminine Female." Social Text 7, 54–68.

Braidotti, Rose. 1986. "The Ethics of Sexual Difference: The Case of Foucault and Irigaray." *Australian Feminist Studies* 3, 1–13.

———. 1991. *Patterns of Dissonance*. Cambridge: Polity Press.

Brennan, Teresa, ed. 1989. *Between Feminism and Psychoanalysis*. London: Routledge.

Burke, Carolyn. 1978. "Report from Paris." *Signs* 3, no. 4.

———. 1980. "Introduction to 'When Our Lips Speak Together.'" *Signs* 7, no. 2.

———. 1981. "Luce Irigaray through the Looking Glass." *Feminist Studies* 7, no. 2.

———. 1987. "Romancing the Philosophers: Luce Irigaray." *The Minnesota Review* 29.

Chalier, Catherine. 1980. "Amante Marine." *Sorcières* 20, 26–30.

Conley, Verena. 1977. "Missexual Misstery." *Diacritics* (Summer 1975), 70–82.

Dallery, Arleen. 1989. "The Politics of Writing (the) Body: écriture féminine," in *Gender/Body/Knowledge: Feminist Reconstructions of Being and Knowing*, ed. Jaggar and Bordo. New Brunswick and London: Rutgers University Press, 52–67.

Fauré, Christine. 1981. "The Twilight of the Goddesses, or the Intellectual Crisis of French Feminism," trans. L. Robinson. *Signs* 7, no. 1, 81–86.

Felman, Shoshana. 1975. "The Critical Phallacy." *Diacritics* (Winter).

———. 1977. "To Open the Question." *Yale French Studies* 55–56, 5–10.

Féral, Josette. 1981. "Towards a Theory of Displacement." *Sub-Stance* 32, 52–64.

Franklin, Sarah. 1985. "Luce Irigaray and the Feminist Critique of Language." *Women's Studies Occasional Papers*, no. 6. Canterbury: University of Kent.

Freeman, Barbara. 1986. "Irigaray at the Symposium: Speaking Otherwise." *Oxford Literary Review* 8, no. 1–2, 170–77.

Fuss, Diana. 1989. *Essentially Speaking: Feminism, Nature & Difference*. New York: Routledge.

———. 1989a. "'Essentially Speaking': Luce Irigaray's Language of Essence." *Hypatia* 3, no. 3, 62–80.

Gallop, Jane. 1983. "Quand nos lèvres s'écrivent: Irigaray's Body Politic." *Romantic Review* 74, no. 1.

———. 1986. "French Theory and the Seduction of the Feminine." *Paragraph* 8.

Gearhart, Suzanne. 1979. "The Scene of Psychoanalysis: The Unanswered Questions of Dora." *Diacritics* (March), 114–26.

Gross, Elizabeth. 1986. "Review of Speculum and This Sex." *Australian Feminist Studies* 2.

———. 1986a. "Irigaray and Sexual Difference." *Australian Feminist Studies* 2 (Autumn), 63–77.

———. 1986b. "Derrida, Irigaray and Deconstruction," in "Leftwright," *Intervention* 20, 70–81.

Grosz, Elizabeth, et al., eds. 1987. *Futur*Fall: Excursions into Post-Modernity*. Sydney: University of Sydney Power Institute of Fine Arts, 118–27.

———. 1988. "Desire, the Body and Recent French Feminisms." *Intervention* 21–22, 28–33.

———. 1988a. "The Hetero and the Homo: The Sexual Ethics of Luce Irigaray." *Gay Information* 17–18 (March), 37–44.

———. 1990. "Irigaray and the Divine." Paper presented at the Society for Phenomenology and Existential Philosophy conference, Villanova University, Philadelphia, Pa.

Holmlund, Christeine. 1989. "I Love Luce: The Lesbian, Mimesis and Masquerade in Irigaray, Freud and Mainstream Film." *New Formations* 9 (Winter), 105–23.

Homans, Margaret. 1986. "Reconstructing the Feminine." *The Women's Review of Books* (March 6), 12–13.

Johnson, Pauline. 1988. "The Dilemmas of Luce Irigaray." *Australian Feminist Studies*, no. 6 (Autumn), 87–96.

Jones, Ann Rosalind. 1985. "Inscribing Femininity: French Theories of the Feminine," in *Making a Difference: Feminist Literary Criticism*, ed. Gayle Greene and Coppélia Kahn. London and New York: Methuen, 80–112.

Kuykendall, Eléanor. 1984. "Toward an Ethic of Nurturance: Luce Irigaray on Mothering and Power," in *Mothering: Essays in Feminist Theory*, ed. Joyce Treblicot. Totowa, N.J.: Rowman & Allanheld, 263–74.

———. 1989. "*Sexes et Parentés*, by Luce Irigaray." *Hypatia* 3, no. 2, 172–74.

———. 1989a. "Introduction to 'Sorcerer Love' by Luce Irigaray." *Hypatia* 3, no. 3, 28–31.

Lorraine, Tamsin. 1990. "Irigaray and Con(fusing) Body Boundaries: Chaotic Folly or Unanticipated Bliss? Paper presented at the Society for Phenomenology and Existential Philosophy conference, Villanova University, Philadelphia, Pa.

Lyon, E. 1979. "Discourse and Difference." *Camera Obscura* 3–4.

McLuskie, Kate. 1983. "Women's Language and Literature: A Problem in Women's Studies." *Feminist Review* 14 (Summer), 51–61.

Nye, Andrea. 1989. "The Hidden Host: Irigaray and Diotima at Plato's Symposium." *Hypatia* 3, no. 3, 45–61.

Plaza, M. 1978. "'Phallomorphic Power,' and the Psychology of 'Woman.'" *Ideology and Consciousness* 4.

Reineke, Martha. 1987. "Lacan, Merleau-Ponty and Irigaray: Reflections on a Specular Drama." *Auslegung: A Journal of Philosophy* 14 (Winter), 67–85.

Sayers, Janet. 1982. *Biological Politics: Feminist and Anti-feminist Perspectives*. New York: Tavistock.

———. 1986. *Sexual Contradictions: Psychology, Psychoanalysis, and Feminism*. New York: Tavistock.

Schor, Naomi. 1989. "This Essentialism Which Is Not One: Coming to Grips with Irigaray." *differences* 1, no. 2 (Summer), 38–58.

Wenzel, V. H. 1981. "The Text as Body/Politics." *Feminist Studies* 7, no. 2.

———. 1981a. "Introduction to 'And One Doesn't Stir without the Other.'" *Signs* 7, no. 1.

Whitford, Margaret. 1986. "Luce Irigaray: The Problem of Feminist Theory." *Paragraph* 8, 102–105.

———. 1986a. "Speaking as a Woman: Luce Irigaray and the Female Imaginary." *Radical Philosophy* 43, 3–8.

———. 1988. "Luce Irigaray's Critique of Rationality," in *Feminist Perspectives in Philosophy*, ed. M. Griffiths and M. Whitford. Bloomington: Indiana University Press, 109–30.

———. 1991. *Luce Irigaray: Philosophy in the Feminine*. London: Routledge.

On Kristeva

Adams, Parveen. 1978. "Representation and Sexuality." *m/f*.

———, with Jeff Minson. 1978a. "The 'Subject' of Feminism." *m/f*, 43–61.

———. 1982. "Feminine Sexuality: Interview with Juliet Mitchell and Jacqueline Rose." *m/f*.

Adriens, Mark. 1981. "Ideology and Literary Production: Kristeva's Poetics," in *Semiotics and Dialectics: Ideology and the Text*, ed. Peter Zima. Amsterdam: Benjamins.

Ainely, Alison. 1990. "The Ethics of Sexual Difference," in *Abjection, Melancholia and Love: The Work of Julia Kristeva*, ed. Fletcher and Benjamin. New York: Routledge.

Allen, Jeffener, and Young, Iris, eds. 1989. *The Thinking Muse: Feminism and Modern French Philosophy*. Bloomington: Indiana University Press.

Andermatt, Verena. 1977. "Julia Kristeva and the Traversal of Modern Poetic Space." *Enclitic* 1, no. 2 (Fall), 65–77.

Atack, M. 1986. "The Other: Feminist." *Paragraph* 8, 25–38.

Barrett, Michele. 1987. "Concept of 'Difference.'" *Feminist Review* 26 (Summer), 29–41.

Barthes, Roland. 1970. "*L'étrangère.*" *La Quinzaine Littéraire* 94 (May 1–15), 19–20.

Bedient, Calvin. 1990. "Kristeva and Poetry as Shattered Signification." *Critical Inquiry* 16 (Summer).

Block, Ed. 1983. "Desire in Language." *Contemporary Literature* 24 (Winter), 512–20.

Bové Carol Mastrangelo. 1983. "The Text as Dialogue in Bakhtin and Kristeva." *Revue de l'Université d'Ottawa*.

———. 1984. "Women and Society in Literature or Reading Kristeva's Desire in Language and Proust." *Dalhousie Review* 64, 260–69.

———. 1988–89. "The Twin Faces of the Mother's Mask: Céline in Kristeva: Julia Kristeva's Powers of Horror: An Essay on Abjection." *Discourse* 11, no. 1 (Fall-Winter), 151–56.

Brant, J. 1987. "The Systematic of a Non-System, Julia Kristeva's Revisionary Semiotics." *American Journal of Semiotics* 5, no. 1, 133–50.

Burke, Carolyn Greenstein. 1978. "Report from Paris." *Signs* 3, 843–55.

Butler, Judith. 1989. "The Body Politics of Julia Kristeva." *Hypatia* 3, no. 3 (Winter), 104–18.

Caws, M. A. 1973. "*Tel Quel*: Text and Revolution." *Diacritics* (Spring).

Champagne, Roland. 1972. "The Words: Le roman du texte: A Response to Julia Kristeva's Reading of Antoine du La Salle's *Le Petit Jehan de Saintré* in Her *Le Texte du roman.*" *Sub-Stance* 4 (Fall), 125–33.

Chanter, Tina. 1990. "Female Temporality and the Future of Feminism," in *Abjection, Melancholia and Love: The Work of Julia Kristeva*, ed. Fletcher and Benjamin. New York: Routledge.

Chase, Cynthia. 1989. "Desire and Identity in Lacan and Kristeva," in *Feminism and Psychoanalysis*, ed. R. Feldstein and J. Roof. Ithaca: Cornell University Press.

Conley, V. 1975. "Kristeva's China." *Diacritics* (Winter).

Coward and Ellis. 1977. *Language and Materialism*. London: Routledge & Kegan Paul.

Creech, James. 1975. "Julia Kristeva's Bataille: Reading as Triumph." *Diacritics* (Spring), 62–68.

Eagleton, Terry. 1983. *Literary Theory: An Introduction*. Oxford: Blackwell.

Féral, Josette. 1978. "Antigone or the Irony of the Tribe." *Diacritics* 8, no. 3 (Fall), 2–14.

Finel-Honigman, Irene. 1981. "American Misconceptions of French Feminism." *Contemporary French Civilization* 3, 317–25.

Fletcher, John, and Benjamin, Andrew, eds. 1990. *Abjection, Melancholia and Love*. New York: Routledge.

Fraser, Nancy. 1990. "The Uses and Abuses of French Discourse Theories for Feminist Politics." *Sub-Stance*.

Gallop, Jane. 1982. *Feminism and Psychoanalysis: The Daughter's Seduction*. London: Macmillan.

Gidal, Peter. 1984. "On Julia Kristeva." *Undercut: Journal of London Filmmakers Cooperative* 12.

Grosz, Elizabeth. 1986. "Philosophy, Subjectivity and the Body: Kristeva and Irigaray," in *Feminist Challenges*, ed. Grosz and Pateman. Australia: Allen and Unwin.

———. 1987. "Language and the Limits of the Body: Kristeva and Abjection," in *Futur&Fall: Excursions into Post-Modernity*, ed. Grosz, Thredgold et al. Sydney, Australia: Pathfinder Press.

———. 1989 *Sexual Subversions*, Boston: Allen and Unwin.

———. 1990. "The Body of Signification," in *Abjection, Melancholia and Love*, ed. Fletcher and Benjamin. New York: Routledge.

Hoy, David. 1980. "Must We Mean What We Say?" *Revue de l'Université d'Ottawa*.

Jacobus, Mary. 1986. "Dora and the Pregnant Madonna," in *Reading Woman: Essays in Feminist Criticism*. New York: Columbia University Press.

———. 1986a. "Madonna Like a Virgin of Freud, Kristeva and the Case of the Missing Mother." *Oxford Literary Review* 8, no. 1–2, 35–50.

Jardine, Alice. 1980. "Theories of the Feminine: Kristeva." *Enclitic* 4, no. 2.

———. 1981. "Introduction to Julia Kristeva's 'Women's Time.'" *Signs* 7, no. 1, 5–12.

———. 1981a. "Pre-texts for the Transatlantic Feminist." *Yale French Studies* 62.

———. 1985. *Gynesis: Configurations of Woman and Modernity*. Ithaca: Cornell University Press.

———. 1986. "Opaque Texts and Transparent Contexts: The Political Difference of Julia Kristeva," in *The Poetics of Gender*, ed. Nancy K. Miller. New York: Columbia University Press.

Johnson, Barbara. 1978. "The Critical Difference." *Diacritics* (Summer).

Jones, Ann Rosalind. 1981. "Writing the Body: Toward an Understanding of L'Écriture Féminine." *Feminist Studies* 7, no. 2 (Summer).

———. 1984. "Julia Kristeva on Femininity: The Limits of a Semiotic Politics." *Feminist Review* 18 (Winter), 56–73.

———. 1985. "Inscribing Femininity: French Theories of the Feminine," in *Making a Difference: Feminist Literary Criticism*, ed. Gayle Greene and Coppélia Kahn. New York: Methuen, 80–112.

Klein, Richard. 1983. "In the Body of the Mother." *Enclitic* 7, no. 1, 66–75.

Kuykendall, Eléanor. 1989. "Question for Julia Kristeva's Ethics of Linguistics," in *The Thinking Muse: Feminism and Modern French Philosophy*, ed. Allen and Young. Bloomington: Indiana University Press, 180–94.

Lechte, John. 1990. *Julia Kristeva*. New York: Routledge.

Leland, Dorothy. 1989. "Lacanian Psychoanalysis and French Feminism: Toward an Adequate Political Psychology." *Hypatia* 3, no. 3 (Winter), 81–103.

Lewis, Philip. 1974. "Revolutionary Semiotics." *Diacritics* 4, no. 3 (Fall), 28–32.

Linderman, Deborah. 1984. "Julia Kristeva: *Powers of Horror*.: Sub-Stance 13, no. 3–4, 140–42.

Lowe, Lisa. 1991. *Critical Terrains: French and British Orientalisms*. Ithaca, NY: Cornell University Press, 136–89.

Marks, Elaine. 1978. "Women and Literature in France." *Signs* 3, no. 4 (Summer), 832–42.

McCallum, Pamela. 1985. "New Feminist Readings: Women as Ecriture or Woman as Other?" *Canadian Journal of Political and Social Theory* 9, no. 1–2 (Winter/Spring), 127–32.

McCance, Dawne. 1988. "Kristeva and the Subject of Ethics." *RFD: Resources for Feminist Research* 17, no. 4 (December), 18–22.

Moi, Toril. 1985. *Sexual/Textual Politics: Feminist Literary Theory.* London: Methuen.

——, ed. 1986. *The Kristeva Reader.* New York: Columbia University Press.

——, ed. 1987. *French Feminist Thought: A Reader.* New York: Blackwell.

——. 1988. "Feminism, Postmodernism and Style: Recent Feminist Criticism in the U.S." *Cultural Critique* 9 (Spring), 3–22.

Murphy, P. 1978. "Vision or Practive: New Poetics of Julia Kristeva." *Essays in Poetics* 3, no. 1, 57–82.

——. 1980. "Ideology or Science in a Mathematical Formalization of Poetic Language: A Close Analysis of Julia Kristeva's 'Pour une Semiologie des paragrammes.'" *Essays in Poetics* 5, no. 2, 84–120.

Nesselroth, Peter. 1976. "Poetic Language and the Revolution." *L'Esprit Créateur* 16, 149–60.

Nye, Andrea. 1987. "Woman Clothed with the Sun: Julia Kristeva and the Escape from/to Language." *Signs* 12, no. 4, 664–86.

Oliver, Kelly. 1990. "Revolutionary Horror: Nietzsche and Kristeva on the Politics of Poetry." *Social Theory and Practice* 16, no. 1.

——. 1991. "Kristeva's Imaginary Father and the Crisis in the Paternal Function." *Diacritics* 21, nos. 2–3 (Summer–Fall), 43–63.

——. Forthcoming, "Traversing Love and Desire: Irigaray and Kristeva on Metaphor and Metonymy." In *Feminism and Language,* ed. D. Bauer and K. Oliver. Bloomington: Indiana University Press.

Pajackowska, Claire. 1981. "Introduction to Kristeva." *m/f* 5 and 6, 149–57.

——. 1985. "On Love and Language." *Free Association* 2, 94–109.

Plaza, Monique. 1978. "'Phallomorphic Power' and the 'Psychology of "Woman,"'" trans. M. David and J. Hodges, *Ideology and Consciousness.*

Poovey, Mary. 1988. "Feminism and Deconstruction." *Feminist Studies* 14, 51–65.

Rabine, L. 1977. "Julia Kristeva: Semiotics and Women." *Pacific Coast Philology* 12, 41–49.

——. 1989. "Essentialism and Its Contexts: Saint-Simonian and Post-Structuralist Feminists." *differences* 1, no. 2, 105–23.

Reineke, M. 1988. "Life-Sentences: Kristeva and the Limits of Modernity." *Soundings* 71, no. 4, 439ff.

Richman, M. 1980. "Sex and Signs: The Language of the French Feminist Criticism." *Language and Style* 13, no. 4, 62–80.

Rose, Jacqueline. 1978. "'Dora'—Fragment of an Analysis." *m/f,* 5–21.

——. 1986. "Julia Kristeva: Take Two," in Rose, *Sexuality in the Field of Vision.* London: NLB/Verso.

Schor, Naomi. 1981. "Female Paranoia: The Case for Psychoanalytic Feminist Criticism." *Yale French Studies* 62.

Silverman, Kaja. 1988. *The Acoustic Mirror: The Female Voice in Psychoanalysis and Cinema.* Bloomington: Indiana University Press.

Smith, Paul. 1989. "Julia Kristeva et al., or, Take Three or More," in *Feminism and Psychoanalysis,* ed. R. Feldstein and J. Roof. Ithaca: Cornell University Press.

Spivak, Gayatri Chakravorty. 1981. "French Feminism in an International Frame." *Yale French Studies* 62, 154–84.

——. 1985. "3 Women's Texts." *Critical Inquiry* 12, no. 1, 243–61.

Stanton, Domna. 1980. "Language and Revolution: The Franco-American Dis-Connection," in *The Future of Difference,* ed. Eisenstein and Jardine. Boston: G. K. Hall, 73–87.

——. 1989. "Difference on Trial: A Critique of the Maternal Metaphor in Cixous, Irigaray, and Kristeva," in *The Thinking Muse,* ed. Allen and Young, 156–79.

Stone, Jennifer. 1983. "The Horrors of Power: A Critique of Kristeva," in The Politics of Theory, ed. Barker et al. Colchester: University of Essex, 38–48.

Suleiman, Susan. 1985. "Writing and Motherhood," in The (M)other Tongue: Essays in Feminist Psychoanalytic Interpretation, ed. Garner et al. Ithaca: Cornell University Press, 352–77.

Taylor, Mark. 1987. "Woman: Julia Kristeva," in Altarity. Chicago: University of Chicago Press, 151–83.

Tel Quel. 1968. Théorie d'ensemble. Paris: Seuil.

Tieszen, Nancy. 1990. "Julia Kristeva's Theory of the Signifying Subject as Presented in La Révolution du langage poétique." Master's Thesis, Miami University.

Van Wert, William. 1974. "Julia Kristeva: Cinematographic Semiotic Practice." Sub-Stance 9, 97–114.

Wenzel, H. 1981. "The Text as Body/Politics." Feminist Studies 7, no. 2.

West, Lois, et al. 1979. "French Feminist Theories and Psychoanalytic Theory." Off Our Backs, 9, 4ff.

White, Allon. 1977. "'L'Eclatement du sujet': The Theoretical Work of Julia Kristeva." Birmingham: University of Birmingham Centre for Contemporary Studies, Stencilled Occasional Paper, no. 49.

White, H. 1976. "Exposition and Critique of Kristeva." CCS Occasional Paper. London.

Wright, Elizabeth. 1984. Psychoanalytic Criticism: Theory in Practice. London: Methuen.

Young, Iris. 1990. Justice and the Politics of Difference. Princeton: Princeton University Press.

Zepp, Evelyn. 1982. "The Criticism of Julia Kristeva: A New Mode of Critical Thought." Romantic Review 73, no. 1 (January), 80–97.

Zeraffa, Michael. 1971. "La Poétique de l'écriture." Revue d'esthétique 24, 384–401.

Ziarek, Ewa. 1992. "At the Limits of Discourse: Heterogeneity, Alterity, and the Maternal Body in Kristeva's Thought." Unpublished paper, 1990. A version of this paper is forthcoming in Hypatia 7, no. 1.

On Lacan

Clement, Catherine. 1983. The Lives and Legends of Jacques Lacan. New York: Columbia University Press.

Coward, Rosilind. 1976. "Lacan and Signification." Edinburgh Review 1.

Felman, Shoshana. 1980. "The Originality of Jacques Lacan." Poetics Today 2.

———. 1987. Jacques Lacan and the Adventure of Insight. Cambridge, Mass.: Harvard University Press.

Gallop, Jane. 1976. "The Ladies' Man." Diacritics (Winter).

———. 1981. "Phallus/Penis: Same Difference," in Men by Women. Women and Literature, vol. 2, ed. Janet Todd. New York: Holmes & Meier.

———. 1985. Reading Lacan. Ithaca: Cornell University Press.

Grosz, Elizabeth. 1984. "Love Letters in the Sand: Jacques Lacan and Feminine Sexuality." Critical Philosophy 2.

———. 1990. Jacques Lacan: A Feminist Introduction. New York: Routledge.

Leavy, Stanley. 1978. "The Significance of Jacques Lacan," in Psychiatry and the Humanities, vol. 3, ed. Smith and Kerrigan. New Haven: Yale University Press.

Lemaire, Anika. 1977. Jacques Lacan. London: Routledge & Kegan Paul.

Macey, D. 1978. "Review of Jacques Lacan." Ideology and Consciousness 4.

———. 1983. "Fragments of an Analysis: Lacan in Context." *Radical Philosophy* 35.

Muller, J. P., and Richardson, W. J. 1978. "Toward Reading Lacan: Pages for a Workbook." *Psychoanalysis and Contemporary Thought* 1, 323–72.

———. 1982. *Lacan and Language: A Reader's Guide to Ecrits.* New York: International Universities Press.

Ragland-Sullivan, Ellie. 1982. "Jacques Lacan: Feminism and the Problem of Gender Identity." *Sub-Stance* 36.

———. 1986. *Jacques Lacan and the Philosophy of Psychoanalysis.* Urbana: University of Illinois Press.

Ragland-Sullivan, Ellie, and Bracher, Mark, eds. 1991. *Lacan and the Subject of Language.* New York: Routledge.

Richardson, William. 1978. "Lacan and the Subject of Psychoanalysis," in *Psychiatry and the Humanities,* vol. 3, ed. Smith and Kerrigan. New Haven: Yale University Press.

Schneiderman, Stuart. 1983. *Jacques Lacan: The Death of an Intellectual Hero.* Cambridge, Mass.: Harvard University Press.

Smith, J. H., and Kerrigan, W., eds. 1983. *Interpreting Lacan.* New Haven: Yale University Press.

Stanton, M. 1983. *Outside the Dream: Lacan and French Styles of Psychoanalysis.* London: Routledge & Kegan Paul.

Stratton, Teri. 1990. "The Lacanian Phallus and Its (Feminine) Slip." Unpublished paper.

Thom, M. 1976. "The Unconscious Structured Like a Language." *Economy and Society* 5, no. 4, 435–69.

Wilden, Anthony. 1981. *Speech and Language in Psychoanalysis.* Baltimore: Johns Hopkins University Press.

Miscellaneous

de Beauvoir, Simone. 1974. *The Second Sex,* trans. H. M. Parshley. New York: Random House.

———. 1980. *The Ethics of Ambiguity,* trans. Bernard Frechtman. Secaucus, N.J.: Citadel Press.

Cade, Toni, ed. 1970. *The Black Woman: An Anthology.* New York: Signet.

Chanter, Tina. 1991. "Kristeva's Politics of Change: Tracking Essentialism with the Help of a Sex/Gender Map," in *Ethics, Politics and Difference in Julia Kristeva's Writing: A Collection of Essays,* ed. Kelly Oliver. New York: Routledge, forthcoming.

Collins, Patricia Hill. 1990. *Black Feminist Thought: Knowledge, Consciousness, and the Politics of Empowerment.* Boston: Unwin Hyman.

Davis, Angela. 1981. *Women, Race and Class.* New York: Random House.

———. 1989. *Women, Culture, and Politics.* New York: Random House.

Foucault, Michel. 1983. "The Subject and Power," in *Michel Foucault: Beyond Structuralism and Hermeneutics,* by Hubert Dreyfus and Paul Rabinow. Chicago: University of Chicago Press.

hooks, bell. 1981. *Ain't I a Woman: Black Women and Feminism.* Boston: South End Press.

———. 1984. *From Margin to Center.* Boston: South End Press.

———. 1989. *Talking Back: Thinking Feminist, Thinking Black.* Boston: South End Press.

———. 1991. *Yearning, Race, Gender, and Cultural Politics.* Boston: South End Press.

Hull, Gloria, Scott, Patricia Bell, and Barbara Smith, eds. 1982. *But Some of Us Are Brave.* Old Westbury, N.Y.: Feminist Press.

Kaufmann-McCall, Dorothy. 1983. "Politics of Difference: The Women's Movement in France from May 1968 to Mitterrand." *Signs* 9, no. 2 (Winter).

Moraga, Cherrie, and Anzaldua, Gloria, eds. 1981. *This Bridge Called My Back: Writings by Radical Women of Color.* Watertown, Mass.: Persephone Press.

Smith, Barbara, ed. 1983. *Home Girls: A Black Feminist Anthology.* New York: Kitchen Table Press.

Terborg-Penn, Rosalyn. 1978. "Discrimination against Afro-American Women in the Woman's Movement, 1830–1920," in *The Afro-American Woman: Struggles and Images,* ed. Sharon Harley and Rosalyn Terborg-Penn. Port Washington, N.Y.: Kennikat Press.

INDEX

KELLY OLIVER is Assistant Professor of Philosophy at the University of Texas at Austin. Her articles have appeared in Social Theory and Practice, Hypatia, Diacritics, Praxis International, and Radical Philosophy. She is author of Womanizing Nietzsche: French Readings of the Figure of Woman and editor of Ethics, Politics and Difference in Julia Kristeva's Writing: A Collection of Essays, both forthcoming.